THE *DAILY EXPRESS*
HOW TO WIN ON THE HORSES

Danny Hall has been a racing man since he saw Lester Piggott on Petite Etoile at the tender age of six. He learned to be a betting man with the colourful bookmaker John Banks and started his journalistic career as editor of *The Racehorse*. He joined the *Daily Express* in 1980 and has been its racing editor since 1986 and 'Scotia' since 1990. He is a racehorse owner and breeder and a keen golfer.

The *Daily Express*
How To Win
On The Horses

Danny Hall
Racing Editor of the *Daily Express*

HEADLINE

Dedicated to the memory of Frank Rowe

ISBN 0 7472 4444 8

Typeset by
Letterpart Limited, Reigate, Surrey
Printed and bound in Great Britain by
Cox & Wyman Ltd, Reading, Berks

HEADLINE BOOK PUBLISHING
A division of Hodder Headline PLC
338 Euston Road
London NW1 3BH

Contents

Acknowledgements

The author is grateful to all those who have assisted in the preparation of this book, and in particular to the following: Guy Butchers, Peter Chapple-Hyam, Calvin Clarke, Barney Curley, Charlie Elsey, Jason Ferens and the team at Computer Sports Services, Jimmy George, Reg Griffin, David Haigh, Bill Heath, Michael Harris and his staff at the Racing Post, Peter Harris, Chris Hawkins, Tony Jakobson, Rolf Johnson, Steve Lee, Anthony Marray, David Powell, Jack Ramsden, Andy Sime, Mike Walker, Neal Wilkins, Colin Woods; and finally my wife Helen for her help, encouragement and patience during the gestation of this book.

Introduction

More than eight million people have a flutter on the Grand National. A million bet on a daily basis, drawn back regularly by the unforgettable joy of victory and that adrenalin rush as their selection hits the front inside the final furlong.

With some 80 per cent of all bets struck at £5 or less, the vast majority stay well within their means. To them it's a harmless form of fun and excitement; the irresistible urge to secure something for nothing. But most of all the attraction is in making a choice and being proved right.

In many ways there has never been a better time for those punters to speculate. Backing horses need not be a mug's game.

The daily newspaper, which once printed just the runners and riders, is now the source of a vast amount of statistical information and analysis. Form books, too, have become far more sophisticated. Meanwhile, the launch of Satellite Information Services (SIS) in 1987, bringing live pictures of virtually every race run nationwide into our 10,000 betting shops, has given the ordinary punter the chance to judge for himself how horses run.

There was also the surprising largesse shown by the then Chancellor of the Exchequer, Nigel Lawson, in March 1987 when he abolished the 4 per cent on-course betting tax.

The odds still favour the bookmaker – if he does his sums right, he should make a profit on every race whatever the result. But the strength of the punters' position has always been, and will always be, that he can pick and choose which races to 'play' in. Betting in every race is certainly a mug's game; being selective gives you a chance to make a profit.

The purpose of this book is to teach the art of betting on horses. I will describe the essential tools of the trade and how to use them; suggest ways of sifting through the vast quantity of data available; define how to make decisions and the best way of turning those decisions into profit; and, with the help of some of the legendary names from the betting ring down the years, guide you through the Do's and Don'ts of successful punting.

Racing is perhaps unique among major sports in that the leading protagonists lose a great deal more often than they win. Linford Christie won all bar one of his fifteen 100 metre races before taking the world title at Stuttgart, while Britain's other athletics gold medallists, Colin Jackson and Sally Gunnell, were undefeated in their long series of prep races; world boxing champion Lennox Lewis took his unblemished record as a pro to 24 with the Cardiff drubbing of Frank Bruno; and Scottish boy wonder of the green baize, Stephen Hendry, once chalked up an unbeaten run of 36 successful matches in world ranking snooker tournaments.

But whether your name is Henry Cecil or Martin Pipe, Richard Dunwoody or Pat Eddery, you will experience failure at least twice as many times as victory, even during a magnificent victorious spell. For punters like you and me, it is no different. We'll be hoping for one winning bet in three. So learning to cope with failure – and wrestling with that fragile concept, confidence – is one of the most demanding aspects about backing horses. You cannot prevent yourself from losing on more occasions than you win; the skill is to end up in the black nevertheless.

A stoic acceptance of the inevitable setbacks, then, is a prerequisite for any punter. It doesn't pay to have too combustible a temperament because that can lose you more than just your shirt. Leslie Spencer, for many years the course representative for bookies William Hill, and therefore the man who stood bets that could have cost his firm a fortune, once told me: 'I have seen many come into this game like lions only to leave like lambs.' Remember, we are not in a contest that can be won with one big hit, so leave the bludgeon at home. Our aim is to show a profit, not on a single day, week or month but over a long period of time. Rather, let's use a stiletto for regular but damaging thrusts against the bookmaker.

A bookmaker refers to the total stakes on his account as the 'sum invested'. Anything less like an investment than a backer's usual bets it is hard to imagine. Certainly the bets of my youth proved no investment for me and it has taken 25 years to eliminate some poisonous habits from my system.

One of them was making wasteful bets. I was amused recently by the advice given by a prominent banker at a high-powered business conference. Someone in the audience asked him how he kept his bank in the black when so many financial institutions were going under. He replied: 'avoid mistakes.'

Obvious, maybe, but how many of us have been guilty of having a bet on something for which we had only a passing fancy? I strongly recommend that readers keep a strict record of their bets, and a simple and effective way of cutting out irrational betting – avoiding mistakes, if you like – is to make yourself write a short explanation as to why a particular horse should be backed. It is amazing how many foolish wagers can be scratched before the damage is done. If I can truly say to myself 'Win or lose, this is a bet,' I am happy to put my money down.

To have come even this far, I must assume that the reader takes betting seriously, and has profit in mind. Those who bet for fun are unlikely to get their entertainment for nothing. But the average reader with a job will have perhaps a maximum of one hour each morning to sort out the day's bets.

Our ever-expanding fixture list – there were about 7,500 races run in the latest complete Flat and jumping seasons – presents an intimidating task for the professional, never

mind the amateur, so an essential word of advice to the
novice backer is *specialize*. You cannot possibly study every
race every day so don't try. I have made a number of
suggestions throughout this book about how to limit your
betting opportunities yet increase your profits. Cutting out
all betting in handicaps, for instance, will reduce the number
of races to be assessed by 40 per cent at a stroke and I
promise you it will have nothing but a beneficial effect on
your account. Concentrating your efforts on two-year-old
races alone – or, during the winter, those for juvenile
hurdlers – will reduce the amount of study time necessary
still further. Or you may prefer to prune the fixture list by
geographical means, studying only those race meetings near
your home, the ones you are most likely to visit. That way
you will build up a valuable mental dossier of local trainers
and their methods.

Alternatively, and I recommend this course of action as
the best of all, you could focus your attention solely on the
new phenomenon of all-weather racing, whose introduction I
view as nothing but good news for the punter.

To be faced with perhaps 50 races spread over seven
meetings on a Saturday, not knowing where to start, is a
daunting task – so specialize.

The majority of punters lose because they are herd animals. They go with the crowd, inevitably backing the most-
tipped horses which then start at shorter odds than are
justified. Horses, as far as I am aware, have no concept of
value, but I find it uncanny how often one that is at far too
short a price – because of the weight of popular money – will
be beaten. Horses who are bad value may win regardless, but
in the long term the punter will lose heavily if he persists in
backing them.

Choosing not to follow the crowd is laudable but being a
maverick for its own sake is just as sure a way to lose your
cash. This is by no means a modern-day problem. In his
classic 1924 book *Men And Horses I Have Known*, the Hon.

George Lambton wrote of Harry Hungerford, one of the leading Turf figures of the day:

> Harry was one of the best fellows I have ever met, clever, and a good judge of horses and racing; he backed his opinion heavily, and at times won a great deal of money. But he had one failing which hurt no one but himself. He always wanted to be thought cleverer than anyone else. I remember Tom Cannon [a Classic winning trainer] saying, as Harry was walking away after talking about some race: 'It is a pity, but I am afraid Mr Hungerford's opinions will cost him a lot'; a prophecy which came true.

Anyone who has backed horses has slipped on that banana skin before – trying to be too clever. But it is only by going it alone that the most satisfying, memorable and profitable coups are landed. If you don't back any 12–1 or 14–1 chances you won't back any 12–1 or 14–1 winners.

There is no short cut to success in betting. It requires much knowledge and considerable concentration. It has taken me many years to acquire the experience necessary to beat the book. I hope the reader will succeed much more quickly and be able regularly to savour the joy of being proved magnificently and joyously correct.

PART ONE
THE TOOLS

Chapter One

The Form Book

I once had occasion to look around the study of a famous bookmaker. Much like any racing man's study, there were framed photographs of victorious horses, mementoes of the successful animals he had owned and shelf upon shelf of form books, dating back some 30 to 40 years. The earlier editions were dog-eared and well thumbed while the recent ones were pristine and untouched.

It was a salutary experience for me. As this man had climbed the company ladder, he had patently lost his enthusiasm for the game which so enthralled him in his youth. He had become a mere accountant – a number cruncher – when once he had been a passionate student of form.

Fortunately I have not travelled the same route. My interest in the form of racehorses is still as vigorous as it was 25 years ago. In the battle against the bookies, one's strongest ally is the book of form, that marriage of fact and opinion which also acts as a diary of the punter's highs and lows during the season.

WHICH FORM BOOK?

There are three principal form books, those published by Raceform, Superform and Timeform. My personal favourite is the *Perspective*, produced by Timeform. Their racereaders, handicappers and comment writers are, I believe, the best in the business.

Timeform was the brainchild of the godfather of modern punting, the late Phil Bull, and for more than 40 years Timeform publications have been the envy of horseplayers

throughout the world. The scholarly *Racehorses* annuals
have achieved such a status that a complete set can fetch a
sum well into four figures and the twice-weekly *Timeform
Perspective* is also a masterly work. Like the other form
books the *Perspective* carries all the basic information: full
finishing order and the distances between horses down to the
last home; weight carried; jockey; position in the stalls;
starting price and official handicap rating. The last point is a
recent innovation and very valuable because while the weight
carried is not of prime importance, the horse's ever-changing
position on the official handicapper's sliding scale (in general
terms 0–140) certainly is.

Three things, though, set the *Perspective* apart from the
opposition: the going recorded; the race synopsis; and the
Timefigure.

Timeform is quite rightly not prepared to rely on the stout
heel or trusty stick of the local clerk of the course as an
accurate means of assessing something as vital as the going.
They take the opinion of their man on the spot, of course,
but principally their recorded going is determined by the
times of the races and how they compare to the thousands of
examples in the Timeform memory bank.

Then there is the superb race analysis. Like any commen-
tator who has the benefit of hindsight, the Timeform team is
occasionally guilty of giving a race result the appearance of
having been inevitable, dragging into prominence the forces
which have triumphed and thrusting into the background
those which have been swallowed up. But all in all, mixing
what was seen by highly experienced race-readers, live at
the track and on SIS back at their Halifax headquarters,
with the handicappers' assessment of the form is a winning
combination.

Thirdly, what of the calculation of race times which gives
this firm its name? How can the race time recorded at one
track have any bearing on the time likely to be taken at
another? A two-year-old can bowl down the five-furlong

course at Epsom in less than 56 seconds, while the average time for the same distance at Beverley, with its severe uphill finish, is six seconds slower. And what about the great British climate, which can produce going as diverse as heavy and hard?

Briefly, all students of time base their calculations on 'standard time', a figure arrived at after scores of races over a particular distance at an individual track have been investigated. Timeform's evaluation of the standards for Newmarket alone involve statistical analysis of more than 4,000 race times.

To arrive at a Timefigure, a sophisticated formula is then used measuring the time in seconds (per five furlongs) faster or slower than the fixed standard. The calculation takes account of such things as track differences, weight carried, going, wind and the distance beaten behind the winner. The most reliable Timefigures are those for races run on good or fast ground over five and six furlongs – distances at which the races are nearly always truly run. Pay no heed to record times; they have usually been set under freak conditions.

A slow Timefigure does not necessarily indicate a moderate horse – the race may have been falsely run or the winner not fully tested by inferior opposition – but only a good horse can put up a fast Timefigure. A fast time is often the first evidence of a good horse's merit.

The busy punter need no longer spend hours compiling his own set of Timefigures. All the form books include their own. I have suggested you use Timeform *Perspective*, and their time calculations are as good if not better than any of the opposition.

Using the time test has, of course, become much more influential since the advent of electrical timing. Racecourse Technical Services (RTS) produce electrical times for the following racetracks: Ascot, Ayr. Chester, Doncaster, Epsom, Goodwood, Haydock, Kempton, Lingfield, Newbury, Newcastle, Newmarket, Salisbury, Sandown and

York. The other courses are hand-timed by expert 'clockers' employed by the respective form books.

My faith in the merit of race times was strengthened further when Britain's racecourses were re-measured recently by laser. Newbury's five-furlong track, for instance, was found to extend to five furlongs 34 yards. No wonder so many of my sprint bets there were caught in the dying strides!

The form book, then, is a marvellous tool; and there are some personal touches which can make it even more useful.

When the day's results are known, turn back to the last race run by each of the day's winners and use a highlighter to mark their names. This colour coding will show up at a glance the races whose form is working out well. If spotted early enough the strongest races can provide you with a rich source of future winners, perhaps as many as ten.

I also like to acknowledge good performances in defeat, particularly those coming after a short lay-off, by again tracing the horse back to its previous race and ticking it in my form book. As a rough guide, beaten horses who happen to have recorded the best Timefigure, as long as it is 70 plus, are ideal qualifiers.

Finding a race that is working out well can often send you spiralling off at a tangent, revealing other worthy performances, but it's a magical mystery tour that is well worth making.

COMPUTERS

I'm a quill pen and ledger man myself; I like the well-used feel of my form book as it gets more battered through the season. It must be something to do with the work ethic, savouring the amount of time and sweat required to give it that grubby appearance. I even like the smell of the rexine cover when the folder and its first few pages arrive at the start of each new season.

But one can't sit Canute-like expecting to hold back the onset of progress and here, creeping sheepishly into the winner-finding arena, are . . . computers. Our very own Computerman has been a popular and successful tipster ever since he approached the *Daily Express* with his methods in 1983. His naps again showed a healthy profit of £20 to a £1 level stake in 1993. Raceform has recently launched a lap-top computer form-book system, among whose pocketful of devotees runs the kind of fanaticism usually reserved for religious fundamentalists.

The principles, of course, make sense. There is no doubting a computer's strength as a store of information, readily accessible at the touch of a button, although I would sorely miss the tactile pleasure of thumbing through my form book.

Anything, however, that could overcome the irrationality of one's moods – what some people call the enemy within – has to be examined carefully. The thought processes required to solve the puzzle set by the 3.45 at Newbury are identical every day. But, for whatever reason – boredom, fatigue, illness, hangover – random errors of judgement creep into our work which decrease the validity of our predictions. And, of course, computers don't get hangovers.

I remain sceptical about the computer as an interpretive tool but owing to the inadequacies of intuition I will have to examine its potential role in the future.

READING THE FORM

Let's now look at the most basic example of form.

In a two-year-old race run over five furlongs in July, Able Alex won by one length from Bright Bob, and Clever Charlie was third, a further length behind. They all carried nine stone.

One month later, they are all engaged in another five-furlong race and again they all carry nine stone.

Taking the July race at face value, Able Alex, Bright Bob and Clever Charlie should again finish in the same order. But racing is never that simple.

Able Alex had already had two races before he won in July; Bright Bob and Clever Charlie had not been out before. Able Alex was probably much the fittest of the three and he certainly had the advantage of experience. Bright Bob and Clever Charlie will have profited greatly from their initial outing; a first race can often bring on a two-year-old by seven pounds or more.

Therefore, it may be argued that both Bright Bob and Clever Charlie should beat Able Alex. But which is the better proposition – Bright Bob or Clever Charlie?

At this point we should summon the interpretive help of the Timeform *Perspective* team and look at their comments under the original race. Which was the most backward – Bright Bob or Clever Charlie – and did either of them run green? Able Alex won the original race by a length, but how much did he have in hand?

Even with the benefit of fact and opinion, Able Alex, Bright Bob and Clever Charlie could each be chosen in the August race by different tipsters and each one could argue cogently that his selection was the form horse.

If we find such difficulty in a simple three-horse, two-year-old race, where there is a direct form line between Able Alex, Bright Bob and Clever Charlie, how much harder must it be when there is no direct form to work on and we have to rely entirely on what is known as 'collateral form'.

There is collateral form when we are able, for example, to relate the form of Able Alex, Bright Bob and Clever Charlie to Dashing Doug. We must assume now that Able Alex, Bright Bob and Clever Charlie have never raced together before but that they have all run in different races in which Dashing Doug took part.

We use Dashing Doug as a yardstick to evaluate our three horses. If there is no single horse like Dashing Doug to rely on, we have to move further afield for our collateral form but the more tortuous the route, the less valid it becomes.

It is far more difficult still to weigh up form when we have to analyse all-aged races, whether conditions events or handicaps.

Broadly speaking, a racehorse reaches its peak on the Flat between four and five years old and then tends slowly to deteriorate. A four-year-old is therefore regarded as superior to a three-year-old and has to concede weight to him. But the concessions vary

(a) according to the distance of the race, and
(b) according to the time of year.

The weight-for-age scale which is set out in Appendix A was created in the nineteenth century by Admiral Rous, one of the Turf's first great administrators and reformers. It is a tribute to his skill that it has been used ever since, with few modifications, as a reasonably reliable guide to assist in deciding the weights to be carried by horses of different ages when competing against each other. The reader should regularly refer to it and its National Hunt equivalent, which is set out in Appendix B.

In the weight-for-age scale for the Flat it can be seen that a three-year-old racing over five furlongs in the first half of March is rated 14 pounds inferior to rivals aged four and above. But by the end of the Flat season, in November, the same three-year-old is deemed to have reached full maturity and should meet those older rivals on level terms.

Similarly, in the jumping scale, a four-year-old hurdler preparing for the Daily Express Triumph Hurdle and running over two miles is rated 12 pounds inferior to an older rival in January; but if he were to meet the same horse ten months later, in November, he could expect the contest to be at level weights.

Weight can also be related to the distance beaten with a

reasonable degree of accuracy and the poundage allowance for distance beaten table (Appendix C) will give readers an insight into how the handicapper makes his calculations.

Here's an example of a result for a three-year-old handicap over six furlongs:

Acer	7st–10lb	....	1
Bermondo	8st–1lb	....	2½l 2
Crobeg	8st–13lb	....	2½l 3

Using the poundage allowance for distance beaten table, we can assess who put up the most meritorious performance. Acer won the race by two and a half lengths, the equivalent of six pounds in our table; but he was receiving five pounds in weight from Bermondo, so he comes out of the race only one pound superior to Bermondo after the weights have been adjusted. Crobeg, meanwhile, was beaten a total of five lengths by Acer, worth 14 pounds in our table, but was conceding the winner 17 pounds, so he comes out a three pounds better horse than the winner Acer and therefore the best horse of the three.

RACECOURSE GRADES

Johann Sebastian Bach, the most mathematical of classical composers, proved that lyrical flights of creative fancy could be produced from the most structured regime.

It would be fruitless and costly to attempt to win money backing horses without working from a solid foundation so, with apologies to certain course executives, I have graded the country's courses, including the three all-weather (AW) tracks, rating them in categories from Class A to Class D. I have also set out some recommended Timefigures which represent a good performance in each racecourse band for Flat tracks.

These gradings for racecourses should not be confused with the British Horseracing Board's restructuring of the Flat programme (Appendix D) in which races come under 14 categories across seven classes from A to G.

Flat

Class A

Ascot, Goodwood, Kempton, Newbury, Newmarket, Sandown, York.

Good Timefigures: two-year-olds, pre-Royal Ascot 85, Royal Ascot to York Ebor meeting 95; York Ebor meeting to end of season 105; three-year-olds (all year) 110; handicappers 100.

Class B

Ayr (Western meeting, Class A), Chester (May meeting, Class A), Doncaster (St Leger meeting, Class A), Epsom (Derby meeting, Class A), Haydock, Lingfield, Newcastle (Northumberland Plate meeting, Class A), Salisbury.

Good Timefigures: two-year-olds, pre-Royal Ascot 80, Royal Ascot to York Ebor meeting 85, York Ebor meeting to end of season 90; three-year-olds (all year) 100; handicappers 90.

Class C

Bath, Beverley, Brighton, Chepstow, Leicester, Nottingham, Pontefract, Redcar, Ripon, Thirsk, Warwick, Windsor, Yarmouth.

Good Timefigures: two-year-olds, pre-Royal Ascot 75, Royal Ascot to York Ebor meeting 80; York Ebor meeting to end of season 85; three-year-olds (all year) 85; handicappers 85.

Class D

Carlisle, Catterick, Edinburgh, Folkestone, Hamilton, Lingfield (AW), Southwell (AW and turf) Wolverhampton (AW).

Good Timefigures: two-year-olds, pre-Royal Ascot 70, Royal Ascot to York Ebor meeting 70, York Ebor meeting to end of season 75; three-year-olds (all year) 75; handicappers 75.

National Hunt

Class A

Aintree, Ascot, Cheltenham, Haydock, Kempton, Newbury, Sandown, Wetherby.

Class B

Ayr, Chepstow, Doncaster, Lingfield (turf), Newcastle, Uttoxeter.

Class C

Carlisle, Exeter, Hexham, Huntingdon, Kelso, Leicester, Market Rasen, Nottingham, Perth, Stratford, Towcester, Warwick, Wincanton, Windsor, Worcester.

Class D

Bangor, Cartmel, Catterick, Edinburgh, Fakenham, Folkestone, Fontwell, Hereford, Lingfield (AW), Ludlow, Newton Abbot, Plumpton, Sedgefield, Southwell (AW and turf), Taunton.

Chapter Two

Watching a Race

Of every £100 bet on horses, £95 is placed off-course. And yet until relatively recently the betting-shop punters' link with the racecourse was a disembodied voice on the 'blower' relaying second-hand commentaries from the track. Now, virtually every race is televised live by SIS in the betting shops, and their coverage is at least as slick and sophisticated as that provided by the Channel Four or BBC racing teams. Whether you are an armchair punter, a betting-shop habitué or a racecourse regular, the things to look out for when watching a race are the same. You will probably see many more races now than you did in years gone by and, if viewed with a purpose, these races can be the source of a regular supply of future winners.

On the track, arm yourself with a pair of binoculars or at the very least watch the race from the stands with the naked eye. Judging the pace at which a race is run is best done when watching the race 'live'. Also, there is nothing more galling than to be focusing on a horse through the race only for the TV director to sanction a change of camera angles, leaving you to guess how your horse may have fared. By all means watch a TV or closed-circuit replay, but do so as a back-up to what you've seen with your own eyes. Artie Edwards, the best-known Newmarket gallops watcher of the post-war years, used an enormous pair of German Beck and Kassel binoculars, big enough almost to need a tripod. Such extravagance is unnecessary – a decent pair of 10 × 50s will do the job satisfactorily.

Not even the best racereaders like Alan Amies of Race-form can watch every horse in a race. Learn the colours of two or three and watch them specifically, while gaining a general impression of how the rest ran.

I strongly recommend that you watch every race in which you have an interest, particularly a financial one. Picking up the results in cold blood from the radio, teletext or the next morning's paper bears no comparison to the adrenalin-pumping sensation that all but the most ice-cool punter knows of shouting your winners home.

What's more, should you have backed a loser, you can console yourself with the knowledge that you may have spotted something valuable for the future.

By studying the race beforehand a number of questions will have been prompted that only the race can answer. The fundamental reason why a horse is beaten is because it is not good enough – and in many cases this is pretty obvious in advance. Horses can't perform to their best abilities if they are not feeling 100 per cent, but there are elements, like the distance of the race, the going and the type of course on which the race is run, which will have a bearing on the outcome and whose influence can, to a certain extent, be predicted.

The horse which was running over the trip for the first time – did it stay? And the horse which had never previously raced on fast going – did it repeatedly change its leading leg as if in discomfort on the ground?

Always watch the race from the start, because the pace at which it is run often determines whether the form can be trusted. A good, even pace, underlined by a fast race time, usually represents the most reliable form; a funereal amble in the early stages, resulting in a headlong sprint over the last two or three furlongs – a typical characteristic of French racing – occasionally produces a false result. A contest in which the pacemakers go off too fast, setting up the prize for something coming from behind, should also be treated with caution. In the latter case, note which of the pacesetters lasted the longest – they have probably run much better than the distance by which they were beaten suggests.

HORSES FOR COURSES

The extensive variety of our 59 racecourses is one of the enduring attractions of British racing. Some horses act on one type of course but not on another. Perhaps the most famous example was the nation's favourite, Desert Orchid, one of the greatest chasers since the war: he won 34 races, but only two of them going left-handed, which explains why his dominance of the sport over six or seven seasons was not consistently underlined at the two major festivals of jump racing – Cheltenham and Aintree, both left-handed tracks.

'Follow horses for courses' is an old racing saying and certainly the idiosyncrasies of our racecourses have thrown up a plethora of course specialists down the years. An arbitrary list includes Lochranza (12 wins at Ayr including two over hurdles), Rapid Lad (12 at Beverley), Operatic Society (seven of his 30 successes at Brighton), Prince Carlton (10 victories at Fakenham), Certain Justice (14 at Fontwell), Twin Oaks (his last eight chase wins at Haydock), Al Amead (nine victories, all at Lingfield), Kilbrittain Castle (11 at Sandown), Eve (eight at Yarmouth), Peaty Sandy (10 at Newcastle) and Suluk, who won 18 of his 22 races on the Fibresand at Southwell.

It seems the more unique the track, the more likely it is to foster course specialists – and a dollop of sea air in the mix doesn't do any harm, either. So be prepared for horses to come back time and time again to run their best races at a specific track, even if they have apparently been out of form elsewhere; similarly, forgive a horse if he patently dislikes a certain track. If an appraisal of Dessie's career were based on his eight runs at the Cheltenham Festival alone, Gold Cup victory notwithstanding, an entire cottage industry of his memorabilia would have been entirely unnecessary.

JOCKEYSHIP

Focusing on jockeyship can prove fruitful for the astute
race-reader, particularly in apprentice, conditional and amateur rider races. There seems little difference in the skill
factor of our top 20 or 30 jockeys under both codes, but in
terms of horsemanship a very wide spectrum of ability is
displayed in boys' races and bumpers.

I keep a list of all apprentices, conditionals and amateurs,
rating them good, bad or average, so I take special interest in
all race finishes that involve raw riders. Potential bets can
easily crop up in events for riders of limited experience and it
is as well to have a sound knowledge of their capabilities. It
pays not to be too dogmatic, though, where young riders are
concerned – this week's sack of potatoes could become next
season's poetry in motion.

Jockeyship over the sticks involves a different set of skills.
Split-second decisions are commonplace in every race on the
Flat and the outcome can be decided by a canny rider saving a
length or two at a vital point. In National Hunt, results rarely
turn on a hair's breadth like that but the qualities of the natural
horseman come to the fore: presenting the horse correctly at
the obstacle . . . and sitting tight if it makes a blunder.

During the winter, concentrate not only on the technique
of the jockeys over the fences but also that of the jumpers
themselves. A horse might manage to collect a sequence of
wins, especially in the early part of the season, despite
indifferent jumping, simply through a distinct lack of competition. The observant race-reader will know not to trust this
horse when it is upped in class.

NON-TRIERS AND ROGUES

Rule 151 (ii) of the Rules of Racing states that 'The rider
of every horse shall take all reasonable and permissible

measures throughout the race to ensure that his horse is given a full opportunity to win or of obtaining the best possible placing.'

It is a rule that is impossible to police comprehensively. Rarely does one see a horse ridden out to finish 11th instead of 12th. But the spirit of the law is there to maintain punters' confidence in the integrity of racing. If the Jockey Club was not vigilant about penalizing non-triers and clamping down on those jockeys who do not ride out for a place – a pernicious habit which, I know, upsets those who specialize in each-way and placepot betting – punters would soon look elsewhere for their 'buzz'.

It is simply part of human nature that the betting shop and racecourse are awash with remarks like 'Did you see that? . . . It was blatant . . . never put in the race with a chance . . . the stewards must be blind'. But the righteous indignation ebbs away when there is some money to be made. That same punter will stab a pen at a racehorse's name in the *Sporting Life* on the betting-shop wall, and say in true nudge nudge, wink wink style: 'A stable lad told me that was stopped at Newmarket . . . I'm having my maximum on today.'

The bulk of talk about non-triers is completely misinformed. Often our betting-stool race-reader may have picked up on the jockey taking things easy in the last furlong, oblivious to the fact that the same pilot had been kicking and scrubbing for all he was worth during the first mile of the race.

There are any number of genuine reasons why a horse has been beaten, the principal one, as I have said before, being that he is not good enough. It is my firm belief that the blatant non-trier – the horse which is prevented from winning a race by a less than zealous jockey – is no longer a worrying phenomenon. Since the introduction of the SIS pictures, a race is covered from every conceivable angle and it is hard for a jockey to pull a stroke without it coming to the attention of the stewards, or at least the professional race-reading organizations like Timeform. The system of retrospective justice, where connections can be reprimanded for cases that were not spotted at the time, has also served to help the crackdown.

That's not to say that non-triers don't ever occur. One of the most celebrated cases in recent years was that of the Dick Allan-trained hurdler Flowing River at Kelso in February, 1991. Jockey Brian Storey was adjudged not to have ridden Flowing River to get the best possible placing, an opinion with which there can have been no dispute. Flowing River raced with the back-markers until making rapid headway under what appeared to be quite severe restraint. He finished third beaten only two lengths and the trainer and jockey in the case were quite rightly suspended for three months. Flowing River won three of his six races the following season. He may have been a difficult ride, often finding little when off the bridle, but the fact remains that those punters who backed him at Kelso were robbed.

The blatant stopping of horses has to be stamped on – especially when it involves doping, which can affect life and limb. But the mild skullduggery necessary in the battle of wits between the owner and trainer and the handicapper – that manipulation of events so that the horse is approaching its peak when the handicapper believes it to be in decline – is one of the game's greatest attractions.

If a horse gets in the grip of the handicapper – in other words, if the official has an unrealistically high opinion of its ability – it can take months and several races before enough clemency is shown for that horse to win. All very frustrating and expensive for the racehorse owner. And I have yet to hear of a trainer who gives a discount on training fees because a horse is harshly handicapped and therefore unable to win.

How does one spot those horses who are being prepared to win on another day?

Here are a few things to look out for: the horse running over the wrong distance, ground or type of course; being ridden by a boy when it's clearly a man's ride; racing when unfit; being asked to set too fast a pace; being dropped out in the early stages and given too little time to make up the ground; being ridden into the 'bottom' of its fences so it jumps with less confidence and loses ground at each jump.

But, frankly, the obsessive search for non-triers is a waste of time. Rather than casting your eye over the also-rans, wondering who is 'busy' and who isn't, you would be far better served watching the business end of the race and seeing how the principal contenders react when the pressure is on in the final furlong. Trainer Henry Cecil is one of the few serious professionals who doesn't use binoculars. He says: 'The vital part of a race usually happens at close range to the stands.' He's right – so concentrate on the finish.

We all occasionally back a horse who wins with its head in its chest but generally they have to work for it. And until you know how a horse reacts in a finish, how can it be a safe bet?

Look for horses who are still travelling strongly rather than weakening at the end of the race. A horse that finishes full of running is a better bet next time out than one that is beaten comprehensively.

Look for horses which respond willingly to a jockey's urgings and be wary of those that appear to be cruising but wander under pressure or just down tools when called upon to battle. The horse may have a terrific 'engine' and flawless conformation, but if it doesn't *want* to win there is little that can be done about it. No horse is born mean, though ill-treatment when young can upset the over-sensitive, but many horses are congenital cowards. Blinkers, a good jockey and a canny trainer with a hundred tricks up his sleeve can help. But training areas around the world reverberate with tales of the fantastically talented rogues who repeatedly beat stable stars in morning gallops. On the track in the afternoon, it's a different matter.

Semi-retired Bill Marshall keeps his hand in training a few winners at Garrison Savannah racecourse in Barbados. Bill is one of the shrewdest trainers and cleverest punters I have come across, responsible, among others, for that marvellous weight-carrying sprinter of the sixties, Raffingora.

One of Bill's favourite expressions has served me well down the years: 'If they've got guts, you can back them.' I couldn't get those words out of my mind as a favourite horse of mine, Prince Pepe, went to post for the David Dixon Gold Cup at York in May 1977. Prince Pepe was a remarkably tough front-runner with a tremendous never-say-die spirit, ideally suited to York. Like most natural front-runners he was always hard on himself at home and at the races, and therefore could not maintain his form over an indefinite period without having a rest to freshen up. But this was his first race of the season, and first for his new trainer Eric Collingwood. Knowing the horse's style, I felt lack of fitness was not going to be a concern. I napped him and the next day watched on TV as he drifted in the market to 33–1. But with Bill Marshall's phrase nagging me, I knew that, win or lose, Prince Pepe would not let me down, and I stepped in.

As I finish this chapter, I can see on my study wall a smashing Don Wallis photograph of Prince Pepe passing the line having made every post a winning one.

Go on my son!

PART TWO
HOW TO PICK WINNERS

Chapter Three

Conditions Races

There are basically two types of race – conditions races and handicaps. In this chapter we deal with conditions races, the area from which the majority of our bets should come.

Conditions races cover a vast spectrum from humble sellers to the five Classic races. The British Horseracing Board introduced a new class structure in 1993 in a bid to produce more competitive racing. Like all innovative ideas it will be tinkered with and improved upon but at the moment it consists of 14 categories, 11 of which can loosely be termed conditions races. They are, in order of prestige: Pattern races; Listed races; conditions stakes; limited stakes; open maidens; rating-related maidens; auction maidens; median auction maidens; sellers; claimers; plus races for apprentices and amateur riders. (Appendix D gives the detailed definition of each type.)

Most two-year-old races are conditions races and they are the ideal betting medium for the novice backer. Juveniles race more consistently than their elders; they have not had time to become jaded, nor have hard races left an impression on them and made them unwilling to give of their best.

Normally, the novice backer who works for a living will not have more than an hour or so in the morning to devote to the study of the day's races. There are usually two races for two-year-olds at each Flat meeting, so you should study the form of every horse engaged in these races and ignore all other races. During the winter you can concentrate on juvenile hurdlers because, like two-year-olds on the Flat, they represent a self-contained microcosm of racing.

This, I know, is the gospel of perfection and will be ignored by 99 per cent of all readers. That's why, during the ensuing chapters, I will make suggestions about races other than juvenile events.

Another means of cutting down the workload for the amateur punter is to let Computerman of the *Daily Express* do some of your preliminary work. The majority of winners appear in the top half dozen on his W-Factor ratings; so don't waste time investigating the dead wood, just concentrate on his top six.

FORM FROM CONDITIONS RACES

Armed with your by now annotated and personalized form book and your memory bank of races seen, as well as a grading system for racecourses, you are ready to put the theory into practice.

The fundamental questions you must ask yourself when assessing each race are:

1 Does the horse have the ability to win it, and is it currently fit and in form?
2 Will it be suited by the ground and, to a lesser extent, the distance?
3 Will it be suited by the contours of the track and the pace at which the race is likely to be run?

As you thumb through the past results, let the form wash over you. You will soon develop a feel or instinct for the right moves. Don't try to force the winner out; if there is an outstanding candidate, it will become obvious.

Ability

It doesn't pay to be dogmatic as to precisely what form can be taken from any particular band of meetings to any other, but here are some general principles to follow:

1 At Class A meetings take form only from Class A meetings. Clearly, form from Class A meetings can be followed in Class B, C and D meetings, although at these weaker fixtures the price is nearly always prohibitive. Regard should also be taken of the value of races. The Tote Two-Year-Old Trophy at Redcar, for example, is run at a Class C track but because of its valuable prize money, only the very best Class A form need be considered.
2 Form from Class B meetings can be taken to Class B, C and D.
3 Form from Class C meetings can be taken to Class C and D.
4 Form from Class D meetings can be taken only to Class D.

Form at Newmarket, Ascot and York is strong all year round. Form from any other meeting, including the remainder of the Class A tracks, should be taken on trust only when it has been boosted by superior *subsequent* performances from its contestants. Class A racing is the best and horses need to be in tip-top form to win. I try to pinch myself whenever I'm thinking of backing a horse at a Class A meeting which did not win last time out. Beaten horses rarely gain compensation at the major tracks but excuses are often found for them; that leaves winners last time out often at surprisingly good odds.

Fitness

On the score of fitness, you will save yourself from backing countless losers it you adhere to the 50-day rule. A horse has only a limited period during which it can be kept in peak condition. When it has been off the course for almost two months, this is usually an indication that it has suffered a slight setback and may therefore need at least one race to bring it back to full racing fitness. There is one exception to this rule: when one of the most successful yards is enjoying a particularly good run of form, they can be trusted to have a horse race-fit despite a lengthy lay-off.

It's at Class A meetings where newcomers with lofty reputations are introduced. 'Never back a two-year-old the first time it runs' is an old racing maxim but still a pertinent one. It's rare to see a newcomer that does not show signs of greenness either at the stalls or during the race, however well drilled it has been at home. Let the supposed 'flying machine' show its worth on the track before you risk any of your cash.

Going

There are seven official categories of going: hard; firm; good to firm; good; good to soft; soft; and heavy.

Most horses are able to reproduce their form on good ground; it is when the going moves to either extreme that we must be very careful. If the horse does not act on the prevailing going, he will not be able to run within pounds, maybe stones, of his true form.

The Kim Bailey-trained chaser Mr Frisk, the only horse to complete the Grand National–Whitbread Gold Cup double in the same season, loved top-of-the-ground conditions and was ineffective as soon as it became wet. Assessor, a courageous stayer handled by Richard Hannon, is the reverse. His form on fast going is ordinary but given very soft conditions – and it was almost unraceable the day he ran away with the Prix du Cadran at Longchamp in 1993 – he was probably the best stayer in Europe.

The limited number of horses which appear indifferent to the state of conditions underfoot tend to have consistent form and are reliable betting prospects. A case in point is the Italian-trained Misil, which in 1993 was placed in Group 1 events on both fast and heavy ground.

As a general rule, don't bet unless the horse has proven ability to act on the prevailing ground. Recalling the going preferences of both the sire and dam of the horse under review may help, but this is unsafe territory.

During the summer when the weather is settled, the results tend to become more predictable. The exception is on very firm ground. Three-year-olds are more inclined to remember a jarring experience on rock-hard going than two-year-olds and are sometimes disinclined to reproduce their form when returned to run on it. For this reason some professional backers strike a line through all potential bets if the ground is fast and will get involved only on going ranging from good to soft to good to firm.

The punter at the racetrack is in a position to check the action of his fancy as it canters to post in order to ascertain whether there are any signs of distress. Obviously horses with a history of leg trouble are not favoured by fast ground.

On heavy going horses find it more difficult to concede weight than on good going. Never underestimate how gruelling it can be to race in heavy ground. The bookies did before the 1980 Grand National, the last time the race was run on officially heavy going, and some friends and I were able to pull off a major coup by betting on the number of likely finishers. We stipulated six or fewer of the 30 starters would make it round and took prices from 16–1 downwards. After a real war of attrition, only the winner Ben Nevis and three others completed the course. As the second circuit ground on and the likelihood of the coup being landed increased, to my shame I was cheering every fall and refusal . . . but there was quite a bit of money involved. The bookies are now rarely so generous as far as these novelty bets on the Grand National are concerned.

Distance

The going will also have an effect on stamina. The six-furlong sprinter which has no trouble seeing out the trip under fast conditions may find itself rolling around with fatigue in the last 50 yards if the race is run on very soft ground.

Most horses have an optimum distance. On the Flat, there are, broadly, four distance categories: sprinters (five and six furlongs); milers; middle-distance horses (one mile two furlongs and a mile and a half); and stayers (one mile six furlongs and above). Over the jumps there are two bands: those who race at up to two and a half miles and those who race beyond that distance.

But it is unwise to be categoric about a horse's distance requirements. An inability to act on the ground will stop a horse from winning, however obvious his chance may otherwise be, while a horse that is fit and in form will often be able to win a race which is not run over its optimum distance.

There are two race distances, however, where it does pay to lay down some hard and fast rules: seven furlongs on the Flat and three miles over hurdles.

I find seven-furlong races a unique division in the racing calendar. Sprinters can rarely sustain their speed for the extra furlong, while milers find the trip on the sharp side. The betting market does not always reflect this fact. The 'in-between' distance of seven furlongs fosters specialists every season, of which two of the more celebrated have been Pitskelly and Salse. In the mid-1970s, Pitskelly was a top-class horse owned by TV magnate David Robinson and trained by Michael Jarvis; he won only at seven furlongs. More recently, the Henry Cecil-trained Salse, after making a successful racecourse debut over six furlongs, achieved the final seven wins of a splendid career over seven furlongs. I therefore back a horse in a seven-furlong race only when it has proven form at the distance. This has proved a rewarding policy over a number of seasons.

The three-mile trip over the sticks is also an interesting one because, in my experience, few horses truly stay it over hurdles, though they may go on to win over three miles plus when switched to chasing. Whether this is because hurdle races are run at a quicker pace than chases, or because it is easier to steal a breather during a chase, I don't know.

Many were prepared to bet that David Elsworth's Muse, who stayed two miles two furlongs well enough on the Flat to have finished sixth in the Tote Cesarewitch, would have the necessary stamina to last out the extended three miles of Ascot's Long Walk Hurdle in 1992. As he swung into the short home straight that day, already at the limit of his stamina, all that could be heard was the sound of his supporters' betting tickets being torn up.

As is the case in seven-furlong races, bet in three-mile hurdles only if your selection has proven form over the trip.

Contours and Pace

The ability of a horse to cope with the contours of a track is not as important a factor as the going or the distance but it has to be addressed nevertheless. In chapter 14, 'Britain's 59 Racecourses', I have highlighted each track's characteristics and which style of runner is best suited to them.

There is also the matter of the pace at which the race is run. If you are faced with two runners of equal merit, both running over their optimum distance, the pace at which the race is likely to be run could supply the casting vote. Firm going, or a small field with the likelihood of a slowly run race, would favour the challenger with the best turn of foot, whereas soft going, or a big field with the prospect of a strong gallop throughout the race, would favour the sounder stayer.

Draw

A final element to consider in Flat races – sometimes the most vital element of all – is the draw position in the starting stalls, which are always numbered from the left as the horses face out. Again, for chapter 14 I have compiled a comprehensive survey on the effect of the draw at our 35 Flat tracks.

Before completing your studies on each horse in a race you may already have unearthed four or five possible 'winners'; at that point strike out the race as a betting proposition. By all means note the outcome of such hard-fought races but wait for the race which throws up only one or two likeable candidates.

Just such a race was the 1993 Coral-Eclipse Stakes, run at Sandown over one mile two furlongs on firm ground and won bravely by Opera House.

4.05—CORAL-ECLIPSE STAKES (GROUP 1)
£147,760   1m 2f   (8)

1	(1)	2010-01 **ARCANGUES (US) (34)(D,T)** A Fabre in France 5 9 7
		T Jarnet	113
2	(5)	0653-62 **ENVIRONMENT FRIEND (30)(CandD)** N Wright 5 9 7
		G Duffield	111
3	(4)	0216-21 **GREAT PALM (US) (48)(D,F)** P Cole 4 9 7.........A Munro	107
4	(3)	10-13131 **KARINGA BAY (13)(D)** G L Moore 6 9 7..............B Rouse	106
5	(8)	0431-32 **MISIL (US)(D,T)** V Caruso in Italy 5 9 7.................L Dettori	110
6	(2)	6231-21 **OPERA HOUSE (30) (CandD)** M Stoute 5 9 7
		M J Kinane	111
7	(7)	11-4215 **BARATHEA (IRE)(S)** L Cumani 3 8 10..............M Roberts	115
8	(6)	111-110 ● **TENBY (31)(D)** H Cecil 3 8 10......................Pat Eddery ★116

PRICEWISE BEST MORNING ODDS: 9-4 Tenby (Ch,C,H,L,Su,T), 5-2 Barathea (D,H,L,T), 11-2 Opera House (D,L,T), 6 Arcangues (C), 12 Environment Friend (C,D), 20 Great Palm (C,D,L), 33 Misil (Ch,C,H,L,S,T), 66 Karinga Bay (CH,L,S).

1992: Kooyonga 4-9-4 W J O'Connor 7-2 fav (M Kauntze 12 ran.

My interest in the race was first aroused the evening before the race when the Pricewise odds from the *Racing Post* came into the *Daily Express* office. The Pricewise column has been one of the great success stories of the *Post* since it was launched. We thought so much of it at the *Express* that we decided to sponsor it. Basically, Pricewise collates the ante-post odds of the leading bookmakers in the principal races, pinpointing for punters the best prices available for each individual horse – and recommending the best-value bet.

When I saw that the Italian-trained Misil was languishing at 33–1 with, among others, William Hill, I was dumbstruck.

Here was a horse in the form of his life with the ability to show it on firm or heavy ground.

In his previous race over one mile one furlong on firm ground at Longchamp in the Group 1 Prix d'Ispahan, he had been beaten just one and a half lengths by Eclipse rival Arcangues at level weights. I had seen a recording of that race on the excellent monthly video magazine *Racing World* and recalled that, though outpaced by the winner when the pace quickened, Misil was hitting back hard when hampered close home. It made no difference to the result, but clearly there was little between Arcangues and Misil.

The time before that, in the Group 1 Prix Ganay, run over an extended mile and a quarter on heavy ground at Longchamp, Misil had finished three lengths behind Opera House when they were respectively second and third behind Vert Amande – the feature of Misil's performance again being the way he battled all the way to the line.

On a strict interpretation of the form book, Misil had a little to make up on both Opera House and Arcangues, but not as much as the odds suggested. Opera House was on offer at 9–2, Arcangues 11–2 and Misil, as I said, 33–1.

British punters and bookmakers alike are often guilty of rampant xenophobia. They have grown reluctantly to respect master French trainers like Fabre, the late Boutin and Head but they distrust the unfamiliar. To most punters Nessun Dorma might well have been the make of an orthopaedic bed until the World Cup 1990 theme came along, and the fact that Misil was trained by Vittorio Caruso, a name more familiar to those in the gods at La Scala than the Silver Ring at Sandown, left them unmoved. Even with popular jockey Frankie Dettori on board, riding at the peak of his powers, there were few overtures about Misil. But clearly he had the necessary Class A form and would not be inconvenienced by the going or the distance.

Opera House, on the other hand, was not sure to appreciate the switch back to a mile and a quarter and firm ground, after winning the Coronation Cup over two furlongs further.

I was getting quite excited about the chance of the genuine Group 1 raider from Milan, and as I told callers to our Bankroll service on the day of the race: 'Rarely do you get the opportunity to back such a good horse at these odds.'

Win or lose, this was a bet, and the 33–1 each-way was duly taken. With a little bit of luck in running it would have been a memorable coup, instead of just a profitable return. Essentially a horse who does not quicken but gallops on resolutely at the one pace, Misil was trapped in a pocket on the rails up the straight and when he got clear late inside the final furlong he could not quite make up the two lengths deficit on Opera House, going down by a rapidly diminishing short head.

FORM FROM HANDICAP RACES

Applying form from handicap races to conditions races, including maidens, is one of the most potent sources of winners that I know. Indeed, if the reader has the patient endurance of Job and would really like to restrict his bets to two or three a week, then throughout the whole season he would be as well to adhere to the rule: *Never back a horse in a maiden or conditions race unless it has shown good form in a handicap*.

What is good form in a handicap? I cannot lay down any precise guidelines but would suggest the reader refer back to our racecourse gradings in chapter 1 on 'The Form Book' and be directed by the following main considerations:

1 Class A conditions events require Class A handicap form;
2 Class B conditions events require Class A, B or C handicap form;
3 Class C conditions events require Class A, B, C or D handicap form;

4 Class D conditions events require Class A, B, C or D
   handicap form.

Note all handicap winners, or horses beaten not more than
four lengths, which carried at least nine stone. That form is
good enough to give them a solid each-way chance in a
conditions event at the grades set out above. The principles
apply to nurseries as well as handicaps for three-year-olds
and over.

The rules are not inflexible and it is for you to use your
judgement as to whether, for reasons of unusually high prize
money or a very good Timefigure, a particular handicap can
be treated as better than the band from which it comes.

For instance, only the very best Class A handicap form can
be considered for the Group 2 Vodafone Nassau Stakes at
Goodwood. On 31 July 1993, the race threw up the ideal
qualifier – Lyphard's Delta.

2.40—VODAFONE NASSAU STAKES (GROUP 2)
£42,490   1m 2f   (9)

1	(1)	523-004 FEMININE WILES (24)(D) P Chapple-Hyam 4 9 2 ..J Reid	99
2	(7)	1121-22 ONLY ROYALE (12)(D) L Cumani 4 9 2 ....R Cochrane	102
3	(2)	511-41 THAKAWIB (IRE)(44) J Dunlop 3 8 9.................W Carson	102
4	(6)	12-2 DANCING BLOOM (24)(F) M Stoute 3 8 6.........L Dettori	106
5	(3)	14-31 INSTANT AFFAIR (US) (14)(D) P Cole 3 8 6........T Quinn	91
6	(8)	4130-46 ● LOVE OF SILVER (US) (24)(D) C Brittain 3 8 6	
		G Duffield ★108	
7	(4)	2111 LYPHARD'S DELTA (US)(24)(D) H Cecil 3 8 6....W Ryan	91
8	(5)	150-100 MARILLETTE (US)(C,D) J Gosden 3 8 6...........L Piggott	102
9	(9)	14-134 SUEBOOG(IRE)(56) C Brittain 3 8 6...........W R Swinburn	105

PRICEWISE BEST MORNING ODDS: 7-2 Dancing Bloom (D,S,T), 4
Thawakib (T), Sueboog (D,H), 6 Only Royale (C), 17-2
Marillette,(S), 12 Lyphard's Delta (C), 20 Feminine Wiles (C,D), 25 Love Of Silver
(H), Instant Affair (C).
1992: Ruby Tiger 5-9-1 T Quinn 2-1 (P Cole) 7 ran.

In her previous race, this Henry Cecil-trained filly had won
the H.E. Limited Duke of Cambridge Handicap at Newmarket worth more than £20,000 to the winner. As I have
mentioned before, there is no stronger form than that
recorded at Newmarket and, in winning, Lyphard's Delta
had also recorded a solid Timefigure of 81.

Her winning weight – eight stone five pounds – was lighter
than ideal, but she did win the race a shade comfortably after

waiting until a suitable gap materialized, having been trapped behind other horses.

She had completed a hat-trick at Newmarket, was clearly still on the upgrade, and was prepared by the most successful trainer of the post-war period, Henry Cecil. Yet, despite these credentials, early birds with Corals could have secured 12–1 about Lyphard's Delta, who eventually started at 10–1.

In the race itself, she maintained her rapid improvement, always travelling smoothly and then producing a better turn of foot than Only Royale who followed her through to be second, beaten one and a half lengths.

In early-season conditions races, punters know little or nothing about the present fitness of horses. Some will have made tremendous strides over the winter while others may not have trained on at all. When the reader refers back to the two-year-old form – as he must – he is advised to pay special attention to form shown in nurseries at the Class A meetings.

When considering the current year's form, he should note particularly any horse that has run well in a three-year-old handicap and, although there will be very few of these early in the season, any horse that has run even reasonably well in an all-aged handicap.

Finally, the reader should make a list of all horses which have distinguished themselves in any three-year-old handicap. In particular he should include:

1 the winners of any handicap giving 14 pounds or more to the second and third horses, and
2 any horse which finished in the first six whose Timefigure is at least 14 pounds better than the winner's.

The really diligent punter can make four separate lists of these qualifiers – one for each class of meeting – and back these horses in conditions races at the same grades.

SELLERS

Selling races are an unreliable gambling medium. Selling platers are the least consistent group of horses, principally because they are often being prepared for coups. The normal criteria of class and time still apply, but the backer should pay particular attention to non-selling form. A horse can finish out of the first ten in a maiden and still be good enough to win a seller.

'Springers' – horses which suddenly plunge from a big price to a much shorter one – form a significant proportion of winners in sellers, especially two-year-old sellers. Readers should complete a list of trainers who successfully exploit this type of race. Merely to start your list, I suggest the following names: R. Akehurst; A. Bailey; M. W. Easterby; P. Evans; S. Kettlewell: J. S. Moore; T. Naughton; J. Pearce; Mrs J. Ramsden; N. Tinkler.

Selling races are occasionally underestimated by the official handicappers and the expert backer will find that form from such races can lead to winners in non-selling handicaps at generous odds. Newmarket sellers are the strongest in the country. Seek out solid handicap form, including selling handicap form.

CLAIMERS

There's a chance here to benefit from the expertise of the Jockey Club handicappers, particularly in the second half of the season when the form has settled down.

A trainer may feel aggrieved at the official rating given to his horse and decide that his only option is to run it in a claimer – a race in which the weight to be carried is directly related to the price at which the horse can be claimed by another owner. The lower the weight, the greater the risk that the trainer may lose the horse to an 'unfriendly' claim.

The Jockey Club ratings are now readily available – both in the *Racing Calendar* and in the *Sporting Life* or *Racing Post* – and it is fascinating to watch how close to the wind a trainer is prepared to sail in a bid to land the prize or a gambling coup.

In search of easy pickings, Jack Berry has regularly run up sequences with horses on unrealistically low weights in claimers, but that avenue was closed in 1993 when the Jockey Club introduced a rule stating that no individual horse could win more than three claimers in a single season.

The ability to recognize at an early stage that a particular race is going to prove a rich source of future winners is fundamental to successful punting. The two-year-old claiming race at Newcastle on Northumberland Plate day is becoming a strong race of its type. Atmospheric Blues, runner-up in 1991, was later placed in Listed company, and the 1992 winner Captain Le Saux subsequently finished second in a £100,000 event in Ireland.

CLASSICS

It would be remiss to conclude any examination of conditions events without a specific look at our five Classic races: the One Thousand Guineas, Two Thousand Guineas, Derby, Oaks and St Leger. In chapter 17, 'Principal Races', I have looked at each race statistically, highlighting any recurring trends, but here I will expand on them more generally.

The first point to underline is that they are a superb betting medium. Classics are run at level weights, apart from any fillies' allowance, and usually the best horse wins. Famous races though they are, they should be treated like any other stakes race. The difference between the winner of a modest three-year-old seller and the Derby is about £445,000 in prize money and the equivalent of 40 lengths in ability, but the methods for selecting the winner in each case are identical.

So our normal rules about class and time apply: only support a horse in a Classic which has excellent winning Class A form backed up by a good Timefigure.

One Thousand Guineas/Two Thousand Guineas

The first two Classics come early in the season and to a large extent we have to rely on juvenile form, in other words form which is several months out of date. Despite this, there are rarely any unpleasant surprises – since 1980 only three horses have won either Guineas race with a starting price longer than 10–1.

The European Free Handicap, run over seven furlongs of Newmarket's one-mile Guineas course, was formerly an important trial for these races, but for some 30 years only Privy Councillor (1962) and the filly Mrs McArdy (1977) completed the Free Handicap – Guineas double. However, this race may just be enjoying a renaissance as a Classic trial, because four of its last six winners have gone on to make the first three in the Two Thousand Guineas, including the 1991 winner Mystiko.

To sum up: look for a horse with very good two-year-old form which has proved his or her well-being with a successful outing in the current season.

Derby

Many pundits believe the Derby is won at stud and it is hard to disagree with this notion. Nine of the last 12 winners have raced in the colours of their wealthy breeders. The Derby is simply never won by a horse that doesn't have the richest bloodlines.

I pass on a formula for finding the Derby winner which has proved successful on 38 occasions since the war. Inevitably, it is based on breeding: *in the Derby, consider only a horse whose sire and maternal grandsire (sire of the dam) both won over ten furlongs or more*.

When thoughts turn to the Epsom course they usually centre on the world-famous downhill run to Tattenham Corner, but it should not be forgotten that not only the finish but also the first five furlongs of the race are uphill. And they never hang about in the early stages of the Derby.

The theory at the core of our breeding blueprint is that horses with suspect stamina do not win the Derby. The predominance of speedier American bloodlines among the winners caused the system to break down during the late 1980s – Shahrastani's dam was by the sprinter Thatch – while back-to-back scorers Kahyasi and Nashwan were non-qualifiers owing to the position in their pedigrees of Blushing Groom, who himself failed to stay at Epsom. But I'm delighted to say that the 1993 Derby result was again a rousing success for the formula with 15–2 winner Commander In Chief and 150–1 runner-up Blue Judge coming from just a handful of qualifiers.

The moral here is to remain faithful to successful betting techniques until the ever-changing character of racing renders them obsolete. As with the Guineas, the Derby is not a race for shock results – there have been only two winning SPs above 10–1 in the last 20 years.

To sum up: look for a successful late-developing type which showed promise as a two-year-old, if not perhaps in the top class, and one which fits the breeding formula.

Oaks

The Oaks is the least predictable of all five Classics, not simply because it is contested exclusively by fillies but also because the fields tend to be smaller than those for the Derby and the race is not always truly run. For that reason, our

Derby formula cannot successfully be adopted. Though the general trend is for market leaders to dominate, there has been a smattering of surprises.

St Leger

If you choose to bet in just one Classic, be sure it is the St Leger. Eight of the last 12 favourites have obliged, making it the easiest Classic in which to find the winner.

Traditionally the Great Voltigeur Stakes, run at the York Ebor meeting three and a half weeks prior to Doncaster, is the best trial, though, Bob's Return in 1993 apart, its influence has been on the wane in recent years. I suspect we should not write off the Voltigeur as a guide, and those who back the York winner and runner-up (unless beaten five lengths or more) will probably show a healthy profit in the Leger over a period of time.

Chapter Four

Handicaps

'There are two times in a man's life when he shouldn't bet in handicaps – when he can't afford it, and when he can.' With apologies for the mischievous plagiarism of Mark Twain, I believe the advice holds good for all but the most accomplished backer.

A handicap is a race in which the horses are allotted such weights as will theoretically give them all equal chances of winning. Handicaps come in three forms: rated stakes; standard handicaps, including nurseries; and maiden handicaps.

The handicapper is a paid official of the British Horseracing Board and is an expert reader both of the form book and of what he sees on the racecourse. Horses are not machines, but the many close finishes we see are a tribute to the skills of the current crop of handicappers – Messrs Gibbs, Tester, Gray, Dangar, Arkwright, Winlaw, Mordaunt, Judge and Gardiner-Hill. Only a super-optimist attempts to 'beat' them.

IF YOU MUST . . .

To the Golden Rule: Never Bet In Handicaps there are, however, three exceptions, but only for the really knowledgeable student of form – which in my view means fewer than one punter in a hundred. All three exceptions apply to form shown in handicaps; under no circumstances take conditions races form into handicaps.

In the old days, the handicapper was required to set weights some three weeks before the actual race, leaving plenty of time for form to be established which was not available to him. Since the recent introduction of the five-day entry system, the incidence of these special cases has been much reduced, but there are still examples of horses which run 'within the date of the handicap' – that is to say, after the weights have been published.

To assist the reader I have compiled the table below which indicates the maximum number of days a horse can have run since being assessed by the handicapper, depending on which day of the week it is racing.

Mon.	Tues.	Wed.	Thurs.	Fri.	Sat.
8	9	10	11	12	6

Use this table in conjunction with the 'days since last ran' figure next to the horse's name in the *Daily Express* race-cards and you will be able to tell at a glance which horses have the potential to upset the handicapper's careful calculations. Runners on Thursday and Friday have had the most opportunities to run since being handicapped; those on Saturday the least, another reason for treading very carefully on the week's busiest day.

Winners since the framing of the weights are often penalized, and occasionally such horses have won so well that the trainer decides to try his luck again before the handicapper has a chance for reassessment. So the first exception to the rule Never Bet In Handicaps is when backing – *a horse whose penalty does not sufficiently reflect the merit of the win*.

Handicaps run over a mile and a quarter to a mile and a half provide the best opportunities under this heading to the informed punter. More horses seem to carry penalties successfully over this distance than over any other. In sprints one is always at the mercy of 'luck in running'. A horse that becomes boxed in during a sprint is handicapped far more than it would be in a long-distance race.

In 1993, Alderbrook was cleverly placed by Julie Cecil to set up an old-fashioned sequence of five straight wins, all of them over a mile and a quarter. On his first outing of the season, 5–1 chance Alderbrook won the Saltwood Handicap at Folkestone on 6 April by a 'comfortable' neck from Here He Comes, with the third horse ten lengths further behind. Here He Comes was receiving 29 pounds and had the benefit of a previous winning performance. Clearly this was an improved effort by Alderbrook and it came as no surprise when, six days later, he was able to defy a five-pound penalty at odds of 11–8 in a similar handicap at Warwick.

A word of warning, though; if the win appeared to come as a surprise to connections (SP 12–1 or better) and reflected a level of achievement out of sync with the balance of the horse's other form, don't back it next time at greatly clipped odds, however captivating the winning performance seems. Or, as the old racing saw puts it more colourfully – If You Missed The Wedding, Don't Go To The Funeral.

Even more soundly based is our second exception, backing – *a winner without a penalty*.

These winners are of three types: winners of races below the value specified to warrant a penalty; horses that after finishing first were disqualified; and winners of apprentice handicaps. A degree of caution is advised in following apprentice-race winners; there is often a wide range of jockeyship on display and they may not always be reliable indicators of form.

At Sandown on 21 July 1993, Joe Naughton's Comanche Companion, the 9–2 favourite, romped home in a 15-runner apprentice race by five lengths. Six days later, on similarly soft going at Goodwood, Comanche Companion was unpenalized in an open handicap with his apprentice rider Tony Garth this time able to claim his five-pound allowance. Backed down to favouritism at 5–1, Comanche Companion was clear halfway up the straight and never looked like losing.

Our last exception is probably the most important, but one that can be of value only to the expert: backing – *a placed horse whose running represented an improvement in form*.

A classic example of the above rule produced one of my most satisfying bets of 1993 – on Friday 13 August as it happens – and fortunately proved a winner for followers of Scotia and Bankroll as well.

5.45—SUTTON APPRENTICE HANDICAP
£2,724　　　1m4f　　　(12)

1	(7)	-42111 **SUNDERLAND ECHO**(15)(D,S) Mrs M Reveley 4 10 0		
			Darren Moffatt	73
2	(12)	00010-P **KHALID**(13)(D) D Gandolfo 4 10 0 ....**V Slattery**		73
3	(3)	0-6001 **MOSHAAJIR**(US)(12) C Smith 3 9 6(5lbex) ....**K Rutter**		73
4	(5)	265003 ● **BIGWHEEL BILL** (27)(D) J Watts 4 9 1		
			Stephen Davies	★74
5	(6)	002220 **KADASTROF**(21) R Dickin 3 9 0 ....**M Thomas**(7)		73
6	(9)	005324 **HILLZAH**(22)(D) R Bastiman 5 8 10 ....**H Bastiman**(3)		65
7	(11)	030245 **WESTFIELD MOVES**(4)(F) H J Collingridge 5 8 9		
			C Hawksley(3)	66
8	(8)	425431 **ROUSITTO** (7) R Hollinshead 5 8 7(5lbex) ....**J Dennis**(5)		60
9	(2)	0-1350 **DEB'S BALL** (21)(D) D Moffatt 7 8 6 ....**L Newton**		62
10	(4)	020203 **BAHER** (161) Mrs A Swinbank 4 8 3 ......**Carol Davison**(7)		73
11	(1)	265603 **GREEN'S CASSATT** (6) W Brisbourne 5 8 0 ....**A Garth**		60
12	(10)	021d35 **DON'T FORGET MARIE** (6) (CandD) A Bailey 3 8 0		
			D Wright	56

Daily Express Betting Forecast:— 13-8 Sunderland Echo, 3 Bigwheel Bill, 5 Rousitto, 7 Moshaajir, 8 Green's Cassatt, Hillzah, 10 others
1992: No corresponding race.

The Sutton Apprentice Handicap at Haydock was a mile-and-a-half race for three-year-olds and upwards. The conditions of the race stated that wins after 31 July should incur a five-pound penalty. Its being run on a Friday meant that any horse to have run in the previous 12 days had not been fully evaluated by the handicapper, and three horses – Moshaajir, Rousitto and Green's Cassatt – appeared to have shown improved form 'within the date of the handicap'.

Moshaajir's win came in a handicap at Lingfield's inaugural Sunday trial meeting, for which no SPs were returned. But the Tote odds of 123–1 suggested the victory came as a shock to all concerned and was to be treated with a degree of caution. So, too, the success of professional loser Rousitto under an artful ride from Walter Swinburn at Redcar seven days previously. The likelihood of his gaining a back-to-back win in the hands of an inexperienced apprentice was slim. Green's Cassatt's chance was another matter. On her previous start, in an interesting four-runner handicap at Redcar on 7 August, she was the outsider at 7–1, a price that seemed accurately to reflect her chance against opponents who had all been in recent winning form.

I saw the mile-and-a-quarter Redcar race and was most taken by the performance of Green's Cassatt. She passed the hat-trick-seeking Essex Girl in the closing stages and was staying on stoutly at the finish, beaten just four lengths by the winner May Hill's Legacy. An improved effort, not surprising for a mare at this time of year. What's more, Green's Cassatt had recently been confirmed in foal to the stallion Hubbly Bubbly, and it is uncanny how impending motherhood elicits improvement in a mare's racecourse achievement.

Win or lose, then, Green's Cassatt was going to be a bet.

Likely favourite Sunderland Echo had been re-handicapped since his latest win 15 days ago and, in any case, as I told Bankroll callers on the day, Sunderland Echo takes some stoking along and is not the ideal mount for an apprentice. I drew up the betting forecast for the *Daily Express*, making Sunderland Echo a 13–8 chance with Green's Cassatt at 8–1. Given that I estimated Green's Cassatt would win the race three times in every 10 runnings, an 8–1 SP would earn a 17 points rating on my expected value grid (see chapter 7, 'The Search for Value'). In other words, she looked a spanking good each-way bet.

I didn't know there was better to come. Moshaajir was withdrawn on the day, yet Green's Cassatt still went off at

12–1, with Sunderland Echo the 7–4 favourite. Under a patient ride from Tony Garth – that boy again – Green's Cassatt had little difficulty in winning by a length and a half. Go on my girl!

THREE-YEAR-OLD HANDICAPS

Three-year-old handicaps are almost as difficult to solve as all-aged handicaps, but here are a few guiding principles.

First, three-year-olds find great difficulty in conceding much weight over a distance further than a mile.

Second, during a severe winter, fillies do not make the same progress as colts and geldings. They appreciate the sun and do not come into their own until the late summer. 'Global warming', the 'greenhouse effect', call it what you will, but the recent mild winters have, to a certain extent, negated the effect of this rule.

Third, horses that have endured busy campaigns as two-year-olds are rarely as effective at three. I suggest that at the start of the season readers make a list of lightly raced colts (up to five runs) that have run well – that is to say, have either won or been beaten not more than four lengths – in five- and six-furlong nurseries at Newmarket, Ascot, Doncaster, Kempton, Newbury, Sandown and York the previous year. Backing these colts blindly in handicaps regularly makes a level-stake profit. Be careful if any qualifier is allotted minimum weight; it may be out of the handicap, a point highlighted in the *Daily Express* racecard. A fancied horse can sometimes get away with carrying a pound or two more than the handicapper intended, but rarely more.

Some three-year-old handicaps are limited to fillies only. They should be avoided, as fillies' form can be mercurial.

NURSERIES

Nurseries – handicaps for two-year-olds – now begin as early as July and have long been regarded as the backers' graveyard . . . with plenty of justification. Given the limited data available, they are the most difficult for the handicapper to assess, especially when it has patently been the intention of the owner and trainer to bamboozle him. A series of easy races in maidens, perhaps over an inadequate trip, leaves the handicapper little option but to give the horse concerned a low rating. Hey presto! Fit to race for perhaps the first time and significantly backed in the ring, our contender lands a gamble – a shock to all except those privy to the coup.

Or so it went until recent years. Since the advent of SIS in the betting shops, with its coverage of racing from many different cameras as well as the race-reading by the Timeform Organization and their ilk, the number of horses entertained unawares has been drastically reduced.

My general advice to the novice, however, remains not to back in these races. The exceptions have been highlighted earlier in this chapter.

MAJOR HANDICAPS

The major handicaps provide irresistible fascination for the average backer. Not for nothing are many of them sponsored by bookmakers. Were they Olympic dives, the major handicaps would have a degree of difficulty of 3.8.

Most of these races are throwbacks to the days before the five-day entry system and are termed 'early closing handicaps'. What this means, in effect, is that there are more qualifiers under our 'form within the date of the handicap' terms. More qualifiers mean more choice; more choice means difficult decisions.

For those dyed-in-the-wool punters who must bet in the big handicaps, I have drawn some conclusions based on the statistical record of previous years' results in chapter 17, 'Principal Races'.

Chapter Five

Hurdles and Chases

When those stalwarts of the jumping game, David Nicholson and Josh Gifford, eventually saddled their first winners at the Cheltenham National Hunt Festival, the winner's enclosure was awash with tears.

For local trainer Nicholson, the exasperating gap in his career record was breached in the most unlikely fashion by 66–1 chance Solar Cloud in the Daily Express Triumph Hurdle of 1986. Two years later Nicholson, more predictably, won the Blue Riband event of the week, the Cheltenham Gold Cup, with Charter Party and since then 'the Duke', complete with trademark red socks, has regularly led in Festival winners.

Gifford's wait had been even longer than Nicholson's. He endured no fewer than eight seconds over 16 years at the Festival until Golden Minstrel won the Kim Muir Memorial Cup in 1988. It was a case of 'after the famine, the feast' for Gifford, who, as if released from some terrible burden, saddled the first and second, Vodkatini and Clay Hill, in the Grand Annual Chase 40 minutes later, and then clinched the top trainer honours at the meeting when Pragada won the Coral Hurdle Final the following day.

National Hunt racing gets under the skin of even hardened pros in a way quite unlike the Flat. There is unquestionably more drama and spectacle in a high-class steeplechase and jump racing's fans can take added pleasure from the fact that their equine heroes are around for that much longer.

Sadly, Champion National Hunt horses often pay the ultimate price: Dawn Run, the Irish mare who assumed almost mythical status when completing the first Champion Hurdle – Gold Cup double, ended her days in a French abattoir after crashing in the Auteuil equivalent of our Champion Hurdle, while big-race favourite Alverton, the 1979 Gold Cup winner, was one of half a dozen horses to be killed as a result of falls at Becher's Brook in Grand Nationals between 1975 and 1989.

The dangers are never far from the minds of those men who ride steeplechasers for £80 a time – £22 more than the Flat boys, which many, myself included, think is not a big enough differential. Is it any wonder that, in addition to injury and weight problems, even the best jump jockeys can eventually lose their enthusiasm for yet another novice chase? Two of the greatest post-war exponents of the art of race-riding, John Francome and Peter Scudamore, were both candid enough to admit that dwindling motivation played a part in their decisions to retire – and we think no less of them because of it.

Whether it is Dunkirk or a local hosepipe ban, adversity binds people together, and there is no greater bonhomie than in a weighing room full of jump jockeys. The sport is full of characters and the appreciation of these hard men and the risks they take is one of its greatest attractions.

Jumping's appeal to the casual racegoer or armchair viewer is self-evident, then, but what about the punter? Despite the fact that obstacles have to be cleared, more favourites win over jumps than on the Flat (39.5 per cent to 36.2 per cent). Many Flat races are palpably unfair, with a horse's chance governed by its position in the draw or whether it picks the best ground on which to mount its challenge. A personal view is that in National Hunt racing you always get a 'good, clean fight' with fair results.

The creed laid out in earlier chapters applies with equal force in jumping. You must still establish whether the horse has the ability to win and is fit enough to do so; if it will be suited by the ground and distance; and whether it is likely to appreciate the contours of the track and the pace at which the race is run. The importance of some of these elements is amplified over the sticks, and there are also a number of new factors which are peculiar to the winter game.

JUMPING ABILITY

The first cardinal rule for punters during the National Hunt season is: Never Back a Moderate Jumper. How many times have you heard a punter say: 'He only has to jump round to win'? In a chase, don't be tempted. The horse may have a stone in hand on the form book, but the number of errors a clumsy jumper will make is usually difficult to overcome.

The availability of the SIS pictures gives ample opportunity to see for ourselves how horses jump. So back only those horses which you know can hurdle or fence well. Winners are not immune from criticism – novice chases in the early part of the season are often so poorly contested that an easy win can be gained despite an inept round of jumping. The winner is sure to meet his come-uppance against more severe competition or when tried at a tougher track. Horses can get away with murder jumping hurdles but not steeplechase fences.

Don't be put off if a horse appears clueless about his jumping early on in his career – young horses have the propensity to improve – but scc the evidence for yourself before risking your cash. Peter Easterby, who has trained winners of both the Champion Hurdle and the Cheltenham Gold Cup, says: 'Give me a horse which gets it wrong to start with; when they get it right, they often end up better than the ones that take to it straight away. The naturals usually have a flaw to appear somewhere.'

The horse who 'pings' every jump on the schooling ground learns nothing. That's why a first-rate schooling jockey like John White, who 'won' the Grand National that never was on Esha Ness in 1993, would deliberately put his horses 'into the bottom' of the practice fences in order to teach them how to 'fiddle'. Any horse can jump well when it meets a fence in its stride but there will be a time in every race when, whether because it has been unsighted or had a disagreement with its pilot on the approach to take-off, the horse will need to improvise. It's here that the beast who looked flashy and extravagant at home, but has not been given thorough coaching, may make a bad mistake and fall. Such an error is likely to destroy confidence and in a young, impressionable horse that could take 12 months to return.

The reader should pay strict attention to those trainers who have excellent chase records, like Mary Reveley, Jimmy FitzGerald and Nicky Henderson. In the Lambourn area, no one schools more regularly than Henderson, and that groundwork pays dividends on the track. After doing a stable swop with Peter Walwyn a couple of years back, some of the early Henderson runners made uncharacteristic mistakes. This Nicky put down to the softer schooling fences at his new base, so he had them rebuilt and very quickly the Henderson jumping polish returned.

Finally, on the subject of jumping ability, be wary about accepting hard luck stories. The horse that falls at the third last with the race at its mercy is inevitably well backed to make amends next time, but these 'unlucky' losers constantly let their supporters down again. So much can happen in the last half-mile of a jump race, it is usually safer to rely on what actually happened rather than what might have been.

JOCKEYSHIP

'Too much is made of all this riding over the last and on the run-in. Races are won and lost out in the country. How many photo-finishes are there over jumps? It is more important to be a good horseman than to be especially strong on the run-in. But of course, it is a help if you can do both.'

The words belong to Jeff King, as uncompromising a jockey as there has ever been.

Undoubtedly, jump races are won by jockeys with, to put it politely, highly individual styles. However, losing rhythm with the horse at the finish is not the heinous crime it might be on the Flat. John Francome, for example, was never considered to be an effective finisher but he more than made up for that by the way he presented his horses at fences – expertise honed in the show-jumping arena – and the tactical race-riding skills he developed throughout his career.

Over jumps, and in particular over fences, a good jockey can make an average horse look good, whereas a good horse can be inhibited by an average jockey. That's not so marked on the Flat, where in many cases the jockey just has to sit and steer to get a result. So if a workaday jockey beats a top one over the jumps, make a special note of that horse's performance.

FLAT FORM

Former Test cricketer Denis Compton also played soccer with Arsenal to the highest level. But the original 'Brylcreem Boy' was the exception; as soccer is to cricket, so Flat racing is to jumping – a totally different sport. Season after season the large sums paid for horses off the Flat rarely prove money well spent. Success at the jumping game is hardly ever bought.

The best Flat horse I've ever known go jumping was Admetus, winner of the 1974 Washington International at Laurel Park when that race carried the cachet now reserved for the Breeders' Cup. On the European classifications for older horses that year, only the brilliant mare Dahlia was rated more highly. Four years later his owner Sir Michael Sobell made the curious decision to put Admetus into training for a hurdles campaign. He could not have chosen more able schoolmasters than trainer Fred Winter and jockey John Francome, but Admetus was not sighted in all four attempts and was then summarily retired to a stud career in Switzerland.

One of the greatest hurdlers of all time was Persian War, winner of the Champion Hurdle in three successive seasons and runner-up when he attempted an unprecedented fourth win in 1971. He was raced a number of times on the Flat during the period he dominated the hurdling scene, and on a couple of occasions he was well backed to win. On the Flat, though, he could hardly get out of his own way – Timeform described him as a 'moderate staying handicapper'.

There are exceptions, of course. Sea Pigeon ran in the Derby, later won the Ebor Handicap and took the Champion Hurdler's title at his fourth attempt. But there is generally little correlation between Flat and jumping form, so wipe the blackboard clean especially when faced with juvenile hurdlers. Horse A may be able to beat Horse B by 20 lengths on the level, but put eight flights of hurdles in the way and the outcome is all too often totally different.

PADDOCK INSPECTION

If you have become attuned to looking at Flat horses over a number of months then switching your focus to big, brawny chasers can be quite off-putting. Compared to their smaller, lighter Flat counterparts, chasers can give the impression of carrying too much condition and winners can easily be missed in the early part of the season through the mistaken belief that a horse is not fit.

This is where the benefit of knowing old friends comes into its own. After a couple of full seasons' racing you should have a clear picture about the preferences, in terms of going and distance, of any handicap hurdler or chaser. It's then a question of deciding when all the positive factors come together to constitute a bet. That old handicapper may look too big and well to do himself justice but if that's the way he looked when winning at a similar stage in previous seasons then the trainer has probably got his condition just right again.

The paddock will also reveal whether your selection is built for the job. Size may be immaterial on the Flat but it is important over jumps, especially at the major tracks, where the fences are more substantial.

INJURIES

Rarely does the steeplechaser not have at least one lengthy period on the sidelines during its career, often losing as much as one year in three. Most are carrying injuries of one sort or another. The 'wheels' are the most susceptible and leg bandages are commonplace, sometimes masking the tell-tale signs of a firing operation which would indicate that a horse has had time off games with a sprained tendon.

Wind problems are the next most common cause of a horse being out of action. The giant Party Politics, who won the 1992 Grand National, has had a chequered history of breathing difficulties. To remedy these he has had the conventional Hobday operation and then a much more difficult one known as the 'tie back'. When his problems recurred before the 1992/3 season, owing to a paralysis on the left side of his larynx, the last resort of 'tubing' was undertaken. As the name suggests, this involves a metal tube being inserted into the windpipe through which the horse can breathe when the oxygen supply from the upper airways is reduced. Such an operation is rarely a permanent solution, though Party Politics won his first race after being tubed and finished an excellent second in the 1995 Grand National.

Don't underestimate the wear and tear on a jumper. If a horse runs a good race after a long lay-off, be very wary about backing it next time. Not only will you have to accept a much reduced price but the patched-up injury will all too often resurface. Remember our 50-day rule – if a horse has been absent for that length of time and there is no obvious reason (unsuitable ground, for instance), then we can safely assume there has been a physical problem and the horse may not be 100 per cent when next it appears.

BREEDING

I have taken an in-depth look at breeding in chapter 12, so here I shall limit myself to its role in jump racing.

The vast majority of what are perceived to be jumping stallions never saw a hurdle or chase fence in their lives (Deep Run being a notable exception). Their assumed role has a lot to do with economics. No breeder looking to produce a jumper would pay more than £2,000 for the services of a stallion, while a top Flat sire can command £100,000 per cover. The guaranteed ability to pass on the admirable traits of stamina and toughness – those staples of the jumper – are just not considered fashionable today.

So in many cases the jumping element in a pedigree has been introduced by the distaff (female) side of the pedigree. There are numerous 'families' that produce winner after winner in the National Hunt division and the reader will profit by making a study of them. One such group which is easy to spot are the horses bearing the 'Dove' suffix – a successful breed for some 30 years now. The latest notable representative is Flakey Dove, who won the 1994 Champion Hurdle. Her dam Shadey Dove won nine races over hurdles, while her granddam Red Dove recorded no fewer than 18 victories.

I have fond memories of Flakey Dove from the Aintree meeting in 1992, when she landed a nice 7–1 touch for Bankroll followers in the Cordon Bleu Handicap Hurdle. Having won cosily the previous week in a competitive Ascot handicap hurdle, she justified a bet as a horse 'whose penalty did not sufficiently reflect the merit of the win' (see chapter 4, 'Handicaps'). Her being a member of the famous Dove family didn't exactly put me off, either.

COURSES

Taking account of the characteristics of a course and how they may affect your selection is not a factor exclusive to jump racing, but it is relatively more important during the winter. Stamina assumes greater significance: if you think of a tough track it will invariably host National Hunt racing. Cheltenham, Hexham and Towcester race only over the sticks, while tough finishing climbs at Ascot, Newcastle and Carlisle share racing under both codes.

It is not just the topography of the track that should concern us, but the type of fences also. Kelso puts on much less valuable racing than Doncaster but the fences at the Borders track are stiffer and take a great deal more jumping. It should also be remembered that on tight tracks like Aintree's Mildmay course, Bangor and Newton Abbot, as well as the three all-weather tracks, the emphasis is on jumping. The pace is usually frenctic, there is little time to relax between obstacles and the fields are never far away from a turn, so jumping errors are more costly than on tracks with long straights. It is for that reason that famous course specialists – Certain Justice, Prince Carlton and Suluk – have thrived on tight tracks.

GOING

The influence of the going is probably more marked at the winter game than during the summer on the level; for one thing the races are longer so the horses spend more time actually racing on the ground. Also, the incidence of extremes of going is greater, with the consequence that more specialists at either end of the going spectrum come to the fore.

The small Chepstow stable of Milton Bradley has enjoyed tremendous success with horses whose legs appeared indifferent to racing on rock-hard going at the beginning and end of the season. Bradley's Grey Dolphin was the most prolific winner of the 1983/4 jumps season, collecting no fewer than 10 handicap chases, while a few years earlier Mighty Marine employed almost identical front-running tactics to record a career total of 23 wins.

The high-class Brown Lad, meanwhile, is not the only Irish chaser to relish a bog, as he showed when winning two of his three Irish Grand Nationals. In the period just after Brown Lad came Master Smudge, whose hippo-like preference for mud happily coincided with two consecutive years, 1979 and 1980, when the Cheltenham Festival was run on heavy ground. On the first occasion, Master Smudge won the Sun Alliance Chase by five lengths at 16–1, and 12 months later this out-and-out stayer stormed up the hill in the Gold Cup to finish a gallant second to Tied Cottage; he was subsequently awarded steeplechasing's top prize when the Irish-trained winner failed a dope test.

FRONT-RUNNERS

There is often an audible groan in betting shops when a popular fancy makes the running on the Flat and in most cases the misgivings are justified. Unless run at Ayr, Sandown or York, middle-distance races are rarely won by front-runners. This is not the case over the jumps, where a higher percentage of pace-setters are successful – and I'm not merely thinking about the runners from the Martin Pipe stable which habitually make the running to capitalize on their superior fitness.

It makes sense to lead in jump races. The jockey can dictate the speed at which he jumps the obstacles and gets a clear sight of every one – very important in novice chases – and he doesn't run the risk of being brought down or caught up in any mêlée as a result of his opponents' mistakes. There is also the not inconsiderable advantage of being able to take the shortest route possible by hugging the inside rail. So do not be put off if your fancy is a habitual front-runner over fences.

RATINGS

In an effort to produce more competitive racing, every jumper in training was raised ten pounds in the official ratings from 9 October 1993. A major review of jump racing found that there had been a marked drop in the level of the average rating in recent years. In consequence, the number of horses which raced off the ten stone minimum weight, but still carried more than the handicapper would have desired in relation to the other horses, increased.

By raising the overall handicap structure artificially by ten pounds and modifying some of the ratings bands for handicaps, a large number of horses have been freed to run off their true rating, which should lead to fewer one-sided races contested by small fields.

BUMPERS

National Hunt Flat races (bumpers) have long been an integral part of Irish racing but are a relatively new phenomenon over here. They are limited to those horses who have not previously run on the Flat and are therefore popular and often oversubscribed, with slow-maturing jumping-bred types taking their first faltering footsteps on the racecourse. Like races on the Flat, they have little bearing on races in which obstacles have to be jumped – after all, the incomparable Arkle's record in bumpers reads two runs, two defeats – and are best treated as a little world of their own. They can, none the less, throw up a decent wager or two.

Of the eight bumper races which have been run at either the Cheltenham or the Aintree Festival, two of them have been won by Jimmy FitzGerald, a superlative effort given the powerful Irish challenge. Watch out for any bumper horse trained by 'Fitzy'.

THE BIG ONES

To finish this chapter, let's have a look at jumping's Classic races, the Champion Hurdle and the Cheltenham Gold Cup, as well as the most famous steeplechase in the world, the Grand National.

The Champion Hurdle

The most vivid memory of my first visit to Cheltenham's corridor of fame concerned the exhibit for the Champion Hurdle, the supreme championship test for our hurdlers. Watching recordings of past Champions rammed home how often it is the same faces battling it out up that final hill.

There have been four triple champions – Hatton's Grace, Sir Ken, Persian War and See You Then – and in the 20-year period between 1968 and 1987 there were only 11 individual champions. High-class winning form is essential, but potential champs are usually kept fresh for the big day with no more than four runs in the current season. Though the familiar names crop up year after year, two historical pointers to remember are that only Comedy Of Errors has ever regained his crown (1973 and 1975) and that not since Sea

Pigeon (1980) has a placed runner the previous year won the Champion.

The Cheltenham Gold Cup

The Cheltenham Gold Cup is our championship race for staying chasers. The record number of wins in the race (five) is held by Golden Miller, but there can be little debate that the greatest chaser of all time was Arkle, winner in 1964, 1965 and 1966.

Bought for 1,150 guineas by Anne, Duchess of Westminster, and named after a Scottish landmark, he was trained by Tom Dreaper of Kilsallaghan and ridden in all his 26 races over fences by Pat Taaffe. He won 22 of them, including the three Gold Cups, and would surely have surpassed Golden Miller's record had not injury ended his career when he was in his prime.

No other chaser has ever come close to matching Arkle's margin of superiority over his contemporaries, but there have been some stirring Gold Cups since his day, none more so than Desert Orchid's only win at the Cheltenham Festival in 1989 and the achievement of Dawn Run, who in 1986 became the first horse versatile enough to complete the Champion Hurdle–Gold Cup double.

From a punters' point of view, remember that, as with the Champion Hurdle, no horse in the last decade has won the Gold Cup after being placed the previous year, and no horse since L'Escargot (1970–1) has won back-to-back Gold Cups. Also, surprisingly for a championship race, only two favourites have won in the last 10 years.

The Grand National

There is always a story connected with the Grand National:

Foinavon emerging from the mêlée at the 23rd fence in 1967 to record the race's most improbable success; Red Rum winning for an unprecedented third time in 1977; victory in 1981 for Aldaniti and his jockey Bob Champion who had fought and won his battle against cancer; and, of course, the confusion at the start of the 1993 race which led to its being declared void. The Grand National's primacy among British chases has slipped since the development of the Gold Cup, but it retains its popular appeal among punters, eight million of whom try to find the winner every year.

Nowadays, thanks to the remodelling (some say emasculation) of the course, it is no longer a lottery, but being a handicap it's still fairly unpredictable – only one favourite (Grittar, 1982) has won in the last 20 years.

Two other facts to note are that no winner in the last decade has carried more than 11 stone, and of the last 44 horses to make the frame, 33 have been in the handicap proper – so you can draw a line through a vast number of no-hopers.

Neither Arkle nor Desert Orchid was risked in the National, but, like Red Rum, the third jumper to achieve hero status in the public's eye, they shared the qualities which draw people to racing and were once admirably summed up by American ace jockey Steve Cauthen: 'Part of why people love racing is they like to see the characteristics in horses they'd like to have for themselves – courage and lots of guts and desire.'

Chapter Six

All-Weather Racing

All-weather racing has provided a burst of sunshine for punters. Not only is it the ideal medium for the novice backer but it is perfect for the punter who, due to lack of time, has to focus his efforts on a limited number of races each day. Form holds up well, winners come from a small pool of predictable and fancied horses, and it fosters course specialists like no racecourse on turf.

The bane of punters is unpredictable going. Results make sense during a prolonged period when the ground remains the same, and there is nothing more infuriating than to see your wager beaten because it has ended up on a part of the course which is palpably slower than elsewhere.

No such problems exist on the Fibresand circuit at Southwell or on Lingfield's Equitrack. The going is almost without fail rated as 'standard' at both venues and is harrowed and prepared before every race so that a uniform, consistent racing surface is provided. With no minor undulations, horses of all actions stride out on it with confidence – good news for the horse and the punter.

All-weather racing as a punters' paradise received a ringing endorsement when the schedules for the SIS televised coverage were drawn up for 1991. With the encouragement of the Jockey Club, the bookies had shown virtually every all-weather meeting since its October 1989 inception. But when it became clear that a high percentage of fancied horses were winning on sand and that punters were growing to like it, was it a coincidence that SIS pruned back all-weather meetings from their filming programme in favour of nondescript jumping fixtures?

Televised races inevitably stimulate betting interest and keeping all-weather events on an audio service only may have helped the bookies to reduce payouts.

HISTORY

During the 1980s the Jockey Club recognized that spells of bad weather, causing abandonments, were having a damaging effect on betting turnover and also, as a result, on the Horserace Betting Levy produced by deductions from punters' bets. A fraction under 1 per cent of all money bet on horse racing – approximately £40 million annually – is returned to the sport to pay for prize money, integrity services (camera patrol, dope testing, etc.), the financing of racecourse building projects and so on.

Bookmakers were able to shore up their falling profits by buying greyhound racing stadia and promoting those meetings on the SIS betting shop service. But the Jockey Club decided to investigate the possibility of building all-weather racetracks which would maintain a racing programme through the deepest winter when it was impossible to race on turf. The contracts were won by Lingfield (in the south) and Southwell (in the midlands), both at one time under the banner of Ron Muddle's RAM group.

The bulldozers moved in – a distressing experience for those who had loved one of the south's prettiest tracks, 'Leafy Lingfield' – and by late 1989 both courses were up and running.

Niklas Angel, trained by Conrad Allen and ridden by Richard Quinn, became the first to win a race on an artificial surface in this country when taking the first of five divisions of a bookmaker-sponsored claimer at Lingfield on 30 October 1989.

Southwell, transformed by the dynamic Muddle from a

rather down-at-heel jumping venue into a modern dual-purpose arena, kicked off just one week later. For its racing surface, Lingfield opted to use the Equitrack compound, already successfully employed in the States and made by the Leicester firm of En Tout Cas; the Muddles, Ron and son Richard, formerly a successful jockey, chose Fibresand, a mixture of sand and fibres which provides deeper going, particularly so during a wet spell.

Both tracks quickly fulfilled their purpose, staging racing when it would have been impossible elsewhere, though Southwell was unlucky to have meetings called off in freak conditions owing to high winds and waterlogging. The early loss of meetings because of the more predictable phenomena, frost and snow, led to some ribald comments about these 'all-weather' surfaces. Indeed, the remarks were similar to those which followed British Rail's famous excuse that train cancellations had occurred because of 'the wrong kind of snow' on the track.

Abandonments at Southwell have now been all but eradicated by an increased investment in manpower and machinery, the enterprising management team ensuring that the course is repeatedly harrowed through the night when there is danger of frost.

The snobbery towards artificial surfaces that was evident among some professionals at the outset has also been dissipated and now most of the major players, be they trainers, owners or jockeys, are happy to have winners on the all-weather.

The scales certainly dropped from their eyes when a number of horses used the all-weather as a springboard to big-race victories on the turf. Amenable and jockey Alex Greaves, a standing dish at Southwell, went on to win the famous Lincoln Handicap at Doncaster; Go South found his enthusiasm rekindled on Lingfield's Equitrack and won the Tote Cesarewitch at the age of seven; and who would have thought that the winner of a novices' hurdle at Southwell in

1990 would develop into one of our top chasers, winner of the Welsh and Scottish Nationals, Run For Free?

All-weather racing remains at the bread-and-butter end of the sport, with countless races of selling and claiming class, but after the success of both Southwell and Lingfield, there has been a distinct lack of dissent about the new £15 million all-weather track at Wolverhampton. Again masterminded by the go-ahead Muddles, the project has been given a £2 million loan by the Levy Board and, more surprisingly, a £3 million grant from the Department of the Environment in an attempt to regenerate the depressed local area. The track opened on Boxing Day 1993, with two of the seven races under floodlights; the first all-floodlit meeting in Britain took place on 8 January 1994, with Saturday night all-weather Flat racing every fortnight subsequently throughout the year.

With an £8,000 race every weekend and a plush 370-seater restaurant, this venture is not being pitched at the lowest common denominator – human or equine. Who knows, it may develop like the popular Meadowlands track in New Jersey, near New York, which specializes in night racing under lights and puts on a number of America's top Grade 1 events. Following the relaxation in 1993 of the laws governing the evening opening of betting shops, it can be only a matter of time before floodlit racing is on show in betting shops the whole year round.

TRENDS

The action happens a bit more quickly on the all-weather and horses have to get used not only to the faster pace of the races but also to the 'kickback' from the other runners. No horse enjoys running through a sandstorm, so the ideal position is either close to the pace so that kickback is not a problem or well out of the line of fire, poised to come with a wide, late challenge up the home straight. This latter manoeuvre is much more easily accomplished at Southwell with its longer straight. I make it a rule never to back a horse having its first experience of the all-weather tracks. They inevitably back off it slightly on their first run but as long as the experience does not prove an unpleasant one, it is surprising how much improvement can be found on the second outing. Horses are more likely to be put off by the sight of their riders who, kitted out in protection against the kickback with helmets, goggles and face masks, look more like Darth Vader than professional sportsmen and women.

Lambourn trainer Charlie Elsey has enjoyed considerable success with his all-weather syndicates, Lingfield and Southwell having created a whole new market in secondhand horses deemed too small to go jumping. His old stager Rapporteur leans into the Lingfield bends like a motorcyclist and has a win total there fast approaching 20. Ten-year-old Rapporteur is a classic example of age not proving a barrier to all-weather success. Elsey maintains that the sand tracks are less punishing than their turf counterparts. 'There are no minor impediments on the surface so horses come back with fewer knocks and sprains. They can recover more quickly from their races than they do on grass.'

Though the going on both tracks is given uniformly as 'standard', on some days, in particular at Southwell, the horses come back as if they had been hosed in mud. There has been enough racing in both places now for the expert backer to gauge the going more accurately from the race times. Elsey says: 'All-weather going doesn't fit along a straight turf line from hard to heavy – it is just off to the side. Lingfield's standard would equate to "good to firm" but with a degree of bounce, while Southwell's standard is slower.'

The way the runners 'stack up' around the home turns is evocative of American racing and, as is the case in the States, in time the 'clock' will rule. Because the going is consistent, a diligent study of race times will definitely profit the reader. In chapter 3, 'Conditions Races', I outlined Timefigures which I would describe as noteworthy from Southwell and Lingfield. At no other tracks in the country is the Time Test more important nowadays.

The normal rules of class and time apply and, as at turf courses, readers should be on the look-out for horses with form in handicaps returning to conditions and maiden company. Incidentally, I've found that if a horse is good at Southwell he is not usually so effective at Lingfield and vice versa. But it is a regular occurrence to see a horse gaining in confidence with a win or two on Fibresand or Equitrack and then being able to maintain that improvement when switched back to turf.

Punters must also be vigilant about the handicap rating of horses on the sand, which can differ quite radically from their turf mark; this is a reminder of the bad old days before centralized handicapping, when a horse could have different weights depending on in which part of the country and under which handicapper's jurisdiction it was racing.

Of course, having two ratings can occasionally work in the punter's favour. Lord Huntingdon shrewdly took advantage of a lenient all-weather mark for the gelding Set The Fashion in the Paris Handicap at Southwell in July 1993. Set The Fashion, with proven ability on the surface in the spring, had improved in the meantime on grass, earning a rating of 58. Yet, at Southwell, he was able to race off a mark of 48. Result: an effortless five-length victory at odds of 11–10.

Set The Fashion races in the colours of Her Majesty The Queen and I shall be taking a more than passing interest in future Honours Lists to see whether a certain handicapper is included!

JUMPING

All-weather jumping was abolished in early 1994, after a public outcry followed a high rate of equine fatalities.

All-weather racing has opened up a tremendous new avenue for the punter and I am positive that with a little dedication you will find some of your most rewarding punts coming at Lingfield, Wolverhampton and Southwell all year round.

PART THREE

THE MECHANICS OF BETTING

Chapter Seven

The Search for Value

Golfer Nick Faldo walks up the fairway after another glorious drive. He's some 140 yards away from the flag and will probably choose to use an 8 iron for his next shot. But he will not base that decision on what his eyes tell him – his 'feel' for the shot – but on the yardage chart compiled by his faithful caddy Fanny Sunesson. Nick knows to within a few feet how far he can hit the ball with every club in the bag; Fanny, having paced out the golf course before the tournament started, can tell her guv'nor exactly how many yards it is to any given target.

What's good enough for the world's top golfer is also good enough for us punters. So, in Appendix E, I have compiled an 'expected value' grid which will enable you to make more of the right decisions in the betting shop; in effect, to tell the difference between a good bet and a bad bet.

One million British adults admit to having a flutter every day, but few of them have any concept of what good value in the betting market means. This is not meant as a criticism of betting shop punters only; one bookmaker has spoken of distinguished clients, some of them company executives and politicians, who 'leave their brains at home when having a bet'.

If your target is a probable but small and steady profit, the chart can help; if you're chasing the remote possibility of a large sum for a small outlay, buy a lottery ticket!

The 'expected value' is based on the most likely results of a large number of bets on which chance will even out. To calculate the expected value one must call upon some elementary mathematics. Maths is a tool to rational thinking; as far as horserace betting is concerned it is impossible to be rational without it. Calculating the expected value is achieved by using the following equation:

amount to be won × probability of winning
MINUS
amount that can be lost × probability of losing.

To obtain the probability of winning and losing, assume the race you have studied is to be run ten times. How many times do you think each runner would win this race over that period, remembering that you have to take the collective chance of the also-rans into account?

Working out the probability of winning and losing is a difficult concept for the novice backer but it will come more easily with practice and eventually take you only a few seconds.

For a real example of a good bet, I'll refer back to the success of Green's Cassatt at Haydock on 13 August 1993, described in chapter 4, 'Handicaps'. I felt that if Green's Cassatt's race were to be run ten times, she would win it on three occasions. Given her starting price (SP) of 12–1 and the notional £10 stake, her expected value was:

amount to be won (£120) × probability of winning (0.3)
MINUS
amount that can be lost (£10) × probability of losing (0.7)
expected value = £29.

A very good bet; you expect to win money. But what about that fictitious filly Lovely Lorna, who is also rated as having a three-in-ten chance of winning, but whose odds are 9–4? Again to a £10 stake, her expected value was:

amount to be won (£22.50) × probability of winning (0.3)
MINUS
amount that can be lost (£10) × probability of losing (0.7)
Expected value = –£0.25.

The result in this case is negative, a bad bet: you expect to lose money.

However confident you are of a horse's chance, under no circumstances place a bet if its expected value produces a negative result. You will lose heavily in the long run. But if there are two 'positive' qualifiers in one race, back them both.

For newspaper tipsters like myself, the chart has another function – it can help to choose which tip is the nap and which the next best. Although estimates of the likely betting forecast 24 hours in advance can sometimes be wildly awry, simply nap the selection with the greatest expected value.

The expected value grid (Appendix E) is a purely mathematical method of establishing whether a horse is a value bet . . . once your selection is made. But there are a number of principles of reasoning which can help steer you towards the type of horse likely to be good value, or signal those which represent bad bets.

The principle that if an event is extreme (either way), the next event of the same kind is likely to be less extreme is known as *regression to the mean*.

We have all been to a restaurant for the first time and found the food to be excellent. We return, or recommend it to friends, but the food doesn't come up to scratch. Chance plays a considerable role in cooking and if the food was exceptional on one occasion, it is likely to revert to the norm on the next. If you had a bad meal at a restaurant you do not return, so you never discover whether the second meal would have been better, which it is likely to be.

If a normally consistent horse puts up a bad performance, look very carefully at its chance the next time it appears. Punters and bookmakers are fickle creatures and the horse will almost certainly start at a much longer price than is dictated by the balance of its form. Similarly, be suspicious of the horse which apparently runs out of its skin. His supporters may be in for a rude shock the next time it runs.

Never base a judgement on a single item of information,

no matter how striking. That leads us to two other concepts of faulty reasoning much discussed by psychologists.

The immediacy and salience of recently presented material should not be allowed to influence you unduly. A horse's form franked on the day before you propose to back it should be given no more credence than form which was boosted a month ago. To do so is to fall foul of the *availability error*.

Lazy newspaper tipsters seem especially fond of bringing very recent evidence to the notice of their readers and such highly visible material assumes greater importance than is merited, often resulting in the horse starting at shorter odds than it should. Another concept to be aware of is the *primacy error*. First impressions are no more valid than second or third impressions, and yet we often stick religiously to them. If we first encounter someone in a bad mood our opinion is prejudiced and difficult to shift, however pleasantly they behave subsequently. Likewise, we may form an instant conviction that the reason a horse weakened in the closing stages of a race was lack of stamina, or that a disappointing performance was the consequence of the prevailing going. Be careful not to distort new evidence in order to support such entrenched views. Keep an open mind: changing your opinion is a sign of strength not weakness. The received wisdom about a horse can dictate its popularity in the betting but that wisdom should be constantly under review.

A well-tried and successful betting method is to uncover those horses whose odds represent poor value . . . and then oppose them. I know of one punter who backs the second favourite in races where the country's national newspaper tipsters unanimously choose the favourite. Cheeky, yes, but effective none the less. The power of the racing press is such that when tipsters are of one mind, the chosen horse inevitably starts favourite and almost as inevitably is returned at very cramped odds. If the favourite is considered to be poor value then there must be some value elsewhere among the other runners.

The skilled backer will, virtually every day, unearth horses which he feels represent exceedingly bad value; some of them may win, but he is definitely working on the right lines in singling out such races as betting opportunities.

No chapter on 'The Search for Value' would be complete without warning the punter how the dice are loaded against him in each and every race. Bookmakers stay in business by quoting and laying prices which ensure them a theoretical profit whichever runner may win.

Their percentage of profit on turnover varies to some extent according to the type of race and the number of runners. Occasionally it may be as low as 6 per cent in races with small fields; but in a handicap with 30 runners it can rise to as much as 40 per cent.

To calculate the percentage each starting price is worth, convert it to decimals using the table in our Ready Reckoner (Appendix F), add one and divide into 100. So, for example, a 3–1 chance becomes $100 \div (3.000 + 1) = 25$ per cent; and an 85–40 chance becomes $100 \div (2.125 + 1) = 32$ per cent.

As an example of how these percentages add up for the bookmaker, let's consider the important Dewhurst Stakes run at Newmarket on Friday, 15 October 1993.

Name	SP	Percentage
Grand Lodge	9–4	30.8
Nicolotte	9–2	18.2
Polish Laughter	13–2	13.3
Redoubtable	7–1	12.5
Stonehatch	7–1	12.5
Psychobabble	15–2	11.8
Mutakddim	12–1	7.7
Alanees	25–1	3.8
River Deep	33–1	2.9
Village Eagle	150–1	0.7
	Total percentage	114.2

The field book for the Dewhurst Stakes is therefore 14 per cent over-round, giving the layers a theoretical profit of 12 per cent (14 divided by 114).

A perfectly round book, with each SP representing the true odds rather than the bookmakers' odds, would total 100. Only in exceptional circumstances would the bookies bet 'over-broke', with the odds totalling less than 100.

Twenty-four hours after the Dewhurst, in one of the most strongly contested handicaps of the season, the Tote Cesare-witch, the field book for the 31 runners was 41 per cent over-round, giving the bookies a theoretical profit of 29 per cent.

A comprehensive at-a-glance odds percentages table can be found in Appendix G.

Chapter Eight

Betting Methods

As part of his submission to the Royal Commission on Gambling in 1977, Phil Bull described the betting shop as follows: 'It is to be as bare and uninviting as possible, to ensure that a person will go into it only if he feels he has to, and will get out of it as quickly as he can. This, doubtless, is the moral way to bet, quickly, furtively and if possible with a sense of guilt – the traditional Christian way of sex, perhaps.'

Times have not changed. Betting shops have become more gaudily coloured, the seats a tad more comfortable and there are now vending machines with instant coffee and soup, but after five minutes in a betting shop I feel like I've been sitting in an ashtray.

The high street betting office is a dinosaur on its last legs. The number of outlets is dwindling and pretty soon hi-tech betting methods will overtake the need for bookmakers to have so much money tied up in prime real estate sites. Already credit betting by dangerously painless Switch cards is a growth area in the industry but before long even that personal contact with the tele-betting girls will be a thing of the past as we simply tap in our bets – and order our groceries – on the telephone key pad.

There can be no substitute for betting on the track – the absence of tax and the ability to shop around for the best prices being two major advantages – but I realize that the majority of my readers will be able to bet only at the track on high days and holidays.

Whatever method you use, don't be suckered into leaving your bet and relying on a favourable starting price. You will be continually disappointed.

No horse represents a bet at any price. Having done your

homework, make sure to bet on your terms, not anyone else's.

It should not be too difficult to get to a betting shop for the two or three races you are interested in; alternatively your bookmaker will be happy to relay the fluctuations of the market over the phone, or you can pick up the shows on the television on Ceefax or Teletext.

One area where punters consistently feel they are being ripped off is what they see as the shaving of odds between the final show and starting price. Vetabet, the independent organization which monitors information sent to betting shops, blasted a hole in that conspiracy theory by producing the following figures for 1992:

Last show same as SP: 76.98 per cent
Last show longer than SP: 11.46 per cent
Last show shorter than SP: 11.56 per cent.

There appears no reason, therefore, for taking the final show. Where the punter can benefit is in the morning-odds market, which has caught on to such an extent that some professionals now bet exclusively on early prices. A recent survey showed that 58 per cent of morning odds were higher than the SP, 16 per cent were the same, with only 26 per cent lower – and that's without finding the best prices.

Some of the credit for the development of this new market can be taken by the Pricewise column of the *Racing Post*, now under the direction of Mel Collier, which the *Daily Express* has endorsed. Nominating their value bets to recommended stakes, the Pricewise team's profit to turnover in 1993 was just over 30 per cent; that's some effort when you grasp that the races the bookmakers choose to lay prices for early are invariably handicaps and often the trickiest of the day.

The reader will know from previous chapters that I am rather allergic to betting on handicaps but when a bet does

arise in such an event the reader is advised to look at the
early prices in a bid to get the best value.

WIN OR EACH WAY?

There is a tremendous difference of opinion among backers
as to the advisability of each-way betting. Many believe that
professional punters bet to win only and that they sometimes
have a saving bet, again to win only, on the horse which they
regard as the main danger to their selection. However, what
is correct for the professional, who has sources of information not available to the ordinary punter, is quite often wrong
for the amateur.

As a general rule, I would advise the reader to bet each
way, particularly in non-handicaps. Whereas in a handicap
most horses have a chance of winning, in conditions races
one can often reduce the number of 'possibles' to two or
three – that's our kind of race.

Maybe it's just my perverse nature but I'm fascinated with
any betting which the bookmakers actively discourage – like
each-way betting. They have, for instance, set purely arbitrary rules, which are entirely in their favour, about the
fraction of odds they are prepared to pay for the place
portion of the bet. Take an eight-runner handicap where the
bookies pay one-fifth of the odds for a place. The true win
odds are 7–1; the true place odds are 5–3 but the bookmakers' odds are 7–5. The advantage is very much with the layer
and escalates in his favour as the number of runners
increases.

The conclusion that the each-way odds are against the
backer is true only on the assumption that all horses have an
equal chance of winning. In practice this is never the case.
The main objection that backers make, however, is that
when a horse starts at a short price, say at less than 4–1, the
place bet recovers only part of the win bet if the horse

finishes second or third. They much prefer to bet each way on a horse at, say, 10–1 or longer, even in a large field.

This view is false. It is much better financial practice to back shorter-priced horses each way and outsiders win only. Readers are advised to keep separate accounts of their win bets and their place bets in conditions races. If they are reasonably knowledgeable they will find that the place bets show a fair profit and, incidentally, form an effective insurance against the inevitable sequence of horses that fail to finish first.

The abolition of the on-course tax has indirectly widened the avenue for each-way betting. How many times do we see a favourite forecast to start at 4–6 going off at 1–3 as investors at the racecourse greedily try to buy money on a horse they believe cannot be beaten? If the favourite starts at such cramped odds, there must be some each-way value among the other runners.

An extreme example of this practice provided one of the bets of the season in the Pershore Novices' Hurdle at Worcester (a Class C track) on 18 March 1992.

The market leader Bean King came into the race after a victory at lowly Class D Folkestone. He was effectively moving up a grade, yet was carrying a penalty. Bean King started at 1–4.

The second favourite, San Fernando, was dropping two grades after finishing a creditable fourth behind Ashfold Copse and Barton Bank at Class A Newbury. San Fernando was unpenalized, carried six pounds less than Bean King but started at 9–2.

Bean King's strength in the market was essentially because of his useful Flat form; but, as I outlined in chapter 5, 'Hurdles and Chases', form on the level has only a very limited application over the sticks. Win or lose, San Fernando, a proper jumping horse trained by Josh Gifford, was a bet; as an extra bit of insurance, a terrific each-way bet – he even paid fractionally more on the Tote. What's more, with the bookies betting to just 104 per cent and going 50–1 bar the front two in the market, you could bet each way on several of the no-hopers plus San Fernando and be sure to come out ahead.

The most profitable each-way betting of all is in each-way doubles and trebles, provided one limits oneself to conditions races, preferably two-year-old events, with between eight and twelve runners.

Backing for a place only can occasionally prove fruitful in a major race like a Classic when there is a short-priced favourite which is truly the form horse. Punters shy away from such horses on the Tote because they fear the price will be too short. This fear is so widespread that the place dividend is sometimes very little less than the win dividend.

On the busiest racing days, with four or more meetings, the reader may find enough bets to warrant an each-way Patent – three horses combining for seven bets: three singles, three doubles and a treble – or an each-way Yankee – four selections combining for 11 bets: six doubles, four trebles and a four-timer.

In any race where he gives a chance to four horses, the reader should clearly have no bet.

In fields of seven, I would prefer to bet win only rather than each way. The only seven-horse races in which I ever bet each way are those where I feel the favourite is a false price. I then bet each way on the Tote, for whenever the favourite is out of the frame, the odds both to win and for a place are excellent.

The question of each-way betting in handicaps is not so simple. I rarely bet at all in handicaps and when I do it is nearly always each way. This is because almost invariably the horse I back has shown good recent form and I therefore expect it to be in the first three.

I would urge the ordinary punter who, despite all the expert advice, insists on betting largely in handicaps, in the main to bet win only. The fields are usually so large that the prices the layers pay for places are rarely good value.

To conclude this section, I make a couple of small suggestions to bookmakers which I believe would inject much
needed extra cash into the betting industry:

1 Treat claiming races as handicaps for each-way purposes –
   these races often have a weight range as large as any
   handicap.
2 Change the each-way rules to one-quarter the odds a place
   in non-handicaps and one-third the odds a place for
   handicaps.

THE TOTE

The Horserace Totalisator Board (Tote) was instituted by an
Act of Parliament in 1928. The fact that 67 years on fewer
than 5 per cent of all bets are struck with the Tote rather than
the bookmakers says much about how this public body has
been run.

The popularity of the Placepot bet – over 50 per cent of
whose tickets are procured off-course – proves there is a
demand for pool betting, so it is scandalous that the Tote and
the Jockey Club between them have so far been unable to
develop a 'superbet' which could effectively compete with
the football pools and see off the potential danger that a
national lottery poses to the racing industry.

I draw an analogy between restaurant chain Wimpy Bars
and the Tote. It seemed that every high street in the 1960s
had its own Wimpy Bar. And yet this position of strength was
allowed to dissipate as more vigorously managed fast-food
outlets like McDonalds muscled in and now dominate the
market.

Should the national lottery seriously erode the amount of
money the punter has to spend on racing it will in part be due
to the wanton short-sightedness of the Tote management

team. They already have in place, with the Jackpot and the Placepot, two pool bets which could satisfy punters' demands for a chance of an enormous payout if only they were developed and marketed more aggressively.

Why, for example, can't the non-punter be encouraged to buy Jackpot and Placepot tickets which throw up a random, computer-derived set of combinations?

The Tote would also attract more business if it was seen to reduce its deductions for operating expenses and profits, which in the case of the Jackpot, Trio and Dual Forecast seem, to me, to be swingeing – see the table below.

Tote pools and deductions

Type of bet	% deduction	Net pool
Win	16	84% of stakes
Place	24	76% of stakes
Dual Forecast	29	71% of stakes
Jackpot	29	71% of stakes
Placepot	26	74% of stakes
Trio	29	71% of stakes

Racing needs vigorous pool betting which is not vulnerable to the manipulation of the major bookmakers, unlike the current SP system. It is a step in the right direction that the Tote has introduced sophisticated betting terminals in all Tote and Corals betting shops nationwide and some independent bookies as well. With a well-aimed kick up the backside, the Tote may yet come into its own.

Before deciding whether to bet on the Tote or with the bookies, the reader must consider the reaction of other backers. Horses representing trainers or jockeys who have large personal followings are normally bad investments on the Tote. So, too, are horses which have good recent form that is easily recognizable or have been selected by the most popular correspondents in the daily papers. On the other hand, runners with a string of 'duck-eggs' are not popular on the Tote, yet those apparently discouraging form figures could mask respectable though unplaced form in superior company.

The same goes for jumping form figures which boast the letters U, F or P indicating unseated rider, fell or pulled up. Such horses should not be instantly dismissed, particularly if the subject has changed stables in the meantime.

The chaser Dandy Minstrel lined up for Windsor's Stora-call Handicap Chase at Windsor on 3 February 1993 carrying the form-figure baggage 3U–PP00. But as any punter who reads the excellent 'Trainer Trace' column in the *Racing Post* knew, Dandy Minstrel was having his first run for the highly successful Nigel Twiston-Davies having moved from Eric Wheeler's yard.

Dandy Minstrel won at 20–1 and paid £32.40 on the Tote!

Horses at the top of the handicap are generally regarded by the Tote backer as having been given too much weight and so attract comparatively little support. Similarly, horses carrying a penalty in handicaps tend to be under-supported, as do horses ridden by little-known apprentices.

Don't be afraid to bet on the Tote in big fields of maidens. The betting load can be spread more evenly and there is more chance of a pleasant freak dividend. Of course, with the computer technology now in place at the Tote's Wigan headquarters, the screens are very accurate at indicating the current state of the various pools. The nearer you bet to the off-time, though, the more closely the Tote display is likely to match the final dividend.

Finally, it seems to me that the growth of corporate hospital-ity at racecourses will have a significant effect on the Tote pools. On-course pools are occasionally so pitifully small that an injection of cash from business clients being entertained in racecourse suites is crucial. Normally well refreshed after a good lunch, these often once-a-year punters rarely stray far from their hosts and are generally accommodated by nearby Tote terminals. They are generally chucking their money away,

but their activities make for some interesting possibilities for
the serious Tote punter.

Dual Forecast and Trio

With a Dual Forecast, which operates in all races with three
or more runners, the object is to select the first two in either
order. The minimum stake is £2 but permutations can be
made to a £1 unit.

With the Tote Trio, which operates only on certain races,
the object is to select the first three in any order. The
minimum stake is £1 but permutations are allowed to a
minimum unit stake of 10p.

I'm especially fond of these bets in the following cases:

1 In a two-year-old race when one or more newcomers are
   well backed: I support my first two or three choices among
   the form horses in the hope that the newcomers will run
   green.
2 In handicaps when there are only two or three runners
   with good recent form.
3 In races where the draw plays a significant role: I may then
   perm the favoured numbers.

Combination bet calculator

| No. of horses | Total cost to £1 stake | |
selected	Dual Forecast	Trio
3	£3	£1
4	£6	£4
5	£10	£10
6	£15	£20
7	£21	£35
8	£28	£56
9	£36	£84
10	£45	£120

Jackpot and Placepot
(with Guy Butchers of the *Daily Express* Placepot Line)

With the Tote Jackpot, the object is to select the winners of all six Jackpot races. The Jackpot operates at one selected meeting a day. The minimum stake is £1 but permutations are allowed to a minimum unit stake of 10p.

With the Placepot, the object is to select a placed horse in each of the six Placepot races. The Placepot operates at every meeting. The minimum stake is as for the Jackpot.

Any horse on which a place dividend is declared counts towards a winning Placepot line. In races of four or fewer runners, you must select a winner. The Placepot qualifications in full are as follows:

up to 4 runners	winner only
5, 6, 7 runners	2 place dividends (1st and 2nd)
8 + runners	3 place dividends (1st, 2nd and 3rd)
16 + runners (handicaps)	4 place dividends (1st, 2nd, 3rd and 4th)

You can either pick just one horse in all six contests, which gives you a single line at your chosen stake – be it ten pence or £50 (the dividend is declared to a £1 unit) – or you can use permutations with a number of horses in each race. To work out how much your bet will cost, simply multiply the number of selections in each race. For example, a 25p Jackpot or Placepot with one horse in the first race, two in the second, three in the third, one in the fourth, two in the fifth and three in the six would be: $1 \times 2 \times 3 \times 1 \times 2 \times 3 = 36$ combinations at 25p each; total stake £9.

Your return is determined by dividing the number of successful tickets into the net pool (after the Tote has retained its percentage).

The Jackpot and Placepot are what the Americans would term 'exotic' wagers. The Placepot is Britain's fastest-growing bet, which is why the *Daily Express* launched its Placepot line on 1 March 1993. We have yet to match the payout one lucky racegoer received at Cheltenham in March 1990 – £22,203 for a £1 stake – but the line is in profit and we have had our notable successes, including individual returns of £1,792, £745, £508, £451 etc. One of the joys of pool betting is that you can win several dividends and at the festival meetings like Cheltenham and Aintree a £100,000 daily pool is guaranteed.

So what about a few clues for cracking the Placepot?

For the time being it makes sense to play the system and stake your bets in shops not linked with the Tote pool. The reason is simple – if you win, your successful entry is not included in calculations to determine the dividend, thus increasing the return on your investment.

In races of up to and including four runners you have to find the winner; it often pays to include all the runners in those races as covering a winning outsider usually bumps up the return. In races with five, six or seven runners, your selection needs to finish in the first two, so more than one selection is a sound idea.

The fewer 'obvious' horses (especially favourites and second favourites) that make the frame, the higher the dividend is likely to be, so avoid them where possible. If two horses have an equal chance, go for the one from the less fashionable yard or which is ridden by the 'lesser' jockey. Keep an eye on apprentices in form. The top jockeys are interested only in winning – they do not have the concerns of the each-way or Placepot punters at heart. Sometimes an apprentice will reward you better by pushing his mount past Eddery or Roberts for third or fourth place.

Consistent horses should be linked with those capable on their best form (like course specialists) when giving multiple selections in a race. And finally, use the effect of the draw to your advantage.

Carry-Overs

The time to attack Tote bets with extra vigour is when the pool is not won outright and is carried over. The Dual Forecast and Trio pools will pass on to races specified by the Tote, the Jackpot pool to the next Jackpot meeting and the Placepot pool to a meeting the following day.

The new pools will therefore be bloated by 'dead money' – cash which will be part of any payout but is not carrying any live tickets. With a £1 stake, a £100,000 pool (£40,000 carried over, say, plus £60,000 in new money), relates to 60,000 live tickets. Each £1 bet is worth, therefore, more like £1.67 and even with the Placepot's 26 per cent deduction it can be seen to be worth £1.24, rather more than the £1 stake and therefore terrific value.

ANTE-POST BETTING

Days, weeks, sometimes even months before a big race, we are tempted by what appear to be generous 'ante-post' prices offered against all the probable runners. In many cases, the races are handicaps and, surprise surprise, many of these are sponsored by bookmakers who promote them heavily.

Readers will know by now my aversion to handicaps and my view is they should not bet in these races on the day, far less at ante-post. I am sometimes tempted at the five-day stage when a reasonably clear picture of the likely field is known, but only under the conditions highlighted in chapter 4 on 'Handicaps'. Betting any earlier, even with the knowledge that a stable has laid out an individual horse for a particular race, is a precarious activity. So much can go wrong with even the best-laid plans when an injury-prone racehorse is involved.

Long-range punters do have the opportunity to 'hedge' their bets, that is to lay off at a shorter price. 'No bet is a good bet until it is hedged' is a wise old maxim on the Turf. As an example, if one is able to strike a bet at, say, 40–1 and the horse shortens in the ante-post market to 8–1, it is sometimes possible to offer it to one's friends at 10s or 12s. If the reader finds himself in this lucky position and lays the bet off, he stands to make 30 points or 28 points profit to nothing, which is a far better proposition in my view than his original bet at 40–1.

The ante-post market in the Classics is really as full of pitfalls as it is in the big handicaps. Nevertheless, on rare occasions I strike an ante-post bet in these races. In chapter 11, 'Information', I will outline the circumstances behind my ante-post wager on Dr Devious in the 1992 Derby, ten days before the race. There, having had an up-to-the-minute report from the trainer and believing that he could not finish out of the frame on form, I was happy to invest each way.

Normally, I make the commission to win only and have a small saver to place because there is always the possibility of the horse being scratched.

RULES AND LIMITS

Backers should always study closely the rules of their book-makers and when those rules are unsatisfactory they should seek to open accounts with other layers. There is great competition among bookmakers and, generally speaking, it is the three major bookmakers – Ladbrokes, Hills and Corals – who offer the public the best deal.

Whoever you bet with, make sure you know the rules which apply to the particular bets you favour. Many, I know, have been caught out by Corals' and Hills' limiting the payout on Dual Forecasts to double their own computer straight forecasts. If you favour multiple bets you had better be clear what the bookies' limits are, because finding out to your cost at the payout counter can be a very sour experience.

Finally, a rule that applies to all punters – Tattersalls' Rule 4c. It is invoked when a horse is withdrawn without coming under starter's orders or declared 'not to have started' and there is insufficient time to reform the betting market. Bookmakers are then entitled to make the following deductions from win and place returns (excluding stakes):

Odds of withdrawn horse	Deduction from winnings
30–100 or shorter	75p in the £
2–5 to 1–3	70p in the £
8–15 to 4–9	65p in the £
8–13 to 4–7	60p in the £
4–5 to 4–6	55p in the £
20–21 to 5–6	50p in the £
Evens to 6–5	45p in the £
5–4 to 6–4	40p in the £
13–8 to 7–4	35p in the £
15–8 to 9–4	30p in the £
5–2 to 3–1	25p in the £
100–30 to 4–1	20p in the £
9–2 to 11–2	15p in the £
6–1 to 9–1	10p in the £
10–1 to 14–1	5p in the £
longer than 14–1	no deductions

When more than one horse is withdrawn without coming under starter's orders, total deductions shall not exceed 75p in the £.

Bets at 'board prices' are affected only if there has been time to form a new market.

Chapter Nine

The Gambling Year

Organizing your betting year is much like planning a success-ful garden. There will be times of prolific growth, periods when some savage pruning is necessary, and weeks when you are simply preparing the ground for the future. Success is down to common sense and, to a large degree, a fundamental appreciation of climate and the weather.

As *Daily Express* gardening columnist Geoff Hamilton might say – work in harmony with the seasons.

MARCH: START OF THE FLAT . . . CHELTENHAM

March is symbolically important to the punter since it encompasses the start of the turf season on the Flat and the great National Hunt Festival at Cheltenham. But it is a time when the serious punter should be relatively inactive.

Timeform supremo Phil Bull once said: 'When the Flat starts the old ticker beats a little faster. I look forward to it every year as an innocent prisoner, wrongfully convicted after a miscarriage of justice, awaits his release from jail.' There is certainly a special buzz for Flat fans when the *Doncaster March meeting* comes around and I have fond memories of making the annual pilgrimage to see in the new season and becoming reacquainted with friends not seen for at least four months.

The introduction of all-weather racing has reduced the impact of the Doncaster kick-off. In these recessionary times, all but an elite group of jockeys, trainers and owners have to keep grinding away to make a living on the sand-based surfaces at Southwell, Wolverhampton and Lingfield.

Wise backers rarely plunge during the first few weeks of the new turf season, when there is a dearth of recent data to work on. There is the all-weather form, of course, and that shown by horses during the National Hunt season, but it is of limited application.

However, to take advantage of the jumpers' fitness edge, I suggest readers make a list of horses that have run well in handicap hurdles at the main meetings (Aintree, Ascot, Ayr, Doncaster, Haydock, Kempton, Newbury, Newcastle, Sandown and Wetherby) since the turn of the year. In this connection 'running well' means either

1 winning a race carrying 11 stone or over, or
2 finishing second, third, fourth or fifth carrying eleven stone seven pounds or more, and being beaten not more than ten lengths by the winner.

When any of the qualifiers runs in an all-aged handicap and is set to carry eight stone seven pounds or less, it is a backable proposition. Remember that two-mile hurdle form equates to between a mile and a quarter and a mile and a half on the Flat, while jumpers with form over two and a half miles plus may find a mile and a half on the level an inadequate test of stamina.

The service provided by the *Daily Express* racing team, whereby the number of days since the most recent run – under either code, Flat or jumping – is highlighted in the card, can be particularly useful. Often a horse is given a pipe-opener over hurdles in preparation for a more specific target on the Flat a few days later . . . or vice versa.

Paddock inspection is vital, especially after a severe winter, as fitness cannot be taken on trust. Pay attention not only to the specific stables whose horses are running well in the early weeks but to the training centres they represent. If one or two stables in a centre are doing well then it is common for the whole area to have its horses well forward.

Concentrating on very recent form pays off with special force in the early weeks of the season. It is amazing how an outing, however lacking in apparent promise, can sharpen a horse up sufficiently to win next time out.

All two-year-old races at this stage are run over the minimum trip of five furlongs. In soft ground, five furlongs on a tough track can be a severe test of stamina for a youngster that may not have reached its actual second birthday. Pure sprint-breds often fail to see out the trip during this period and two-year-old races can be won by juveniles bred for seven furlongs, a mile or beyond – occasionally at fancy prices.

The middle of March sees the three-day *National Hunt Festival* meeting at the home of steeplechasing, Cheltenham. It is quite the most exciting and fascinating meeting of the year with a unique atmosphere, provided in part by the vast and vociferous Irish contingent. They are over to back and cheer on their contenders in many of the championship races, including the Champion Hurdle and Cheltenham Gold Cup. For many it is a 72-hour party with a few hours' sleep grabbed between the racing, carousing and card schools. Stamina is a prerequisite not just for every Cheltenham horse, but for the punter, too, if he is to last the pace of a demanding week.

For the serious backer, there are a number of lessons to be learned at Cheltenham which apply to all the major festival meetings like Aintree, York and Royal Ascot. They are the most glamorous meetings, but also the most difficult, and those punters who pull on their betting boots just four or five times a year at these meetings should be committed.

There is a strong element of machismo about the desire to back a winner at Cheltenham but a 5–1 success at Sedgefield on the same day will provide the same return from your bookmaker as a 5–1 winner at Cheltenham. To me at least, it is no less satisfying and much easier to find.

Ken Cundell, father of the current trainer Peter, and a

very astute punter and trainer in his day, set himself a rule never to back a horse at less than 9–2. I believe that policy can wisely be adopted during the festival meetings, perhaps even moving the threshold up to 6–1. Big fields of runners, many of them recent winners, and all of them trained to peak on the day – the problems set seem insoluble. As a result, I rarely find a good betting opportunity and content myself with small wagers on attractively priced, lightly raced horses that have shown form at the highest-class meetings.

The rule concerning the backing of only last-time-out winners at a Class A fixture, detailed in chapter 3, 'Conditions Races', should be hewn in rock and never broken as far as the festivals are concerned.

As Cheltenham is my local track, it is a busy week for socializing. I must confess this is the one meeting of the year when I allow professional betting standards to slip a little. But the Festival is unique so I am happy to take any losses on the chin . . . and enjoy the crack.

APRIL/MAY: CLASSIC TRIALS . . . AINTREE

In early April, the Newmarket season – and for many fans the Flat season proper – opens with the three-day Craven meeting. I strongly advise readers to bet sparingly, if at all, in the two-year-old races there, as it is rare to find any early-season form good enough to merit a win at Newmarket.

At the second Newmarket meeting, follow the two-year-old form shown at the Craven meeting. It is a sound policy not to back any horse at less than say, 3–1 or 4–1. Very short-priced favourites in two-year-old races at Newmarket show a large loss in most years.

Throughout this period the reader should rate form from Newmarket and Sandown as the most reliable guide to two-year-old races. I have little regard for form shown at

Chester and Epsom, as, although these races are sometimes valuable, the peculiarities of the courses generally render the form suspect.

Spring sees the various three-year-old *Classic Trials*: avoid them, as they produce more than their share of shock results. Recent examples include: Dante Stakes (Environment Friend, 20–1), Lingfield Derby Trial (Bob's Return, 14–1), Sandown Classic Trial (Gulf King, 25–1), Dee Stakes (Infantry, 16–1), Predominate Stakes (Ibn Bey, 20–1).

It should also be remembered that fillies, particularly after a severe winter, are slower to come to hand than colts. Don't rely on them to reproduce their two-year-old form in the spring.

Despite the healthy weight-for-age allowances, it is rare to see a three-year-old sprinter beating his elders in the early part of the season; if you do, it is usually the sign of an exceptional performance. Paddock viewing signals this inferiority: a three-year-old is unlikely to have the muscular development of the powerful, mature four- or five-year-old speedster. Middle-distance three-year-olds, who do not require such explosive power, are not at such a disadvantage.

The three-day *Grand National Meeting* at the under-used Aintree is another feast of National Hunt racing, but my remarks concerning punting at the Festival fixtures apply here with even greater force. The meeting begins a fortnight after Cheltenham, but there are three good reasons why it does not usually provide a mere lap of honour for Cheltenham winners:

1 Cheltenham horses have usually been involved in gruelling finishes and have perhaps lost their edge.
2 The contours of the Aintree course are radically different from those at Cheltenham; if a horse appreciated Cheltenham, it is by no means certain to relish Aintree.
3 Horses trained to peak at Aintree often surprise Cheltenham horses who have come on to Liverpool as an afterthought.

The balance definitely swings in favour of the punter from Aintree onwards, when the National Hunt season runs alongside the Flat. Horses who have perhaps been rested during the soft-ground spell of winter reappear in April and May when the going is on the fast side countrywide. Try to maintain your enthusiasm for the jumpers at this stage, despite the long season, because well-backed, fancied horses win the majority of races.

The arrival of the final Cheltenham meeting of the season – the evening fixture for hunter-chasers – is a sure indication that the winter game is drawing to a close. This is a fun meeting and an ideal opportunity to catch up with many of the year's best hunter chasers and point-to-pointers on a single programme. Double Silk, the 1993 champion, won his last five hunter-chases, including the Foxhunters double at Cheltenham and Aintree, and concluded his campaign at this meeting in scintillating style.

JUNE/JULY/AUGUST: ROYAL ASCOT . . . YORK

The midsummer months, when the weather is more settled and the ground more consistent, is in consequence the period when we must make the most of the predictable results. We should now bet more frequently and perhaps even slightly increase our stakes if the results seem to justify it.

Concentrate on conditions races rather than handicaps, and two-year-old events in particular. Although one hears of two-year-olds becoming jarred up on firm summer ground, juvenile races remain the most reliable betting medium during this period. But what we gain in consistency, we lose in the shaving of the odds; inevitably, the horses with the soundest credentials start at the shortest prices.

In terms of reliability, the form registered at Newmarket and Sandown has now been joined by that of some of the other Class A meetings – Ascot, Goodwood and York. With agreeable regularity the National Stakes at Sandown is one of the strongest two-year-old races in the early part of the season and an excellent pointer to the juvenile events at Royal Ascot. Three recent winners of the Queen Mary Stakes – Risky, Lyric Fantasy and Marling – either won or finished second in the National Stakes.

The *Royal Ascot meeting* itself, when fashionable society discovers racing for one week a year, puts on four days of the most absorbing Flat racing to be had anywhere in the world. But the reader should take heed of the advice made with regard to betting opportunities at the Cheltenham Festival meeting. In addition, although the Royal meeting takes place on some of the longest days of summer, the peculiarities of the English climate frequently conspire to dump a biblical deluge on Berkshire during the week. What was an assault course becomes a minefield as downpours on top of artificially watered ground throw into disarray preconceived ideas about the effect of the draw.

One point to remember, though, is that if a horse is good enough to run well at Royal Ascot it is usually able to return and repeat the feat: the legendary Brown Jack, for example, won at the meeting seven years running!

In July and August, we begin to see the leading stables introduce their more choicely bred colts and fillies with Classic potential. These youngsters were not precocious enough to run at Royal Ascot, which is no longer the accepted route to Classic success. The top yards do not entertain their best prospects unawares and the betting market will provide an accurate guide to their chance.

It is also at this time of year that we enter a danger zone for all except the expert backer: the introduction of the first seven furlong and mile races for juveniles.

Form shown over five and six furlongs often has little relevance in these races and a sound understanding of pedigrees is as important as a knowledge of the form book. Not only does one have to be satisfied that the horse has the necessary ability to win, but one also has to be confident that it will not be found wanting when faced with the greater examination of its stamina. The problems are compounded when five- and six-furlong winners are required to carry a penalty over seven furlongs. At sprint distances, two-year-olds appear able to concede weight pretty well but the reader must always try accurately to assess the merit of the race that occasioned the penalty.

During this period look out for those three-year-olds that make abnormal progress, the ones who seem able to keep a step ahead of the handicapper and the weight-for-age scale. They may have found it tough against their elders in the spring, but during the autumn they come into their own.

Also in August, we have the wonderful *York Ebor meeting*. It's a superb gala of racing run over one of my favourite tracks, which has rightly been judged Racecourse of the Year on a number of occasions. Yet while the facilities may be superb, it has not been the kindest of meetings for punters down the years. The only blemish on an otherwise magnificent 18-race career for Brigadier Gerard came with his 3–1 *on* defeat by Roberto in the 1972 Benson and Hedges Gold Cup at York. It was a bloody battleground for punters again in 1993 with shocks a plenty and an average price for the 21 winners of 17–2!

My advice about the major meetings bears repeating at this stage. Confine yourself to small wagers on good-priced horses who have recorded form at the Class A meetings and have not been over-raced. Don't feel too depressed about missing out on the glamorous venues: your bank balance will look healthier if you concentrate your efforts on the Class B, C and D fixtures where there will be many good opportunities.

Of course, the Royal Ascot, Glorious Goodwood and York Ebor meetings will still have a significant effect on your punting because the results there bear the closest inspection and following handicap form over the succeeding fortnight can pay off handsomely.

From summer 1995, jump racing will continue through June and July rather than taking its traditional break. It is likely that jumping in June and July will be similar to that which usually takes place in August. The fields are generally small and the racing uncompetitive. Fast-ground specialists dominate, none more than on the West Country circuit.

SEPTEMBER: ST LEGER

September is the fillies' month, that time of year when the breeding season is long gone and fillies and mares leave their previous form behind. This improvement may have started as early as mid-August because fillies, even more so than colts and geldings, seem to thrive in the sun. Pay attention to the chance of all fillies and mares, especially those coming back after a break, having been out of form in the spring.

The *Doncaster St Leger meeting* signals a watershed in the Flat season, and my advice to all readers below the expert class is either to stop betting or reduce stakes from this point. The length of our season and the ever-expanding number of fixtures means that there are a lot of jaded horses by the end of September. Horses can lose their form in a twinkling during the autumn, so it is essential to follow recent form – and by recent I mean in the last few days rather than weeks.

As in the spring on the Flat, paddock inspection is important. Racegoers are beginning to wear heavier coats and the same is true of the entertainers. If a horse is 'going in its coat' it can signal a deterioration in performance. In two-year-old races the time test is of much less value than earlier in the year as the ground softens up. The best technique to apply now is to follow good nursery form into maiden and conditions race company.

As always, Newmarket and Ascot nurseries throw up a host of subsequent winners and close attention should also be paid to two-year-old handicaps at the Doncaster St Leger meeting and the Ayr Western meeting. Form from the Leger meeting and the one-day Festival of British Racing at Ascot – the richest single racecard of the year – is reliable across the board. It can be followed with profit for the next fortnight or so. The British Festival puts on two of the more prestigious events for potential middle-distance horses, the Fillies' Mile and the Royal Lodge Stakes.

OCTOBER/NOVEMBER/DECEMBER

The period from October to Christmas provides the punter with his best chance of building up winnings. Who says so? The bookmakers do. My friends in that noble profession tell me it is the most difficult time of the year to make a book and a profit.

The fast-ground horses have now been put away and we get more typical jumping ground with plenty of give. The classier National Hunt horses are therefore tempted to race and establish their credentials before perhaps having a short break when the weather turns in the New Year, ready to be brought to a peak again for Cheltenham and Aintree. The hurdling is also enlivened by a number of recruits off the Flat that are still fresh enough to make the most of their fitness advantage before the demands of the long season take their toll.

National Hunt form becomes more predictable and a large proportion of well-backed horses seem to oblige. Just as we attempted to do during the three midsummer months on the Flat, we must capitalize on this period when the punter has the edge. Bet more frequently and perhaps even increase the stakes if the results warrant it. The jumps season is almost 1,000 races old by the time of the first major race of the season, the Mackeson Gold Cup at Cheltenham. From this point the racing really steps up a gear and so should the punter.

As the Flat winds down, the incidence of heavy ground – also present during a wet spring – is more common. Horses find it much more difficult to concede weight in heavy ground and the number of horses who can carry nine stone or more to victory in genuinely heavy ground is limited.

So, for handicaps on heavy going, draw a line through those horses in the top half of the handicap and concentrate your studies on the featherweights.

The Flat turf season goes out with a whimper these days at Folkestone on the Monday after the William Hill November Handicap at Doncaster, the last domestic Flat race of any substance. But, of course, all-weather Flat racing continues at Lingfield, Wolverhampton and Southwell, which is dealt with in chapter 6.

JANUARY/FEBRUARY

The bookies start to rub their hands in January, not simply because of the cold snap. It is now the run-up to Cheltenham, when they expect to make some healthy profits. Frost and snow play havoc not only with the fixture list but with training programmes as well. Even if there is not a prolonged break, the racing programme can stutter from one abandonment to the next with the result that the form becomes unpredictable.

It is a time for reducing our stakes or perhaps shutting up shop altogether. If you must bet during a really cold spell, stick to very recent form. Frost can hold up even the most basic roadwork and steady cantering, never mind the full-tilt gallops, so it is possible that horses which have been race-fit before the snap can lose a little condition. Leave nothing to chance and just back horses that have run within days – their fitness is guaranteed.

There could be pockets around the country which are more, or less, severely affected than others, so monitor those yards and training centres which are sending out winners despite the difficulties caused by the cold weather. One point to note is that small yards are often able to find more enterprising means of keeping their horses on the go. It would be unfeasible for a yard with as many as 100 horses to ferry them to a beach for exercise but by no means out of the question for a stable with 10–15 inmates.

It is also now that thoughts turn to Cheltenham. A small pointer for our race, the Daily Express Triumph Hurdle, is that more often than not the winner has not made its hurdling debut until after 1 January.

A little meeting that I never miss on the run-up to the Festival is the Warwick fixture, which boasts a couple of good trials, notably the Regency Hurdle. It is no surprise that this meeting has been designed to attract Cheltenham horses as both meetings are under the direction of the enterprising Edward Gillespie. Cheltenham winners Rolling Ball, Dusty Miller and Thetford Forest all prepped at this fixture before winning at Cheltenham.

ALL YEAR ROUND: A BAD RUN

The classic blues song 'Born under a bad sign', written by Booker T. Jones and William Bell, contains the line: 'If it wasn't for bad luck, I wouldn't have no luck at all.' We punters know only too well what is meant. Photo-finishes go against you, your bet finishes full of running after being stuck in a pocket or falls at the last fence with the race at its mercy. Perhaps most aggravating of all is the 'winner' that has the race taken away in the stewards' room. We can't budget for that sort of bad luck but, in truth, according to the law of averages, we will have just as many such incidents going our way, too.

What is more worrying is the Bad Run, that string of losers that we have all experienced, and that we must anticipate in the future, which are not just pipped or unlucky but never hold any hope of success in the race. It can happen at any time during the betting year. Confidence is shaken, if not rocked to its very roots, and a quiet afternoon watching the racing on the box becomes a prolonged torture as you watch a series of selections or bets that you *know* are going to lose. I suspect I'm not alone when I say that during these inevitable losing runs I prefer the sudden death of the teletext or radio results service in the evening to the protracted agony of death by a thousand cuts, monitoring the results through the afternoon.

Unfortunately the newspaper tipster cannot approach his editor with the suggestion that a three-week sabbatical in the sun may be the answer. The punter, in comparison, does have the option to draw stumps and wait until his luck changes. Confidence is a fragile thing and when it goes, it goes good and proper. As soon as you recognize that you are not seeing things as clearly as you should – *quit*. Remember, the target is to make a profit not over a week or a month but over a long period of time. Maximize your profits by increasing stakes and the number of bets when things are going well, but minimize losses by reducing your stakes or stopping altogether when the results are bringing you nothing but grief. Log the bets you would have had, because it is only by keeping a strict record that you will be able to judge when you are ready to step back into the fray.

Peter Walwyn has twice been champion trainer and enjoyed a golden period in the mid-1970s when he guided the career of the young Pat Eddery and handled that marvellous racehorse with the flaxen mane and tail, Grundy. But Peter also knows the downside and has seen his number of winners dwindle to just 17 in 1993. When he won the 1993 July Cup with Hamas, it was his first victory in a Group 1 race for eight years. In the winner's enclosure that day, Walwyn summed up his feelings: 'I've always said that if you do the right things and keep plugging on, it always comes back.'

I couldn't agree more.

Chapter Ten

Secrets of the Professional Punters

There is definitely the whiff of the carbine and the manner of the Wild West gunslinger about the man who backs horses for a living. Often a man alone, his shoot-outs with the bookmakers become legend . . . and sometimes get distorted in the telling.

The fact that there have been, and still are, professional punters who have taken on the system and won – men whose betting skills have earned them fabulous riches – is an inspiration to anyone having a daily flutter.

Many backers have regularly bet in bigger stakes than the quintet I have chosen to investigate – Dorothy Paget and Terry Ramsden, for example – but the qualification for joining my select band of hombres was that each of them made their money from backing horses . . . and all have stood the test of time.

Where possible, I have talked to these men or their associates, recording the major coups and, I hope, gleaning a lesson or two along the way which might benefit the average punter.

Phil Bull, Jack Ramsden, Alex Bird, Barney Curley and Paul Cooper . . . we salute you.

PHIL BULL

The man who founded Timeform made his fortune as a punter, not as a publisher.

An unmistakable figure on racecourses – small, bow-tied

and with greying whiskers stained by an endless stream of his favourite Bock panatellas – it is hard to imagine that his passion for the stopwatch began when, as a kid, he used to time his sisters as they raced round the kitchen table. A more sophisticated use of the 'clock' and the application of mathematics to race times led to a lifetime of successful punting. By his own estimate, he took the bookies for more than half a million pounds.

A coalminer's son from Hemsworth in Yorkshire, Bull won a scholarship to Leeds University, where he graduated with a BSc in mathematics. Moving to London in the thirties, his £173-a-year schoolteacher's job left him with the time to go racing and he launched a weekly sheet of horses to follow under the pseudonym William K. Temple.

'My recommendations were based on the time figures recorded by my own stopwatch and the conclusions I drew from them,' said Bull.

Eventually he gave up the Temple service to devote more time to his own betting as well as to writing a series of hardback annual publications (*Best Horses of* . . .) which were the precursors of today's Timeform annuals. The early volumes remain some of the finest books about racing and racehorses ever written – vivid, lucid and littered with gems of insight which are just as pertinent today. Even in those far-off days, when the fixture list was half the size it is now, the work necessary to keep up with all the form proved too much for one man. Timeform was therefore set up to serve Bull's needs as a punter and, as he said: 'For 40 years I've never made a bet without it.'

Bull's success as a backer brought him the full trappings of wealth including a 10-bedroomed mansion, The Hollins, set in 66 acres of woodland a few miles from his Timeform base at Halifax. A miniature castle with turrets and battlements, The Hollins boasts an Adam fireplace and a snooker room where he occasionally scored notable triumphs over his friend, snooker champion Joe Davis.

About the time Reg Griffin, Timeform's managing director for the past 25 years, joined him, Bull dispensed with his chauffeur-driven Jaguar and bought his first Rolls-Royce – not from his winnings but as a company car, an expense of the business. The fact that he had the Midnight Blue model returned to the factory in favour of one a shade of Bolshevik Red gave a clue to his political leanings. It's unlikely you would have found a copy of the *Daily Telegraph* on the seat of Bull's roller. But like many a man of leftish opinions, he had an ambivalent attitude to wealth and saw nothing incongruous in commissioning Asprey's of London to produce two personal leather covers for the Timeform race card, monogrammed in gold for Griffin and himself.

'The racecourse was the perfect battleground for me,' said Bull. 'It was an exhilarating place where you could pit your abilities and your nerve against those of everyone else – because that is what it amounts to, every punter against every other punter – and only the best-equipped would survive.

'I wanted an arena, and here was one ready-made for me, with all the elements for testing myself already created and a marvellously varied and fascinating cast of characters.'

That in part explains his lifelong opposition to a Tote monopoly. 'The presence of a live betting market on every race – provided by the bookmakers – gives a vitality and excitement to racing here that is absent abroad.'

Like many a punter before and since, he adopted a stable in the beginning – in his case the horses of Lord Derby. But, appropriately for a man based in Yorkshire, his first major coups involved the north's last Derby winner, Dante. Bull clocked Dante's first win as a two-year-old at Stockton in the spring of 1944 and knew from the time that the colt had enormous potential. Dante was beaten only once (in the Two Thousand Guineas) during a brilliant career whose climax was his 100–30 win in the

1945 Derby; Bull backed him substantially every time he ran.

Bull had a particular affinity for the Two Thousand Guineas and Derby winner of 1949, Nimbus. At one time personal assistant and then bloodstock adviser to the legendary bookmaker William Hill, Bull was responsible for the breeding of the colt. Nimbus won the Guineas at 10–1 in the first English Classic race to be decided by a photo-finish, and went on to take the Derby at 7–1. He did not go unbacked on either occasion.

For Bull a £1,000 bet was commonplace and a £5,000 stake very rare. His turnover was as much as £500,000 a year and he reckoned on a profit of 8 per cent. In later years, though, he had to settle for about 4 per cent owing to the introduction of betting tax, the progressive weakening of the betting market (yes, even in those days) and, ironically, the result of his life's work. Bookmakers and punters who studied his publications could know almost as much as the man himself. As Bull put it graphically: 'I have soiled my own nest.'

Reg Griffin recalls Phil making a consistent profit year in and year out. 'He was invariably successful but I remember a particular Flat season soon after I joined him when he made a profit of £32,000.' At the current rate of exchange that would amount to £360,000.

Perhaps one of Bull's secrets was his temperament. 'Phil was never one to shout his selections home,' recalled Griffin. 'One day at Ayr, Phil had a bet of £5,000 to £2,000 about a two-year-old of Ernie Davey's: It crossed the line locked together with another youngster and I was getting in a desperate state until the result was announced in Phil's favour, but he hadn't turned a hair.

'At the end of the afternoon, I might ask him how he'd got on. He'd just say "£5,000 up" or "£2,000 down", before falling asleep in the back of the car on the drive home.

'He took the day's results with equanimity – it was the season as a whole that counted.'

Of course, it was not success all the way. In a penetrating interview with Ken Hurren for the *Daily Telegraph Magazine* in 1970, Bull told of the day he chartered a plane to Hamilton Park in Scotland to back a two-year-old that was a certainty on form. He expected the odds to be prohibitively short, but that was not how things turned out.

'The more I bet on the horse, the longer the odds became,' he said. 'I lost £6,500 and ended up giving myself a lecture on my folly. I had been so carried away with the horse's theoretical chance that I had not noticed the obvious indications that something was wrong with the horse – which everybody seemed to know except me. On the racecourse, eyes are usually more valuable than ears, but on this occasion the ears had it.'

Asked once by Griffin at what point he might become concerned if his punting were going badly, Bull said: 'I suppose if I was £20,000 down.' After a particularly bad run, he had reached just that threshold in 1963 on the eve of the big York August meeting. As was often the case, he took his form books with him to the bath and determined to find the winner of the big race the following day, the Ebor Handicap. Much like another mathematician some 22 centuries before, he leapt from the bath crying Eureka! The solution turned out to be the Irish-trained three-year-old Partholon, who had been runner-up in the race sponsored by Bull, the Timeform Gold Cup, the previous year. The next morning he had £1,000 on Partholon at 20–1 – and his debts for the season were erased as the colt held on with the utmost gameness in a pulsating finish.

All races came alike to Bull. He regarded a race as something which required examination. If, having studied it, there was no bet, so be it. Every race was treated on its merits; but he did draw up the following list of don'ts:

DON'T bet unless the odds are good value – a matter of individual judgement. 'If I am offered only evens about what I judge to be a 6–4 chance,' he said, 'I do not bet. If I can get 2–1, I bet. And 3–1 about the same horse is a Bet with a capital B.'

DON'T bet beyond your means or try to make your fortune in one day.

DON'T concern yourself with staking systems – increasing stakes after a winner or so many losers and so forth. Vary your stakes only according to the chance of the horse and the odds.

DON'T buy tips or systems: geese that lay golden eggs are never for sale.

DON'T fail to read your bookmaker's rules, especially the small print.

DON'T bet ante-post (before the day of the race) unless you know that the horse is an intended runner.

DON'T bet each-way in handicaps or other races with big fields: a place bet at one-fifth the odds is rarely good value.

By following these principles, Bull felt the punter at least had a chance. 'It is not possible for the majority of punters to make a profit in the long run,' he said, 'for they are betting against one another with the bookmakers acting as middle men. There is so much information available that nobody has the edge. I am not saying that a punter can't make it pay any more, but he needs to be very good.'

In the context of his life as a whole, the three-times-married Bull once said: 'Racing is a triviality, but I'm hooked on the game.' His library may have been dominated by books on philosophy, sociology and humanism, his leisure time spent on his other passions, chess and the music of Mozart, but it was to racing that he devoted 50 years of his life.

Rarely can that be said about anyone of his towering intellect and only one such, Bull himself chose to champion the cause of the punter. His abrasive anti-establishment views and an inability to listen to any opinions other than his own prevented him from wielding any real influence in racing politics, but the legacy he bequeathed to punters was the superb Timeform publications.

The clock stopped for Phil Bull, aged 79, on 11 June 1989. The debt punters owe him is incalculable.

JACK RAMSDEN

To call Jack Ramsden the scourge of the bookmakers is not strictly true. He bets with only one – Colin Webster – and sees his relationship with the leading northern rails layer as a partnership.

'It's years since I have had any betting accounts closed,' says Jack. 'Now I bet personally with Colin. He's an honourable man and we work as a team. He has the problem of getting the money on and in doing so he knows the horses I fancy, so we both benefit.'

Ramsden's individual punts are not the sort to send shudders around the ring. The biggest single bet he ever had was £5,000 – 'and that got stuffed' – but ever since he quit his job as a stockbroker in 1980 he has had 13 consecutive winning years as a full-time professional backer. Some of those years have been very profitable indeed. It is a record of which he is fiercely and justifiably proud. 'I like to think I adopt an intelligent approach to backing horses and it has served me well for 30 years.'

The betting-shop punter knows Ramsden as the husband of Lynda who trains with success from Breckenbrough House, Sandhutton near Thirsk in Yorkshire, a once derelict farm that is now a plush, modern training establishment for 50 horses. In the spring of 1993, Lynda saddled the first and third – High Premium and Will Of Steel – in the William Hill Lincoln Handicap, the first big competitive handicap of the season.

Jack, who studied accountancy for eight years – 'I learned how to read a balance sheet but little else' – is the business brain of the outfit, and running a racing stable is a very expensive business. He is also perceived as a Svengali figure, pulling the strings (and the horses) in order to mastermind gambling coups. The truth is somewhat different. Jack says he hardly ever backs the horses trained by his wife. 'Whereas we used to get 14–1 about a horse that should have been 5–1, it's now the other way around. When they drift to a more realistic price and are beaten, people say they are not off. Someone, somewhere, is always prepared to smell a rat.'

Of course, there have been some well-engineered gambles. Jack fondly remembers two from the days before Lynda was a trainer – Cheapside (backed from 33s to 10–1), which Albert Davison saddled to win a Wincanton handicap hurdle in 1973, and Hidden Talent (14s to 5–1), trained by John Sutcliffe to win a claimer at Glorious Goodwood the following summer. 'You could say neither had much form,' added Jack with a chuckle. 'But in those days if a horse finished 7th, it might as well have been 19th because only the first six were recorded in the form book. Now nothing is missed.

'They were the dark ages as far as punters were concerned.'

Ramsden's biggest payday on a horse trained by Lynda came in 1989 when Arbory Street (14s to 13–2) won a selling handicap at Leicester. 'The thick end of my bet was £2,000 to win and £1,000 to place and in total I cleared £35,000,' said Jack. 'That paid for the equine swimming pool in the yard.

'Arbory Street was a moderate two-year-old and no better at three. He did improve in the spring of his four-year-old career but by that time he had become a very well-handicapped horse. We simply made sure he was fit for his reappearance.'

The success for Colin Webster-owned Daring Times first time out as a five-year-old in a handicap at Doncaster was another notable plunge from 33s to 5–1, while in 1993 Jack had reason to thank the two-year-old Multi National.

'Our two-year-olds have the reputation for needing the run so we used that to our advantage. Multi National had been working well at home but we also gave him a racecourse gallop to make sure. We found a race for him against a large field of maidens at Beverley and he lapped them, backed from 8s to 9–2.

'We can only pull that sort of stroke once a year or the bookies would be waiting for it every time one of ours runs.'

The majority of Jack's bets, though, are on outside horses, and the result of diligent work on the form book. He gets the Timeform *Perspective* twice a week, makes some adjustments to their renowned Timefigures, and then his personal assistant logs the ratings in the Ramsden computer. A weights-adjusted print-out is then produced for Jack each morning.

'I cannot stress more strongly the importance of race times. They bind my whole approach together.

'There are fewer good times recorded over jumps but everyone seems to know about those horses and they are too short to back.

'Even cutting out the endless looking up of form books, I still spend two or three hours every day working out my bets. I then watch races on SIS at home in the afternoon, so it's a full-time job.

'I'm constantly on the look out for the 3–1 chance which starts at 8–1. There are 30 or 40 of them a year and they are there to be seen. At those prices you don't have to be right all the time.

'We've all fallen for backing the 6–4 certainty and had too much on, only to see it beaten. I don't do that any more. One of the greatest disciplines the pro backer must learn is to stand back and watch when those short-priced horses win.'

Rather surprisingly, Ramsden is an advocate of multiple bets – doubles, trebles and accumulators – the sort considered the province of the mug punter.

'I can't see why people knock multiple bets. They are an extension of my philosophy to go for big prices. On a busy Saturday I might average seven or eight selections which I pool in trebles and accumulators – I drop the doubles to cut down on the stakes because I'm only looking for a major return.

'I usually average about ten nice touches a year and on four occasions in my career I've won over £200,000. That pays for an awful lot of losers.'

That other staple of the mug punter, the each-way bet, is frowned upon, but Jack can't quite erase it from his accounts. 'I'm a cautious punter and my natural reserve makes me have £700 to win and £300 to place when I know I should have £1,000 on the nose.

'I analysed my betting a couple of years back and found that if I had doubled my win stakes instead of having each-way bets, I would have been much better off. I think every punter would benefit by cutting out all each-way bets.'

As can be seen from some of his spectacular coups, Jack doesn't shy away from handicaps. 'I like them, especially when I'm able to take an early price. The form is there to be seen. I can't understand punters who take short prices in big fields of maidens when they know so little about some of the runners.'

As for his staking plan, there are no hard and fast rules. It could even be called haphazard . . . but it works. 'If I get a gut feeling for a horse that I really fancy, I'll steam in. I don't always bet to the same stake.'

Ramsden has come a long way since, as a 17-year-old at Stowe public school in the late 1950s, he was part of a small gambling syndicate which successfully raided a local betting shop in Buckingham. There were also a couple of firms that took postal bets on evening racing. 'A friend and I used to take it in turns to post off our bets and towards the end of a summer term we landed a nice little touch. Unfortunately, the cheque, made out to my confederate, didn't arrive until during the holidays and was opened by one of the masters. 'My pal was promptly expelled.'

Then, as now, Britain's most successful, active pro punter had the happy knack of being in the right place at the right time.

ALEX BIRD

Epsom racecourse, 22 April 1947 – an important day in the annals of the Turf. The prestigious Great Metropolitan Handicap that afternoon, in which Pahelion beat Salubrious by a head, was the first race decided by a photo-finish.

It also began the phase of Alex Bird's calling as a punter when he regularly had a turnover of £2 million a year.

In those days, the photo-finish film took five minutes to develop and during that time an active betting market was formed. Bird, who was racing six days a week, noticed that as the horses flashed across the line together an optical illusion favoured the runner on the far side. He found that by keeping his head perfectly still and closing one eye, he could, with uncanny accuracy, predict the outcome. When he believed the unfavoured (and therefore longer-priced) near side had won he would back it.

Until a combination of betting tax and more rapid film development effectively closed this avenue of betting, Bird took up the same position on the line for 20 years. During that time he claimed to have registered a phenomenal 500 consecutive successful bets at an average of £500 a time. Watch the birdie, indeed!

It was a method which brought him immense wealth and an ostentatious lifestyle: the fifteenth century moated manor house in Cheshire; house parties at which orchestras from Manchester's Midland Hotel would play until the early hours for guests including his great friend Sir Matt Busby; a string of luxury cars and successful racehorses; his own private plane; a box at Old Trafford; a riverside suite at the Savoy; and a diet of oysters and caviar, washed down by his favourite Krug champagne. Not bad for a man whose father was a coal merchant from Newton Heath on the outskirts of Manchester who also ran a small bookmaking concern in the days of bookies' runners, clock bags and the close attention of the police. Who says gambling does not pay?

Bird was still a teenager when he had his first betting account closed and landed his first major touch, aged 21, on the 1938 Grand National winner Battleship. He put on £10 at 40–1 and scooped £410. But it was only after he had served in the Pacific with the Royal Navy and flirted briefly with the family bookmaking business that he decided punting was his game.

Battleship was not to be his only triumph in the National. Bird was very fond of the race and had a private dining room at Aintree. Freebooter's success in 1950 netted him £70,000 and two years later he backed the winner Teal to win £50,000. With his own horse Signification winning later on the same card, and netting a similar sum in bets, it was his biggest single payday.

But, as for so many punters, the coup of a lifetime – again in the National – was the one that got away. It was the one occasion when this man, who had the discipline not to have a bet after chartering a plane to Newmarket on four consecutive days, allowed his opinions to run away with him. Backing Tudor Line originally at 40–1 and continually pressing his bets until the day of the race, he stood to win £500,000. But for a vital piece of Tudor Line's tack being dispensed with, Bird would have collected.

Tudor Line had a tendency to jump to the right and

wore an attachment to his bit called a brush pricker which helped to correct the problem. In the mistaken belief that Tudor Line's wayward fencing had been cured, trainer Bobby Renton left the pricker off at Aintree. In the race the gelding forfeited so much ground by jumping to the right that as they passed the stands with a lap to go he was so far behind it looked as if he might be pulled up. Miraculously he got back into the race and actually led at the second last. Surrendering the lead with another erratic leap at the last fence, he managed a final rally on the run-in but was beaten a neck by Royal Tan, the middle leg of Vincent O'Brien's hat-trick of wins in the race.

The introduction of betting tax at 2½ per cent in 1966 caused Bird to alter his betting strategy. At a stroke, the tax had wiped out his profit margin. Bookmaker William Hill, for one, believed it would mean the end of the professional backer; but Bird wasn't prepared to take flight. He reduced his annual turnover to £250,000 by cutting out 80 per cent of his wagers. The ones he had, he made count.

One horse on which he never put a foot wrong was Mill Reef. And it was Bird's passionate interest in race times which alerted him to the colt's exceptional talents. 'Mill Reef broke the clock on firm ground and won the Gimcrack Stakes in the mud. That's the mark of a good horse.' Bird's biggest bet in 1970 – £20,000 at 4–6 – was on Paul Mellon's little bay in the Dewhurst Stakes. Mill Reef won by four lengths. The following season Mill Reef became the seventh Derby winner in eight years backed by Bird. In total he won £123,000 on Mill Reef.

Of course, Bird didn't always get it right. He took an over-optimistic view about the ability of star two-year-olds Tromos, J. O. Tobin and Gorytus, all of whom failed to fulfil early promise, and endured a seemingly endless run of losers in the Breeders' Cup when backing British flops – Dancing Brave, Indian Skimmer and the unlucky Dayjur, who jumped a shadow with the race at his mercy.

But in 1990, the year before he died, Bird summoned up one last coup. A popular racecourse saying during his heyday went: 'Alex Bird won't go to bed with his wife the night before a big punt in case he talks in his sleep.' It was the money that talked when his friend Peter Hurst owned a runner in the Ayr Gold Cup, a race Bird himself had won three times and which he affectionately dubbed 'Scotland's Derby'. Backed from 40s to 12–1, the winnings were never in doubt. The name of the horse? Final Shot.

If you want to Follow the Bird – here are the axioms of Alex.

DON'T BET WHEN THE GOING CHANGES. If the going changes from firm to soft, keep your money in your pocket. Nothing upsets form more regularly than a significant change in the ground.

FOLLOW UP-AND-COMING JOCKEYS. Look out for promising apprentices. I saw Kevin Darley show the utmost coolness riding his first ever winner and told his guv'nor Reg Hollinshead: 'That boy is better than money in the bank.'

DON'T BET WHEN THE BOOKMAKERS' PROFIT MARGIN IS UNFAIR. At some small meetings, particularly on a bank holiday, the bookmakers will bet massively over-round – almost so the figures are 60 per cent or 70 per cent in their favour.

BET EACH WAY IN NON-HANDICAPS WITH 8–10 RUNNERS. Pick races where there are a limited number of form horses, oppose the favourite and combine your second and third fancies in each-way combination bets.

DON'T BET FIRST SHOW. The bookmakers' profit is never higher than when they are sparring for an opening. Almost all runners increase in price, especially where the market is weak.

ONLY RELY ON ELECTRICAL TIMES. Stopwatch holders for the press are not 100 per cent reliable. Never compare times for races run on different days, even if the going is the same.

NEVER BET IN HANDICAPS. The handicapper makes few mistakes; when he does, the bookmakers are only too aware of them.

DON'T BET IN THREE-YEAR-OLD MAIDENS. When betting tax was introduced in 1966, I had to rethink my betting strategy. The biggest saving I made was to stop betting in three-year-old maidens, especially those for fillies.

BARNEY CURLEY

The reason Barney Curley has been the bane of bookmakers and the most celebrated punter of modern times can be traced back to an evening at Belfast's Celtic Park greyhound stadium some 40 years ago. It was the night Barney's father, a grocer from Irvinstown, Co. Fermanagh, went for the gamble of his life on one of the dogs he owned. At the first bend, the dog fell and broke its neck.

The sight of his dad walking back up the track, cradling the dead dog, has haunted Barney ever since.

Curley senior took Barney, the eldest of six children, out of school and into self-imposed exile in Manchester where the two of them worked double shifts in a plastics factory for 15 months until enough money had been raised to clear the gambling debts. 'My father wouldn't come back until everyone was paid and he could hold his head high in the local community,' said Barney. 'But it left him wounded deeply.'

Every gamble Barney lands is a form of retribution for the way bookies made his father suffer. He has accumulated closed betting accounts like a pony-mad schoolgirl collects rosettes at a gymkhana, but he drew a perverse pleasure when William Hill decided in 1988 they no longer wanted his business after he had taken them for £200,000 in the previous two years.

Barney persistently harangues bookmakers, saying: 'My priority has been to lessen the influence of the Big Three – they wield far too much power.

'There are only four or five bookies I'm interested in betting with – the ones who will lay me a substantial bet – and they don't represent the majors.'

With his large, distinctive fedora and his menacing countenance, he looks as if he would have made a mean adversary for Eliot Ness in prohibition-era Chicago. Yet underneath the daunting surface lies a congenial family man, with three grown-up children and a charming wife, Maureen, who, ironically, is the daughter of a bookmaker.

Get him off the subject of bookies and Barney speaks almost in a whisper, his conversation peppered with pregnant pauses as he carefully chews over his thoughts. Ask him what his greatest touch was and he unhesitatingly admits it was the day he was pronounced clear of the tuberculosis which struck him down as a lad of 21. At the time he was studying for the priesthood with the Jesuits – the shock troops of the Catholic religion, he calls them – at Mungret College in Limerick, a former school of Vincent O'Brien.

'I'd been getting pains in my chest and when they examined me I was riddled with TB. I spent the next 12 months on my back in a special hospital in Northern Ireland. Fortunately they'd just discovered a cure but plenty in there did not survive. I was lucky.'

It was another 18 months before he had a clean bill of health but he realized he would not be strong enough for the gruelling studies of the seminary – and that's when he drifted improbably into the pop music business. At 24, he began to manage showbands – a phenomenon curious to the dance hall circuit in Ireland at the time. He diversified by buying a handful of pubs and betting shops but sold up and went south of the border to start punting.

'I wanted to prove myself,' he says. 'You have to be out of the ordinary to make money as a punter.

'I fancied myself as a race reader and I thought I could crack the system.

'My first big win was about £80,000 and within six weeks it had vanished. I was drinking; I soon discovered drinking and gambling don't go together so from that day I've never touched a drop.'

The biggest gamble he masterminded in Ireland was the infamous Yellow Sam coup, which netted almost £300,000. The race was the Mount Hanover Amateur Riders' Handicap Hurdle at Bellewstown on 25 June 1975. Bellewstown is a small country track north of Dublin, which, at the time, had just one phone line. Curley and his team got to work backing the horse off-course in stakes of up to £50, while another associate kept the single phone at the course out of commission. In the days before mobile phones and a sophisticated 'blower' system, the bookmakers were unable to notify their representatives at the track that a coup was going down. Yellow Sam, who had shown little form in his nine previous runs, started the complete outsider of the nine runners at 20–1 and won by two and a half lengths.

Curley calls it a 'marvellous stroke'; the bookies thought otherwise. The bold Irishman defends his operation: 'The racecourse is a dog-eat-dog world where there are no rules and only the toughest survive.

'Bookmakers are up to every trick in the book. If you have a horse and you can keep something up your sleeve from them and then go to the well and draw at the right odds, there's nothing morally wrong with that. Remember, gambles come unstuck as much as they come off.'

Not surprisingly, Curley found the bookies in Ireland shutting him out; so he moved to England in 1984 and added a new hat to his wardrobe, that of racehorse trainer.

Previously, Jimmy FitzGerald and Michael Dickinson had trained his horses over here and he spent some time with the legendary 'Bald Eagle' Charlie Whittingham in

California. Two shaved, domed heads on the backstretch at Santa Anita. Barney was keen to demystify the art of racehorse training. 'I'm not a half-hearted person, I always give 100 per cent. But anyone can train – I did it in my spare time. The secret is to get your horse fit. Too many trainers send their horses to the track unprepared.'

He proved his training talents were as acute as his flair for punting after he had backed himself to saddle ten winners in 1987. During the 1985/6 season, he had sent out just one winner, so it was a deeply satisfied Curley when on 22 December 1987 Experimenting became his tenth winner, landing the Sellindge Handicap Hurdle at Folkestone. Curley won £275,000.

Like all the professionals in this chapter, Curley has made a very comfortable living. His house is a seven-bedroomed mansion at Stetchworth near Newmarket, complete with indoor swimming pool, and there's a top-of-the-range Mercedes in the driveway with the personalized number plate 1 BET.

Ever the punter looking for value, Curley bought his current home at a knock-down price from Terry Ramsden when the flamboyant financier and mega-punter fell on hard times.

But Curley is not very encouraging about any punter's chance of following in his own footsteps: 'It is impossible to make it pay with 10 per cent tax.

'The important thing is to control your emotions and don't chase your losses. There's always another day. I know my knowledge and judgement of form will pay off in the end.'

And he's not one to spread his chances around. 'I only ever bet on one horse in any race – for me, it's the whole duck or no dinner.'

Fifty-five-year-old Curley's influence in the ring is perhaps on the wane, and he cuts a rather disenchanted figure after his failed attempt to unite the country's one million punters in his punters' organization.

'Do you know how many joined me? Just 300. I'm afraid I'm not in the business of helping people who can't help themselves. I feel I've wasted the last three years.'

Then, rather chillingly for any bookmaker, I suspect, he added: 'I made a New Year's resolution to look after just one person's interests – my own!'

PAUL COOPER

Betting on tricasts seems an improbable means to punting profit but professional backer Paul Cooper, at 35 one of the young turks of the betting ring, used it to win nearly £400,000 on a series of bets at Thirsk.

Cooper was one of the first to capitalize on the fact that horses drawn high seemed to have a pronounced advantage over the straight sprint course at Thirsk. There are a number of tracks around the country where, in soft ground, a particular draw can prove an enormous asset, but at Thirsk the same was true on lightning-fast going. It appears that the inadequacies of the course watering system left a strip of ground under the stands rails 'unsprinkled' which was significantly faster than the rest of the track. By perming the five or six highest draw numbers – those most likely to grab the favoured ground – Cooper was able to pull off a number of major coups.

It is entirely appropriate he should have made a killing at Thirsk, since he was brought up on a farm close to the racecourse; but it was at the local point-to-point that he was first seduced by the excitement of betting. As a four-year-old lad, he was taken there by his father and, like many a tot on a day out at the races, he was invited to nominate a horse he wanted to back. A beast called Paul's Diamond seemed to pick itself and when it came in at a good price, he'd set off on the path which was to lead ultimately to his current luxury lifestyle.

The stake on Paul's Diamond was a couple of bob, but in

the 13 years that Cooper has backed horses for a living, he has staked over £30 million and had more than 40 betting accounts closed.

'I was hooked on betting from a very early age,' admits Cooper. 'But even then I understood that you had to be in control of it, or otherwise it would gain control of you.'

His masters at Stowe public school – also Jack Ramsden's alma mater – would have been delighted that his affinity for maths was being exercised during his holidays, but perhaps not so pleased that the problems solved were those set by the 3.30 at Newbury.

When the time came to consider a career, Cooper decided to join bloodstock magazine *Stud and Stable*, then moving on to *The Statistical Record*, the publication whose stallion statistics are required reading for leading breeders and owners. But a dreary office job on the periphery of racing only whetted his appetite for his real passion – punting.

'I took my courage in both hands and decided to back horses for a living,' he told Colin Fleetwood Jones in a *Daily Star* interview. 'I started off with small stakes and the new ITV Seven caught my eye. One of my first wagers was a £1.90 bet which won over £800. I was in business.

'A couple of years later, I collected £13,365 on a £3 accumulator and I was really on my way. After that the staking plan went up to £100.'

Cooper is still fascinated by multiple bets – the prospect of huge returns for a small outlay – and believes serious punters should not treat them in such a cavalier fashion.

'The Lucky 15 is a value bet – it is a yankee that also has four win singles and the different bookies offer a variety of bonuses and consolations. For instance, if only one of your selections wins you may get double the odds so just one 7–1 winner virtually guarantees you your money back.'

Cooper's penchant for what Barney Curley calls 'miracle bets' is not his only apparent similarity with the man in the street – like all betting-shop regulars he is irresistibly drawn to competitive handicaps where they bet 6–1 the field . . . but he hits the target far more often.

'Paul is an ace at working out handicaps,' says one racing insider, admiringly. 'He's out on his own. He may back more than one horse in the race but he inevitably finds the winner.'

Cooper insists that studying trainers is the key to his whole operation. The fact that, as an owner, he has chosen to have horses trained by Barry Hills, Jimmy FitzGerald and Robert Williams gives a clue to the men he most respects in the game.

'There are certainly some trainers I much, much prefer to back,' he insists. 'What I'm really looking for is someone who is perhaps underestimated and as a result their horses start at a bigger price than they should do.' Just such a trainer is Yorkshire-based David Chapman, who won nine handicaps in 1988 with star sprinter Glencroft, improving the gelding four and a half stones during the season according to the official handicapper. Cooper's instinctive feel for a good horse helped him to spot Glencroft's rise early and on that single horse he won more than £100,000.

'And that takes into account a bet of £22,000 on him when he was beaten in the Bovis Stakes at Ascot,' adds Cooper. That day the responsibility for steering heavily backed Glencroft seemed to affect jockey Stuart Webster. After losing ground by coming out of the stalls crookedly, clattering into the heels of the leaders at one stage and then hanging badly in the closing stages, Glencroft was still beaten less than three lengths.

Handicap king Cooper has also enjoyed some notable triumphs in the Derby, including a truly blessed run at Epsom during the 1980s.

'I put £8,000 on Reference Point at 10–1 after he won the William Hill Futurity at Doncaster as a two-year-old. I had

Shergar at all rates down from 8–1 to 7–2 – he won at 10–11. I saved on Secreto in 1984. Golden Fleece was my only bet on the race in 1982 and I took 20–1 about the 1980 winner Henbit.'

So what then can we learn from the fastidious, immaculately turned-out Cooper, who admits: 'If it wasn't for betting tax, I would be a very, very rich man indeed'? Here are ten do's and ten don'ts – Cooper's Law.

DO stay cool, calm and collected when making a selection and don't go in head down. Weigh up all the possibilities and then have the nerve to go through with it.

DO bet only when you are getting good value.

DO, if possible, bet on the racecourse where there is no tax.

DO, alternatively, shop around for the best early-morning prices.

DO back horses who have winning form; shy away from maidens.

DO bet in sprints – the form is more reliable than in long-distance races.

DO always check that your selection has recorded good times.

DO find a small, competent yard to follow; because it isn't fashionable, you'll get a better price. If the stable uses a capable apprentice, all the better.

DO look at the horses in the paddock, especially in the spring and autumn. You can usually discard quite a few which are obviously not ready.

DO bet within your means. Reduce your stakes when having a bad run, increase them when things are going well.

DON'T get drunk at the races. You need your wits about you to back winners.

DON'T back short-priced favourites. The return simply isn't good enough and they often get turned over anyway.

DON'T chase your losses – there is always another day.

DON'T bet heavily when there has been a sudden change in the going.

DON'T back out-of-form stables.

DON'T back jockeys carrying overweight.

DON'T back heavily at Chester – the tight track is a law unto itself.

DON'T bet in races where the horses split into two or more groups, effectively making it two or three different races, e.g. Wokingham, Royal Hunt Cup, Stewards' Cup and Ayr Gold Cup.

DON'T listen to whispers; rely on your own judgement.

DON'T bet in too many two-year-old races. There is more evidence concerning older horses.

These are the principles Cooper uses not only for his own betting but also on the premium line tipping service, Fonaview, which he has set up from his company offices in Guildford, Surrey.

Sadly, the recession has forced him to spend much of the winter in the States where, incidentally, the nose defeat of Paseana cost him a mammoth payout on the last Breeders' Cup Pic 6 bet, and to diversify into the more salacious end of the phone line market. Let's hope this doesn't signal the end of Cooper as a prime mover in the domestic betting market. The bookies may applaud his temporary withdrawal, but for punters he has proved an inspiration, showing that it is possible for one gifted young man to take on the vast multiples and win.

PART FOUR
OTHER FACTORS

Chapter Eleven

Information

'The most valuable commodity I know is information . . . the public's out there throwing darts at a board; I bet on sure things . . . staying up all night analysing charts; where did it get you? . . . if you're not inside, you're outside . . .'

The words belong to Gordon Gekko, fictional creation of Oliver Stone in the Oscar-winning movie of the 1980s, *Wall Street*.

Gekko was archly named and as ruthless a monster as any of those overgrown reptiles in 1990s blockbuster *Jurassic Park*. But was he right? The ordinary punter certainly yearns to be on the inside track. Tell a friend you have spent three hours unravelling a difficult handicap and have concluded that X will win and he will ask: 'But what does the trainer say?'

It's a frustrating experience and one every newspaper tipster knows only too well. There is a regular flow of tips from 'impeccable sources', but I would estimate that fewer than 15 per cent of them actually win. Backing favourites blindly on the Flat yields a 36 per cent success rate. So perhaps it's not surprising that I lean more towards Phil Bull's aphorism – *Believe what you see, not what you hear*.

Well, who would you trust – Gekko or Bull?

Information is no substitute for form, but it can be used in tandem with it, helping to predict the likely betting moves. By information I don't mean some third-hand hearsay passed down over the pool table at the local pub but a direct line to the gallop watchers. That's where the *Daily Express*'s network of regional reporters, especially our three men in the key training centres of Newmarket, Middleham and Lambourn, are invaluable. They are expert readers of the form book and have a comprehensive knowledge of the stables in their areas.

In the case of our Newmarket man that's more than 2,500 racehorses. On a balmy, good-to-be-alive summer's morning, Newmarket can be heaven on earth for anyone interested in racehorses. But when the wind and rain come horizontally off the North Sea, and one layer of oilskins is simply not enough, I can think of few more depressing places. Our correspondent has to be out in all weathers every morning, and without the luxury of the jockeys' colours he must identify the horses from a white sock or snip on the nose. I have reproduced below a page from his 'work book' to show how little data he needs to identify a horse looming out of the early morning mist.

ARDKINGLASS	b.	v ft*	———
ARMIGER	ch.	big bl	$\dfrac{}{st}$ st
BARRATRY	ch.	bl	$\dfrac{st\quad st}{}$
BIG SKY	br.	w/c	———
COMMANDER IN CHIEF	b.br	snip	———

Here a selection of Henry Cecil's three-year-old colts is listed. Their name and colour are logged in the first two columns. The third column refers to markings on the head; the fourth shows an imaginary body line with markings on the legs arranged thus:

off fore	*off hind*
near fore	*near hind*

The abbreviations used are: b: bay; bl: blaze; br: brown; ch: chestnut; s: sock; snip: white snip on nose; st: stocking; w/c: whole coloured (no markings); *: star on forehead. Ardkinglass, therefore, is a bay colt with a very faint star on his forehead but no markings on his legs; Armiger is a chestnut colt with a big blaze and stockings on all legs apart from his off (right) foreleg.

What our correspondents see on the gallops is privileged information, unavailable in any form book, and a potent weapon in the punter's armoury. Just how potent can be gauged from the following list of winners given as Training Hints in the *Daily Express* by our three main regional contacts during July, August and September in 1993: Herr Trigger (25–1), Lindon Lime (25–1), Hannah's Music (16–1), Bob's Return (16–1), Pigeon Island (16–1), Norman Warrior (16–1), Candi Das (16–1), Water Gypsy (14–1), Danger Baby (14–1), Jaazim (14–1), Admiring (13–1), Charity Express (12–1), Alpine Skier (12–1), Cumbrian Rhapsody (12–1), Margaret's Gift (12–1), Jokist (12–1), Persiansky (12–1), Glimpse (12–1), Embankment (12–1), Side Bar (11–1), Jess Rebec (11–1), Chatoyant (11–1).

A fine record, I think you will agree – and there were many, many more. It underlines the fact that it is during these summer months that the punter should be maximizing his profits.

As impeccable sources of information go they don't come any better than a trainer ten days before his first triumph in the Derby. Peter Chapple-Hyam, the son of a wholesale greengrocer from Leamington Spa, has made a rapid rise to the head of the trainers' profession and members of the *Daily Express* Marie Curie Racing Club have reaped the benefit of his skill since he trains one of our Club horses, the exciting prospect Charity Crusader. In the furtive world of racing, where stable secrets are kept as close to the chest as any vest, Peter is as open and accommodating as any trainer I know.

It seemed to me that his Dr Devious had an excellent chance in the 1992 Derby. A tenacious bulldog of a horse, Dr Devious had Group 1 winning form as a two-year-old and proved he had trained on when finishing second in the Craven Stakes in the spring. The Two Thousand Guineas was bypassed for a bold, if misguided, attempt to win the Kentucky Derby. But to my mind it didn't diminish his chance at Epsom. Being a son of the sprinter Ahonoora, however, there had to be a doubt whether Dr Devious would stay the mile and a half. A make-or-break gallop was planned at Manton with big-race jockey John Reid in the saddle.

Dr Devious worked with two lead horses, Relentless Pursuit and Spanish Grandee, over a mile and a quarter on the Bank Bend gallop. A searching pace was set but at the finish Dr Devious had come eight lengths clear on the bridle and showed no signs whatever of stopping. I happened to speak to Peter within a couple of hours of this trial and his mood was . . . effervescent. The animated conversation ended with my asking him: 'Are you telling me to take the 14s about Dr D?'

The unequivocal reply was: 'Yes.'

Within minutes my bet of £1,400 to £100 each way was struck with Hills; ten days later Dr Devious put up a typically courageous display to win the Ever Ready Derby.

Insider dealing, maybe; but in this market they can't touch you for it!

FUTUREFORM

The entries an owner or trainer makes in major British races, both Flat and jumping, have long been readily available for anyone who subscribes to the *Racing Calendar*. But it was only when Peter Gordon's Cambridgeshire firm, Future-form, set about indexing those entries, and those of British horses in races abroad, that this information became a fascinating new colour on the punters' palette.

The basic premise of Futureform is that you can share the innermost thoughts of trainers – the equivalent of having your own mole in every stable yard. You can establish how much potential a particular horse has in the trainer's eye, based on future entries, perhaps weeks before it makes its racecourse debut.

Futureform's proponents make extravagant claims for it as a winner-finding system; but it falls down because it is based on the optimism of owners and trainers and what a horse has been doing on the gallops, not on the hard fact of results in racecourse competition.

There are two further problems: the block-booking methods of the leading Arab owners, in the hope that a star will emerge from their top-heavy caravans, and the fact that some horses are entered for big races at the late supplementary stage, when they are sure to run, rather than incurring a large entry fee months in advance which could prove wasted if the horse does not come up to expectations or gets injured.

Like most 'inside' information, Futureform's principal use is in helping to estimate the starting price of a horse for whom we have little or no racecourse data. It is a novel idea, good enough to have been picked up by racing's two daily trade papers, who now run weekly entries' columns along Futureform lines.

I began this chapter on information with the words of fictional Wall Street trader Gordon Gekko. To finish, here is a much more cautionary verse by Hilaire Belloc:

> Lord Hippo suffered fearful loss
> By putting money on a horse
> Which he believed if it were pressed
> Would run far faster than the rest
> For someone who was in the know
> Had confidently told him so.

Chapter Twelve

Breeding

'Mate the best with the best . . . and hope for the best.' So the old saying goes. Perhaps the quest to breed the Classic racehorse is that simple.

But when wealthy men are prepared to pay up to $13.1 million – the world record price for a yearling, paid for Seattle Dancer at Keeneland, July, 1985 – a pithy little maxim is just not enough. Nowadays no self-respecting stud operation decides on the matings of its mares and stallions without logging into an ever-expanding bank of computer data: stallion statistics, mare statistics, fertility figures, complicated formulae relating to progeny earnings – it is all available on your VDU screen.

But one group that has a legitimate reason to expand their knowledge of breeding has not been catered for. Punters.

No race has ever been won because of breeding alone; but many have been lost by a horse – perhaps a well-backed one – that has been asked to run over an unsuitable distance. An elementary knowledge of pedigrees – which is the most, I think, to which my readers will aspire – is therefore useful less for finding winners than for avoiding losers. But, as I will outline later in this chapter, there are a number of new statistical works which could revolutionize the way the expert backer goes about this area of his work.

Much in the way that a horse's appearance in the paddock has just a superficial effect on its odds, so the breeding of the horse is perceived to have a negligible effect on its chance. Some of the exciting new data available may show that view to be due for revision.

The basic breeding information available about each runner consists of the names of the sire, the dam, and the sire of the dam (maternal grandsire). The bare bones of that information are fleshed out in a publication like the Timeform weekly *Black Book* with a number of other interesting snippets of information: date of birth; Timeform's best recorded rating for the sire, dam and maternal grandsire; cost of the horse if sold at public auction; the number of foals the dam has produced; and any notable achievements by that offspring as well as a précis of the dam's racing record.

Until a horse has put up enough performances to establish categorically his racing characteristics, the above information is all we have to go on in trying to deduce what level of ability the horse might attain, and what preferences he may have in terms of distance and going.

Using the 1993 dual Derby winner Commander In Chief as an example, let's examine the basic pedigree information available to us before he set foot on a racecourse to see whether we could have made any accurate judgements about the way his career might have panned out. The benefit of hindsight will not, I hope, have affected this analysis.

Commander In Chief's sire was Dancing Brave, at 140 one of the best horses ever rated by Timeform. He won the Two Thousand Guineas and the Prix de l'Arc de Triomphe, and looked an unlucky loser in the Derby. Commander In Chief's dam, Slightly Dangerous, was also top class, if not quite so brilliant, and like Dancing Brave she finished second in an Epsom Classic when beaten a length by Time Charter in the 1982 Oaks.

The sire of Slightly Dangerous, Roberto, did win at Epsom in that memorable whip-cracking finish against Rheingold in 1972.

To an earlier mating with the miler Known Fact, Slightly Dangerous produced the brilliant miler Warning and after a covering by the Derby winner Shirley Heights, she foaled Deploy, placed in the Irish Derby.

The majority of pedigrees are a blend of speed and stamina, leaving the reader at a loss in deciding which element will be uppermost in the offspring; in Commander In Chief's case there is an embarrassment of high-class middle-distance form on both sides. With Dancing Brave, Slightly Dangerous and Roberto as the three principal names in his pedigree he was always going to improve with age, be a stayer rather than a sprinter, and have every chance of being a top-drawer performer. An 18 May birthdate compounded this likely lack of precocity.

History points out that Commander In Chief did not race at two, was never asked to race at less than ten furlongs, won the English and Irish Derbys, and finished third in the King George VI and Queen Elizabeth Diamond Stakes – middle-distance form of the highest class, and quite predictable after examining his breeding.

That's all very well when the names in a pedigree are well known, as is the case with Commander In Chief. But what does the punter do when the names are not so familiar?

The merit of a stallion as a racehorse is covered by the catch-all Timeform rating, but the serious backer will be keen to know how successful a stallion has been and over what distances his progeny excels. The average winning distance of any sire's or maternal grandsire's progeny, originally compiled by *The Statistical Record*, but now available in a number of publications including the daily racing press, is a good basic guide. At the moment, however, there is no universally accepted method of measuring a sire's ability as a producer of good racehorses. The best information to hand is to be found in the sophisticated stallion statistics in *The Statistical Record* and *The Stallion Focus*, published by Weatherbys. It is with grateful thanks to the team there that I reproduce a number of facts and figures in the tables below.

SIRES

The sires championship is decided on the basis of prize

money won by progeny, and as such is of only marginal benefit to the punter. The number of sales-related bonus races these days, in which vast sums of money can be won by relatively modest performers, completely distort the figures. Just one very successful racehorse can be enough to push his sire into the top ten.

Leading Sires of 1994, in order of money won

Rank	(1991 rank)	Name	Top earner	Races won	Win/place prize money (£)
1		Sadler's Wells	King's Theatre	67	1,478,336
2		Chief's Crown	Erhaab	9	919, 986
3		Green Desert	Owington	60	730,759
4		Caerleon	Moonax	37	639,492
5		Last Tycoon	Ezzoud	39	630,351
6		Storm Bird	Balanchine	19	626,547
7		Danzig	Maroof	30	552, 589
8		Alzao	Bobzao	41	516,314
9		Bluebird	Blue Siren	39	457,485
10		Night Shift	Midnight Legend	57	454, 916

Every one of the top ten sires represents the Northern Dancer sire line. Four years after the great horse's death in 1990, it is still the most dominant sire line in the world and Erhaab, a great grandson of Northern Dancer, gave him his ninth Derby success at Epsom last June. Recognizing Northern Dancer's potential at an early stage helped Robert Sangster and Vincent O'Brien to become the leading owner–trainer combination for almost a decade from the mid-1970s. Their Northern Dancer stallion Sadler's Wells is currently the best sire at stud in Europe and justifiably tops the charts.

He has proved a tremendous influence for stamina: of the first 35 Group races won by his older stock, 32 of them were over a mile and a quarter or more. Another statistic which has the owners of his stallion sons smacking their lips with anticipation is that his good horses are virtually all colts – of his first 17 individual Group winners, only Salsabil was a filly. Since then, almost inevitably, his fillies have made a bit of a comeback with Spring, Intrepidity and dual Classic-placed Royal Ballerina all hitting the headlines.

Incidentally, the Coolmore Stud has tried to ensure that Sadler's Wells remains pre-eminent by allowing him to cover an unusually high number of mares for a top Flat stallion.

Another significant aspect of the leading sires data is the strength of the Never Bend line, represented by Riverman and Irish River, and most famous for its Mill Reef branch. This sire line is one successfully patronized by His Highness The Aga Khan, one of the world's top owner–breeders.

Leading Sires of 1994, in order of percentage of winners to runners

Rank	Name	Top Earner	% Winners to runners	% Stakes winners to runners
1	Storm Cat	Elrafa Ah	69.23	7.09
2	Danzig	Maroof	67.74	12.90
3	Topsider	Tethys	62.50	0.00
4	Mon Tresor	Kindergarten Boy	60.00	0.00
5	Storm Bird	Balanchine	59.09	4.56
6	Conquering Hero	Quintiliani	58.33	8.33
7	Silver Hawk	Lower Egypt	57.89	21.05
8	Mr Prospector	Distant View	56.52	8.70
9	Beldale Flutter	Halkopous	54.55	0.00
	Vaigly Great	Can Can Charlie	54.55	0.00
11	The Minstrel	Theophanu	53.85	0.00
	Nijinsky	Munnaya	53.85	15.38
13	Warning	Piccolo	52.27	6.82
14	Nureyev	Mehthaaf	51.72	20.69
15	Most Welcome	Kissair	51.52	0.00
16	Sadler's Wells	King's Theatre	50.65	14.29
17	Cadeaux Genereux	Hoh Magic	50.00	5.00

	Lugana Beach	Autumn Affair	50.00	0.00
	Rousillon	Vintage Crop	50.00	2.50
	Shahrastani	Cajarian	50.00	10.00
	Valiyar	Swynford Flyer	50.00	0.00
28	Gulch	Harayir	46.67	13.33
40	Zilzal	Monaassabaat	45.00	10.00
42	Theatrical	Broadway Flyer	44.44	11.11
	Trempolino	Dernier Empereur	44.44	11.11
46	Doyoun	Karikata	43.48	13.04
57	Bluebird	Blue Siren	42.00	10.00
65	Manila	Time Star	40.00	10.00
	Song	Lochsong	40.00	10.00
84	Top Ville	Beneficial	36.84	10.53
100	Chief's Crown	Erhaab	35.00	10.00

The ability to forge a successful career when given only indifferent mares to cover is the sign of the truly great stallion. Probably the classic stallion of this type has been Ahonoora, runner-up in the 1992 sires' list. To have known of Ahonoora's exceptional talents at an early stage would not only have given potential breeders an edge, it would have been a boon to the serious backer.

Ahonoora has been a dream of a stallion because he is so predictable. Not only does he improve on the record of his mares, but the optimum distance of his offspring seems to be determined wholly by the mare. To an Alleged mare, speed horse Ahonoora bred Derby winner Dr Devious; to a mile-and-a-quarter winner, he produced a high-class winner at that trip in Ruby Tiger; and to two sprinting dams he sired top-class speedsters Indian Ridge and Statoblest, both now embarking on promising careers at stud themselves. Indian Ridge has made a tremendous start with his first two crops, and Statoblest made the top ten first-season sires in 1994.

As Jimmy George, the knowledgeable editor of the *Pacemaker Update and Thoroughbred Breeder* once said to me: 'Dayjur had two shadows in his career – one was at Belmont

Park, and the other was Statoblest.' The latter's career as a sprinter was certainly blighted by racing at the same time as Dayjur – Statoblest chased him home on a number of occasions – but, as a son of the exceptional Ahonoora, I look forward to his stud career with immense interest.

The list of leading sires in prize money terms may decide the outcome of the stallion championship, but the table of leading sires in terms of percentage of winners to runners has greater value in assessing stallion abilities. As you look at it, be reminded of the opinion of James Delahooke, perhaps the most gifted bloodstock agent currently working, and former adviser to Khaled Abdulla. Delahooke maintains that any sire with a 10 per cent winners to runners ratio in stakes (Group and Listed) races is a world-class stallion. I have therefore included the stallions outside the top 20 who met this standard.

DAMS

What about the mare in the breeding equation? If the balance of statistical data is to be believed, she has little say in the matter. In many ways, though, the mare is the most vital element.

In 1992, there were 1,048 stallions registered in the UK and Ireland, the majority of them from a narrow (high-ability) band, boasting respectable pedigrees. During the same period there were 23,300 mares at stud, ranging from Classic winners to those who were too unsound or slow to make an impact on the racecourse. That varied assortment of mares produced no fewer than 12,193 Thoroughbred foals in 1992, many more than was necessary to service the racing industry.

As far as judging a mare goes, the same criteria exist as with the sire: what sort of racemare was she and over what distance do her offspring excel? The simple entry in the Timeform *Black Book* is usually sufficient for our needs, particularly with regard to the offspring of the dam, which amount to just half a dozen or so.

The expert backer will be able to recollect, even if only briefly, the majority of domestic stallions from their racing careers. Understandably he will know nothing about the bulk of the 23,300 active broodmares. When he does come across a dam he has heard of, it is a gold nugget of information and to be cherished.

Just such a mare was Mrs Moss, bought as a six-year-old at the 1975 Newmarket December Sales for just 2,100 guineas by the Marchioness of Tavistock. Though by the excellent broodmare sire Reform, Mrs Moss did not look underpriced after a short racing career which yielded just one maiden race win and a modest Timeform rating of 81. But the Marchioness obviously has an eye for a bargain, because the first ten foals produced by Mrs Moss all won. They included Queen Mary Stakes winner Pushy; multiple Group winner Jupiter Island; the unbeaten sprinter Precocious; and the National Stakes hero Krayyan, who, like Jupiter Island and Precocious, is today at stud.

Mrs Moss is now immortalized in a Philip Blacker bronze in the grounds of the Tavistocks' Bloomsbury Stud at Woburn Abbey.

MATERNAL GRANDSIRES

Leading maternal grandsires of 1994: in order of total money won

Rank	Name	Top earner	Winners	Races won	Win place prize money (£)
1	Habitat	Grand Lodge	60	97	1,502,383
2	Riverman	Erhaab	17	23	747,698
3	High Top	Turtle Island	33	66	744,873

4	Affirmed	Balanchine	11	21	674,244
5	Princely Native	King's Theatre	2	3	612,180
6	Bustino	Maroof	26	40	603,131
7	Northfields	Arcadian Heights	33	50	581,385
8	Sharpen Up	Mister Baileys	25	34	580,657
9	Mill Reef	Hawajiss	36	56	526,416
10	Star Appeal	Bolas	24	40	501,600

NATIONAL HUNT BREEDING

The breeding of Flat racehorses is not an exact science. But I sometimes feel those professionals who spend any time wrestling with the intricacies of National Hunt matings might be better employed at meetings of the Flat Earth society.

Examine the pedigree of any Derby winner and there is never any surprise that a top-class racehorse resulted. Look at the antecedents of the winners of steeplechasing's Blue Riband, the Cheltenham Gold Cup, and you are left scratching your head. Jump racing's top prize must have been the furthest point from the minds of Jimmy Burridge and Stan Riley, breeders respectively of Desert Orchid and Burrough Hill Lad, two of the finest chasers since the war. And as for 1990 winner Norton's Coin . . . owner–trainer–breeder Sirrell Griffiths bought the sire Mount Cassino for a princely 700 guineas after its undistinguished racing career. Mount Cassino only sired a handful of foals, while the dam, Grove Chance, never raced and died shortly after producing her only foal. And yet it was that foal, Norton's Coin, which came up the Cheltenham hill more stoutly than Toby Tobias to record an emotional 100–1 triumph.

Having said that, there are families that regularly produce jumping winners as well as stallions who consistently sire money-spinners, as can be seen from the leading National Hunt sires' and maternal grandsires' tables.

Leading National Hunt Sires 1993/4, in order of total money won

Rank	Name	Winners	Races won	Win/Place Prize Money (£)
1	Strong Gale	91	171	1,018,618
2	Deep Run	57	92	706,382
3	The Parson	37	66	552,743
4	Oats	27	47	371,504
5	Furry Glen	41	69	359,177
6	Kambalda	19	32	329,979
7	Buckskin	28	56	299,435
8	Le Moss	32	59	250,710
9	Over The River	25	33	248,554
10	Callernish	23	44	240,833

Leading National Hunt Maternal Grandsires 1993/4, in order of total money won

Rank	Name	Winners	Races won	Win/Place Prize Money (£)
1	Deep Run	60	98	577,595
2	Bargello	30	54	499,177
3	Menelek	36	58	456,078
4	Arctic Slave	16	29	223,738
5	Raise You Ten	19	35	212,889
6	Busted	24	43	203,108
7	High Top	30	59	187,757
8	Prince Hansel	21	36	172,307
9	Northfields	20	31	171,871
10	Choral Society	6	13	159,500

The problem with the National Hunt statistics is that by the time sufficient data have been amassed – and by that I mean a number of crops reaching a mature age for chasing, say nine years old – the stallion is often dead.

Deep Run, who died in 1990, dominated the National Hunt scene as champion sire for 14 consecutive years, but his era is drawing to a close. The figures in the leading NH sires' table for 1993/4 show that Deep Run has given way to his natural successor, Strong Gale. Deep Run has been a superb stallion – helped understandably by having huge 'books' of mares to cover, but I think he would have been pre-eminent even on a level playing field.

Strong Gale has been the most popular jumps stallion with mare owners – in his 12 years at stud he has covered more than 1,800 mares. He has already proved to be a good stallion but I have my doubts that he is a great one. Sheer weight of numbers will doubtless keep him at the top, though.

The covering season of the NH stallion can go on well past the normal boundaries. Unlike Flat racing it is of no real concern whether you have a January foal or a July foal when you are trying to produce a potential jumper six or seven years down the line. But there is no doubt that Strong Gale is a busy boy at the height of his exhausting covering season with anything up to five coverings in a single day.

Readers sufficiently interested in the fascinating but vexed subject of breeding as an aid to finding winners should be able gradually to compile their own favoured lists of stallions to follow. Merely to start the collection, I would offer the following suggestions in various categories, both as sires and maternal grandsires:

Influence for Speed – Early Winners

African Sky, Ballacashtal, Bay Express, Belfort, Burglar, Decoy Boy, Indian King, Jukebox, Krayyan, King Of Spain, Lochnager, Mummy's Pet, Music Boy, No Mercy, Petong, Primo Dominie, Realm, Song, Tina's Pet.

Influence for Stamina – Late Developers

Alleged, Ardross, Blakeney, Busted, Celtic Ash, Commanche Run, Ela-Mana-Mou, Grey Dawn, High Line, Law Society, Mill Reef, Nijinsky, Niniski, Rainbow Quest, Reliance, Rheingold, Run The Gauntlet, Sadler's Wells, Sassafras, Sea Hawk, Shirley Heights, Theatrical.

Fast-Ground Sires

Dara Monarch, Kalaglow, Known Fact, Persian Bold, Waajib, Warning.

All horses act on good going and the modern use of artificial watering has limited the opportunities for racers who really prefer the going like a road: so much so that I found it difficult to compile this list. But I have no hesitation in including Warning on the limited amount we know of him – the signs from his extremely successful first two crops are that his offspring definitely have a preference for a sound surface.

Soft-Ground Sires

Absalom, Darshaan, High Top, Kampala, Lear Fan, Precocious, Rainbow Quest, Risk Me, Rousillon, Sharpo, Sadler's Wells, Vaguely Noble.

Tough Sires

Alzao, Fairy King, Glenstal, Nebbiolo, Night Shift, Petong.

Fairy King proves that the lack of a racing career – he was injured in training – is no bar to producing sound, reliable performers. Turtle Island, Prince Babar and Fairy

Heights have all helped enhance Fairy King's reputation in the last two years. Conversely, Rainbow Quest, despite having a 14-race career over three seasons, does seem to produce rather delicate specimens. His two best three-year-old colts of 1993, Bin Ajwaad and Blue Judge, both broke down in the first half of the season, while his top three-year-old-filly Rainbow Lake blossomed only briefly in the summer.

I am loath to label any stallion a sire of rogues; there is usually a perfectly good reason why a horse turns it in and I have discovered that in many cases it is simply down to a hatred of the prevailing ground. I will, however, mention that the brilliant Zafonic is not the only headstrong animal I have noted sired by Gone West, while Shirley Heights, though himself as genuine as they come, does throw an inordinate number of tail-swishers. What's more, his son Arcadian Heights is famous for trying to take a chunk out of an opponent during a race at Doncaster.

Broodmare Sires

Derring Do, Graustark, Habitat, Levmoss, Lord Gayle, Lorenzaccio, Nijinsky, Reform, Relko, Sassafras, Silly Season, Tamerlane.

Nicks

In breeding parlance a 'nick' is when a certain sire line appears to mingle successfully with another one. As an example to the reader, I suggest you note when sons of Northern Dancer are mated with mares by Auction Ring. This combination has produced a trio of speedy stars recently: Lyric Fantasy (by Tate Gallery), Fair Crack (Fairy King) and Bradawn Breever (Salmon Leap).

Jumping Sires

Andrea Mantegna, Bold Owl, Broadsword, Celtic Cone, Deep Run, Faraway Times, Gala Performance, Goldhill, Idiot's Delight, Kemal, King's Ride, Le Coq D'Or, Lucky Brief, Mazaad, Montelimar, New Brig, Over The River, The Parson, Politico, Precipice Wood, Roselier, Sharrood, Strong Gale.

Much as one should look out for underrated trainers to follow, I have had quite a bit of profit seeking out under-estimated stallions. In 1993 I felt sure I had unearthed a good staying sire who had the makings of a successful career as a producer of jumping stock – Sharrood. But I was soon to discover that he, like Commander In Chief's more celebrated sire Dancing Brave before him, had been exported to Japan leaving only three crops behind.

Two aspects to take into account when assessing National Hunt sires are their ability to pass on stamina and whether they are likely to produce hurdlers rather than chasers.

Idiot's Delight has proved the most gifted home-grown sire of jumpers in the last decade and despite his untimely death in 1991 his influence is sure to be important for another decade to come. His record is particularly note-worthy given that he was an unprepossessing individual, well short of top class in terms of ability, and received poor patronage in his early years at stud. Being a mile-to-ten-furlong horse himself, he was never going to be a sire of three-mile chasers, but he has sired a string of prolific winners over two miles, including Sea Merchant, Prideaux Boy and Clever Folly.

It is early days in the stallion career of Broadsword, who was a modest performer on the level but twice finished in the first four of the Champion Hurdle. The signs are already there, though, that his progeny do not shine until they are sent over fences.

NEW DEVELOPMENTS

The Statistical Record

The success of a stallion is, like all sexual congress, a matter of opportunity. Hot NH sire-of-the-moment Executive Perk – like Strong Gale a son of the excellent Lord Gayle – is almost guaranteed to do well given that he covers more than 200 mares a season. We know about the quantity; what about the quality? As far as I am aware no one has attempted to give a stallion's book of mares a qualitative rating . . . until now.

In their *Stallion Focus* of 1993, the *Statistical Record* wizards at Weatherbys have refined their mares index, which indicates the quality of broodmares a stallion has covered. As with the average earnings index, a mares index above 1 is better than average and below 1 is worse than average. The higher the figure, the better the quality. In addition, they have introduced a computer analysis of stallions' progeny in terms of their ratings in the International Classifications which, used in tandem with the mares index, gives punters the first chance to judge sires accurately on performance and opportunity.

Raceform

One of the most interesting features of the lap-top computer form book available from Raceform is its breeding statistics, and none more so than the unique stallion ratings. Raceform have come up with the simple yet effective idea of totalling their best handicap ratings for every single member of a sire's progeny and then working out the average rating figure. To base this index figure on the ratings of a highly respected team of handicappers rather than on the basis of earnings or the very variable 'black type' from sales catalogues, looks a sure-fire winner to me. And again it must have a positive application for the punter.

Timeform

Timeform entered the murky arena of breeding statistics with the introduction of their statistical companion to the *Chasers and Hurdlers* annual in 1993. They are now producing a full list of successful progeny indexed under each sire; it includes not only the runner's best Timeform rating but also the ground on which it gained its wins.

These statistics will have limited appeal until they encompass more than just a 12-month period. But when the sages of Halifax get their act together and draw some conclusions over, say, five years, then we will really have a valuable addition to the punters' arsenal, perhaps the most valuable of all. To be able to say with conviction backed by fact that an individual stallion's stock prefer fast or soft ground would be invaluable.

For years mathematicians and students of breeding have addressed the subject of how accurately to measure the success of a stallion at stud. It is commonplace, after all, to have our racehorses rated, and the signs are that we are on the verge of a major breakthrough in the information regarding sires and dams. When it happens, one man sure to benefit is the diligent punter.

Chapter Thirteen

At the Track

Punters are forever driving themselves crazy, invariably going off their game plan as they become distracted at the races. Malcolm was one of those chaps you would find talking to himself at the end of the day. He believed in betting on only one or two races and making them count. He only backed horses that he had noted running well, and which had been recorded religiously in his black notebook. Malcolm swore by this book. Every time he saw me at the course he would greet me with its open pages, pointing to a recent 10–1 or 12–1 winner.

Yet Malcolm was a loser. He always had a sad story about how he let the horse get away. He wouldn't even have a £2 saver on it!

His excuses were always the same: the owner hadn't bothered to make the journey; he'd noted some idiosyncrasy at the paddock which he didn't like; the horse had gone to post 'like a crab'; or, most often of all, there didn't appear to be a penny for it in the ring. Malcolm ate his heart out every day, and yet still continued to second-guess his little black book.

It is maddening to be right when studying in the privacy of your own home only to be put off horse after horse by some flood of new information which emerges in the last 15 minutes before the race-time.

The moral of this tale is: if you know you pick more winners at home than at the track, you owe it to yourself to stick with the horses you pick at home.

Of course, the paddock *can* prove a valuable source of information. In my experience, the racecourse market responds in only the most superficial way to how horses have looked before the race, consequently the genuine paddock judge can have what we are all looking for at the races – 'an edge'.

THE PADDOCK

Anyone can learn to interpret the form book and read a race, but very few have a genuine eye for livestock, and for the Thoroughbred racehorse in particular. Crowds dutifully troop down to the paddock before every race to see the horses parade, but for most of them it is a complete waste of time. I have met just three really good paddock judges and their talent has nothing to do with diligence or perspiration – it's a gift.

The ability to look at a horse whose form is on an apparently irresistible upward curve and to state categorically: 'It can't win . . . it has lost so much condition since I saw it a fortnight ago,' and then to be proved joyously correct as the well-backed favourite puts up a miserable performance which even connections are at a loss to explain, is truly awe-inspiring.

But there are few judges with such a rare gift.

The basic principles of conformation are no deep mystery, just common sense. The most important part of the horse, though, is that part you cannot see – the 'engine'.

And even the best make mistakes judging a book by its cover.

At the Keeneland July Selected Sale in 1983, the highly paid advisers of Dubai's defence minister, Sheik Mohammed Bin Rashid Al-Maktoum, were in unanimous agreement that the choicest lot in terms of pedigree and looks was No. 308 – a Northern Dancer colt out of My Bupers. The oil-rich Sheik determined to have him and would not be denied in an epic, some would say obscene, bidding duel against Robert Sangster and Vincent O'Brien. The gavel of auctioneer Scott

Caldwell came down at a staggering $10.2 million. Subsequently named Snaafi Dancer, the colt went into training with John Dunlop at Arundel in Sussex.

One morning on Dunlop's picturesque gallops, I was among a group of breeders who watched Snaafi Dancer work. It is said of morning work-outs that any horse can look fast going past trees. Snaafi Dancer was the exception to the rule. He was totally useless and never raced. When he was sent to stud in an attempt to salvage some of his value, he proved infertile!

One day in the future a machine will be devised to measure a horse's 'motor' and wealthy men will be prevented from making embarrassing and costly mistakes. Until then, if we want to pick a winner as the runners are parading in the paddock, we have only our eyes.

At the paddock, the first essential is to get yourself a good vantage point as you try to establish two things:

1 general make and shape (conformation);
2 fitness and well-being.

A slightly raised viewing position near the paddock rail is best; it guarantees a view uninterrupted by hordes of owners as the horses walk across your vision from left to right in the middle-distance and then again from right to left as they pass close up. Try always to keep the sun behind you.

Tree-lined paddocks are anathema to the paddock judge. The parade rings at Haydock and Windsor, for example, may be pretty but their sheer size and the dappled light created by the trees make them a far-from-ideal place to give horses the once-over.

Congratulations to Cheltenham racecourse whose new pre-parade ring is a model for every racecourse. Perfect for the student of horseflesh, it is rectangular, not too big, and with good, well-sited viewing steps.

Having found a good vantage point, the next thing to bear

in mind is to approach the task in hand with an open mind. Try to avoid obtaining information that would bias your judgement. Remain oblivious to whose horse you are looking at until you have formed an opinion. Knowing it is from a prestigious yard will inevitably affect your assessment.

The contestants are about to embark on an athletic activity, so while they are on the far side of the paddock look out for those horses which are alert and yet relaxed and have a good swinging walk. As a mechanical guide to the latter, the prints made by the hind feet should pass those made by the fore feet. As you would in any beauty or body-building contest, compare the contestants while they are in view together for size and physique, looking particularly for balance and grace.

When the horses come to your side of the paddock, home in on more specific elements. Does the horse have a confident expression and look at ease with its world? Just because every rib is showing does not mean that the horse is fit; usually the reverse. Look for a tight, well-muscled neck; a firm line under the ribcage with no evidence of fat or loose flesh and well-defined quarters. Then take in the condition of the coat – is it gleaming with good health or dull and lifeless?

A lot is made of horses hanging on to their longer, winter coats in spring or when they grow them prematurely in the autumn. It is not the length of coat that matters but whether the horse is doing well physically. Muscle tone is usually associated with a good coat, but in early spring it may not be, because sometimes horses build muscle and benefit from training before they let go of their coat.

Close up at the paddock you also pick up those negative points such as a horse neighing through immaturity, restlessly grinding on its bit, having a protracted and debilitating tugging match with its lad or lass, or sweating up. Beware, though. Some horses need to get themselves worked up before running to their best. Green God, a top sprinter of the early 1970s, used to sweat buckets before winning such prizes as the Vernons Sprint Cup at Haydock: it was of more concern if he looked cool and unfussed in the parade.

In the back of your mind when assessing physical type you should always be aware of the track and going conditions. A neat, well-balanced horse is likely to have an advantage over a tall, gangly individual on Epsom's gradients, for instance; while the big-boned, heavy-topped horse is certain to have more problems coping with mud than his wiry, light-framed counterpart.

And remember, you are not just sifting through the runners looking for today's bets. That attractive horse which could be made a lot fitter, or that leggy, immature colt – they could both be a completely different proposition from a betting point of view in two months' time. Make a mental note to look out for them in the future.

Conformation is not so important when assessing established hurdlers and chasers – their predilections should be clear from the form book – but size does play a role in the jumping game. Often you are faced with a horse which, having run up a sequence of early-season chase wins, is made favourite on his first appearance at one of the bigger meetings – Cheltenham or Ascot. The fences at more prestigious tracks are altogether bigger and stiffer, requiring size and scope to cope with them adequately. One glance in the paddock may reveal that the market leader does not boast the physical attributes necessary to win at an Ascot or a Cheltenham, however measured his jumping has been at the gaffs.

Ultimately, the most valuable role paddock inspection can play is to help supply the casting vote when your form studies have indicated there are only two or three potential winners.

Back in January 1989, I vividly remember going to Ascot undecided as to which of two up-and-coming jumpers, Slalom or Sir Blake, would win the Peter Ross Novices' Chase, for which there were only four runners.

In the ring, Sir Blake was a solid 8–13 chance while Slalom

was easy to back, drifting out at one point to 3–1. But from the moment Sir Blake came up the walkway from the saddling boxes and entered the paddock, I was convinced all was not well with him. I couldn't put my finger on it exactly but he certainly didn't fill the eye. In comparison, Slalom, a big slab of a horse, looked fit and well – so I helped myself to all the 3–1 I could get.

Sir Blake made a monumental mistake in front of the stands, started to labour from Swinley Bottom on the second circuit and was pulled up before the last fence with a broken blood vessel; Slalom came home alone.

A sad postscript to this story is that Sir Blake, who had almost limitless potential, was put down after breaking a leg on the gallops just two months later.

Sir Blake's well-being was especially telling because his trainer was that maestro David Elsworth. From his early days training out of converted pig pens and cow byres at Figheldean near Salisbury, and long before Desert Orchid came on the scene, David has simply been one of the best conditioners of a horse in the game. For a horse of his not to fill the eye in the paddock is rare indeed.

Not only can the paddock provide clues to equine winners today and in the future, then; it can pinpoint the best trainers, too. And we cannot finish our look at the paddock without a brief nod in the direction of the human personalities under scrutiny there – the owners and trainers. It is difficult to maintain maximum confidence in one's selection when it has been accompanied to the track by only its groom and an apparently disaffected travelling head lad. Owners naturally like to be on hand when one of their horses wins; and most trainers, too, enjoy regaling the waiting gentlemen of the press when another victory has been logged. But don't be like our friend from the beginning of this chapter, Malcolm, trying to second-guess why an owner has not bothered to turn up to welcome his good thing. Concentrate on the horse.

Goethe said that the eyes are the mirror of the soul. In the paddock, look at the horse's eye and see if you can find the will to win.

CANTERING TO THE START

The canter to post provides the punter with a final piece of information before he goes off to the ring to place his bet. It is of special benefit on extremes of going and in sprint races – I've seen horses with the most extraordinary actions win long-distance events and National Hunt races. But in general terms, look for the horse which goes to post keenly and under control and seems at ease on the prevailing going.

Broadly speaking, a horse with a high, round action, which hits the ground hard, will best be served by going with a good deal of give; while it cannot be too fast for the horse with a light, daisy-cutting gait that appears to float above the ground.

Two-year-olds whose joints are barely fully formed are susceptible to getting jarred up on fast ground. Don't take it on trust that a young horse will act on firm ground just because it has done so in the past; willing and enthusiastic, it may have strode out purposefully to post only to return sore. Next time the canter to the start may reveal an altogether less extravagant action and a commensurate loss of performance.

As they go past the stands, inexperienced two-year-olds may show signs of greenness which are often exaggerated in the race itself. Like kids on the first day at school, they give the impression of being totally unaware of what is required of them. And yet that immaturity is not always reflected in the ring.

Watch out for the horse that takes charge of its jockey and loses the race before the off. Check, also, the animal which was getting warm in the paddock – it may be awash with sweat by the time it reaches the start.

THE RING

The stallholders of the betting market are open for business every day there is racing on one of our 59 racecourses. Their pitch is in front of the Tattersalls enclosures, exposed to all the elements – though in Doncaster's case there is an interior betting hall for use during bad weather.

'The ring', as it is called, is where the odds makers (bookies) meet the odds takers (punters). Like the floor of the Stock Exchange, it plays host to the major transactions in the dealing and trading.

The ring has a cast list, past and present, of lively characters with names like Jack the Judge, Fingers, The Asparagus Kid, Dodger, Dennis The Chest, Lights, 11–10 (so called because he had one shoulder set slightly lower than the other) and a duo dubbed FBI – 'they know everyone's business'.

In fact, if the bookmakers' intelligence network had been at work in Dallas on that fateful day in November 1963, I suspect 'Who killed JFK?' would not still be a mystery today.

It is not the role of this book to engage in polemic about the betting industry, but a brief look at how the ring works and the current state of the market is, I think, apposite.

At the beginning of trading on each race, bookmakers have the benefit of the 'tissue', a set of odds compiled by a very experienced professional. Nowadays, the tissue can take account of the ever-growing amount of morning business done in the betting offices. From the time the bookies first chalk up their odds, the forces of supply and demand dictate the fluctuations.

The betting shows which the punter sees in his high street shop are unofficial in that they are transmitted by agents of SIS simply to give the punter a guide as to how the market is taking shape.

The official starting price (SP) is the joint responsibility of a group of representatives from the Press Association and the *Sporting Life*. Each operator in this group covers a designated group of bookmakers – one on the boards, the other on the rails – constantly making notes on all price fluctuations and recording any significant bets. At the 'off' of each race, the representatives form a huddle to discuss openly the betting movements and, following a brief discussion, an agreed SP return is set.

It is perhaps surprising that the contract between the punter and the bookmaker in this billion-pound industry revolves around the subjective assessment of a few experienced individuals, but it is a method that has stood the test of time since its introduction in 1923 and has the complete faith of both sides.

It goes without saying that the SP reporter has to be the most incorruptible man on the racecourse. Neal Wilkins has been doing the job on the Press Association for the last 20 years and claims he has only once been approached by a bookie to fiddle the SP. 'He told me he would be betting longer odds about the likely winner than anyone else and would I take notice. I said "I shall forget we ever had this conversation" and he's respected me ever since.'

Sadly, Wilkins's patch is no longer the vibrant and exciting place of old. Betting was the last industry to feel the current recession, and it looks as if it is going to be the last to pull through. Despite the abolition of on-course betting tax in 1987, the racecourse betting market has never been so weak and a vulnerable market is certainly not in the interests of racing.

Ladbrokes, the firm named after a sleepy village near Warwick racecourse, are the most active of the Big Three bookmakers in terms of manipulating the weak market to their own ends. Using a 'pyramid' system, they monitor key shops to discover how much money is being bet on particular horses. If they believe a price is too generous, word is passed to their course representative who backs the horse, thereby shortening up its odds. For example, at a Yarmouth meeting in August 1993, the course agent for Corals was told by his head office to place £3,500 on the 9–4 chance Sun Grebe. This had the effect of forcing the favourite down to 6–4, potentially saving the country's 10,000 betting shops hundreds of thousands of pounds. In this case, Sun Grebe lost.

A stronger market would be able to withstand such influence. But while the outdated, closed-shop method of bookmaker pitch allocation remains in place – frustrating the newer breed of bookie who would not be afraid to lay a big wager but who is unable to trade in the main ring – the racecourse market has the look of a terminally ill patient. 'The market is absolutely moribund,' says Wilkins. 'The public thinks there is no such thing as a bankrupt farmer or a skint bookie, but that is not the case these days.'

We're only a few years away from the twenty-first century, and yet punters are expected to bet with the bookmakers outdoors, exposed to all weathers. Advocates of the present system and anti-Tote monopolists point to the 'colourful atmosphere' of the ring. Such a rose-tinted viewpoint is stuck in a time-warp. Current racegoers will find the ring desolate, while the racecourse betting office is teeming with action, punters apparently choosing to pay 6 per cent tax instead of nothing with the course layers.

As another professional told me: 'Racecourse bookies have the mentality of the street trader – they are gruff and impolite. Is it any wonder punters choose the familiar surroundings of the course betting shop where they can have their doubles and trebles and bet in small stakes, both denied them by the men in the ring, or that they prefer the pleasant, smiling face of the lady in red behind the Tote window?'

He added: 'The Big Three have already imposed their computer straight forecasts and would be quite happy to let the course market die and produce their own SP from charts.'

To stave off that unpalatable prospect, racecourse layers must smarten up their act and move with the times. The punters must also insist, in the loudest and most unified voice possible, that they are not prepared to accept such a scenario.

Given the parlous state of the betting ring, an experienced hand like Neal Wilkins firmly believes that, with bookmakers chasing so little money, there is tremendous value on offer. As the market seesaws in the 15 minutes or so of betting activity before the race, an astute professional can bet on all the runners and be sure of a profit, when the full set of prices is said to be over-broke. More realistically, he may back two or three horses at what he deems attractive odds. I suspect the average reader has more of an emotional investment in the horses he supports and therefore calculating to what degree the market is over-broke or over-round is unnecessary.

By the time you enter the ring you should have a firm idea of the price you are prepared to accept about your selection. The price can never be too high. If you have done your homework you should be delighted if the odds offered are longer than you expected. Gratefully accept the price, perhaps even increase your stake if it appears exceptional value – such instances come around all too rarely. Whatever you do, don't torture yourself with the thought that the horse can't be 'off' if it is starting at that price. Even if the horse runs for a gambling stable, an apparent lack of interest in the ring is no foolproof sign that the horse is not fancied.

A final piece of advice: always 'take the fractions'. If you are backing a 12–1 chance, ask for £1,000–£80 or a 16–1 chance, £1,000–£60; the extra pounds saved can build up to a tidy sum over the season.

The principal advantage of betting in the ring, apart from paying no tax, is to obtain the best possible odds. In the celebrated Casbatina case that meant accepting a price *eight* times higher than the one first offered to the betting shop punter.

At the Doncaster St Leger meeting of 1988, Newmarket

trainer Jeff Pearce introduced the two-year-old filly Casbatina. The initial bets recorded on the course were at 25–1 but in those betting offices taking the Extel service, the first show was 7–1; six minutes later SIS deigned to send out their first show about Casbatina . . . 3–1! She started at 2–1 and won by three-quarters of a length but most off-course backers were blissfully unaware that one of the great on-course gambles had taken place.

Chapter Fourteen

Britain's 59 Racecourses

One of the inherent pleasures of racing in Britain is the infinite variety of our 59 racecourses. No two tracks are alike; some appear to be set in an industrial wasteland, while others boast the most magnificent scenery imaginable. All of them have characteristics which are of importance to the punter as he weighs up his bets.

In addition to basic information – whether the course is right-handed or left-handed, the length of the home straight and the total circumference – my colleagues Rolf Johnson, Colin Woods and I have endeavoured to pinpoint idiosyncrasies which may steer the reader towards winners or help him avoid losers. Is the course sharp or galloping in nature? Are the fences stiff or soft? Which jockeys and trainers are to be noted?

We have also tackled the troubled question of the draw on our 35 Flat courses. Where conclusions can be drawn, we have drawn them. Unless otherwise stated, our Draw Data refer to races at sprint distances or those run over a straight mile.

The top half dozen trainers and jockeys at each track have been listed in order of races won. For the Flat, those figures take in the last five seasons from 1 January 1990 until 31 December 1994. For the jumps, the period covers five full seasons from 1 July 1989 to 30 June 1994. The two figures published are: total number of winners during the period and percentage strike rate.

Finally, I have listed the percentage success rate of favourites over the last five seasons.

The course diagrams have kindly been supplied by the *Racing Post*. For National Hunt tracks, the steeplechase courses are shown blocked out in black, the hurdle courses in outline. Water jumps are marked 'W', and open ditches are marked 'OD'.

RACECOURSE MEASUREMENT

During 1991, the Racecourse Inspectorate measured all steeplechase and hurdle race distances at every racecourse. Measurements were taken down the centre of each track with a land wheel, which has an accuracy of ±1 per cent.

Some fascinating findings emerged – including some strikingly inaccurate race distances at the home of National Hunt racing, Cheltenham. A famous race like the Tripleprint Gold Cup (formerly the Massey-Ferguson Gold Cup) is actually run over two miles five furlongs and not two miles four furlongs, as has been believed down the years; while our own Daily Express Triumph Hurdle is, it seems, contested not over the minimum hurdling trip of two miles but over two miles one furlong.

There were some more alarming discrepancies in long-distance chases round the country. The three-and-a-half-mile distance at Bangor, the three-mile-one-furlong at Kelso, the three-and-a quarter at Stratford and the four-mile at Uttoxeter were each found to be a quarter of a mile longer, and race descriptions have now been adjusted accordingly.

A similar survey, this time with measurements carried out by laser, was also tackled for Flat courses. To highlight just a couple of incongruities, Ayr's two-mile-one-furlong track was found to measure two miles, one furlong *and* 105 yards, while (perhaps of greater significance) Newbury's five-furlong track in fact extends to five furlongs and 34 yards.

Given the narrowness of his famous last-gasp wins at Epsom on The Minstrel and Roberto, it is probably just as well for Lester Piggott that the true length of the Derby course turns out to be one mile, four furlongs and 10 yards.

FAVOURITES

During the period 1989–94, 35.1 per cent of all Flat races were won by favourites; in non-handicaps 42.4 per cent of favourites obliged, while in handicaps the figure dropped to 27.3 per cent.

Over five National Hunt seasons between 1989 and 1994, 40.7 per cent of all favourites were successful.

As an easy-to-use guide, here is the league table showing how favourites do at each course, compiled by the *Express* statistical guru Calvin Clarke. It shows percentages for both Flat and National Hunt over the last ten seasons. It would appear that Perth's jumping track (47.6%) offers the favourite backer the best percentage chance of success, while on the Flat, Kempton (28.6%) is a bit of a graveyard for the 'jolly'.

National Hunt	On the Flat
1. Perth 47.6%	1. Edinburgh 43.1%
2. Fontwell 47.3%	2. Catterick 40.0%
3. Lingfield 47.2%	3. Hamilton 39.7%
4. Edinburgh 46.3%	4. Pontefract 39.2%
5. Cartmel 45.7%	5. Folkestone 39.0%
6. Haydock 45.6%	6. Brighton 38.2%
7. Exeter 44.6%	7. Wolverhampton 38.2%
8. Plumpton 44.3%	8. Chester 38.0%
9. Ayr 44.3%	9. Newcastle 37.4%
10. Doncaster 43.9%	10. Ripon 37.2%
11. Chepstow 43.1%	11. Nottingham 37.1%
12. Newcastle 43.0%	12. Beverley 36.9%
13. Sedgefield 42.5%	13. Redcar 36.8%
14. Hereford 42.2%	14. Yarmouth 36.8%
15. Kelso 42.2%	15. Bath 36.5%
16. Wincanton 42.1%	16. Ayr 36.1%
17. Newbury 41.4%	17. Chepstow 35.9%
18. Wetherby 41.4%	18. Southwell (AW) 35.1%

19. Folkestone 41.0%	19. Newbury 35.0%
20. Southwell 40.6%	20. Thirsk 34.5%
21. Carlisle 40.3%	21. Windsor 34.1%
22. Newton Abbot 40.2%	22. Lingfield (Turf) 33.8%
23. Hexham 39.9%	23. York 33.6%
24. Ludlow 39.9%	24. Leicester 33.5%
25. Sandown 39.9%	25. Lingfield (AW) 33.5%
26. Fakenham 39.5%	26. Newmarket 33.4%
27. Bangor 39.4%	27. Warwick 33.2%
28. Huntingdon 39.4%	28. Doncaster 33.0%
29. Uttoxeter 39.4%	29. Sandown 32.9%
30. Kempton 39.3%	30. Carlisle 32.5%
31. Leicester 39.3%	31. Salisbury 32.2%
32. Nottingham 38.7%	32. Goodwood 32.1%
33. Warwick 38.5%	33. Haydock 31.0%
34. Cheltenham 38.1%	34. Ascot 30.6%
35. Wolverhampton 37.9%	35. Epsom 29.9%
36. Taunton 37.5%	36. Kempton 28.6%
37. Worcester 37.2%	
38. Market Rasen 36.9%	
39. Towcester 36.9%	
40. Stratford 36.4%	
41. Windsor 35.3%	
42. Aintree 33.9%	
43. Catterick 33.8%	
44. Ascot 32.3%	

DRAW DATA

On many courses, although the draw is of some importance in sprints, it is not decisive and we must bet regardless of it. But on others its effect is so marked that our entire punting strategy must be built around it. The following list shows how the advantage falls at the most infamous tracks in Britain as far as the draw is concerned;

in most cases it is the presence of soft ground which causes
the exaggerated bias.

   Beverley: high numbers on soft ground
   Hamilton: high numbers on soft ground
   Kempton: high numbers on soft ground
   Sandown: high numbers on soft ground
   Thirsk: high numbers on fast ground
   Warwick: high numbers on soft ground

Readers should continue to monitor the effect of the draw as
artificial watering and poor drainage can upset even the most
established patterns. Don't lose your money before the start!

AINTREE
Class A (NH)

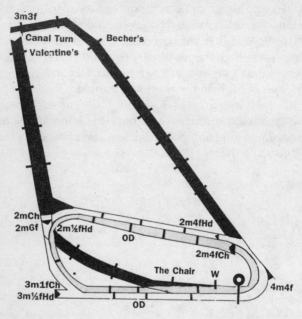

All eyes turn to Aintree in spring for the greatest race in the world, the Grand National.

Few horses have the stamina to gallop four and a half miles and the ability to jump 30 steeplechase fences including the mighty Chair and hair-raising Canal Turn. Following recent modifications, Becher's Brook is no longer the daunting fence of old.

Red Rum's incredible three wins in the contest proved beyond all doubt the old 'horses for courses' adage. No single stable has a stranglehold on the race, but the fancied horses have an excellent record in recent years; stick with the first half-dozen favourites and you won't go far wrong.

The majority of the other steeplechases are run on the much less testing Mildmay course (the white track on the plan), whose fences are not nearly so stiff. Despite this, these 'upturned dandy brushes' can cause appalling mistakes because horses fail to respect them.

The left-handed hurdle course is a level, sharp and fast track where races are normally run at a helter-skelter pace. Try to avoid long-striding types who take an age to get into top gear.

The Irish love to raid Aintree. They enjoy nothing more than launching huge on-course gambles, often allowing other well-fancied contenders to start at attractive odds

Statistics, 1989–94 (NH)

TOP JOCKEYS: R. Dunwoody 12, 16%; L. Wyer 5, 15%; A. Maguire 5, 14%; G. McCourt 4, 12%; M. Dwyer 4, 12%; C. Maude 3, 33%.

TOP TRAINERS: M. Pipe 10, 12%; J. Fitzgerald 8, 32%; D. Nicholson 7, 16%; K. Bailey 6, 35%; G. Balding 6, 15%; M. W. Easterby 4, 36%.

FAVOURITES: 33.9%.

ASCOT
Class A (Flat)   Class A (NH)

Racing of the highest quality, and not just at the Royal Ascot meeting in midsummer. Ascot form can be trusted at any other track. The right-handed round course is uphill throughout the last seven furlongs from Swinley Bottom; only those

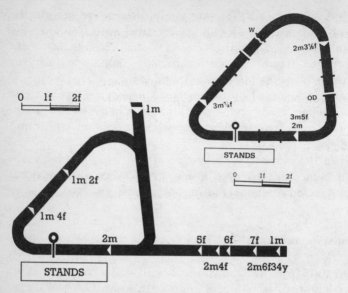

horses who truly get the trip win at Ascot. There is an equally testing straight mile and all races of less than a mile are run on this course.

The going can get very wet in spring and autumn, which leads to patchy ground and unpredictable results. On very fast ground, those horses in front at the start of the short two-and-a-half-furlong straight can last home.

Henry Cecil has a fine record and is especially dominant at the Royal meeting.

It was the Duke of Norfolk who said jump racing would take place at Ascot 'over my dead body'. Introduced in 1965, it actually takes place largely over the dead body of Hurst Park; many of the sods of that defunct Thames-side track were relaid at Ascot, and contribute to what is often testing going. Set this alongside stiff fences and an uphill finish to a galloping track, and you need a good horse to win round here. The last fence offers plenty of heart-in-the-mouth action.

Trainer Jimmy FitzGerald knows what is required to win here; he and stable jockey Mark Dwyer have a good record on their infrequent visits.

DRAW DATA: No appreciable advantage, though in soft ground it pays to race against the stand rail.

Statistics, 1990–94 (Flat)

TOP JOCKEYS: Pat Eddery 42, 17%; L. Dettori 32, 13%; W. Carson 32, 13%; M. Roberts 28, 11%; W. Swinburn 23, 12%; T. Quinn 17, 10%.

TOP TRAINERS: M. Stoute 27, 15%; J. Gosden 23, 17%; H. Cecil 22, 22%; P. Cole 20, 19%; R. Hannon 19, 8%; L. Cumani 17, 16%.

FAVOURITES: 30.6%.

Statistics, 1989–94 (NH)

TOP JOCKEYS: J. Osborne 21, 22%; R. Dunwoody 16, 12%; M. Perrett 10, 17%; D. Murphy 9, 10%; J. Frost 8, 15%; G. McCourt 7, 17%.

TOP TRAINERS: M. Pipe 24, 24%; J. Gifford 15, 11%; O. Sherwood 12, 21%; N. Twiston-Davies 12, 19%; G. Balding 11, 12%; Mrs J. Pitman 10, 22%.

FAVOURITES: 32.3%.

AYR
Class B (Flat)   Class B (NH)

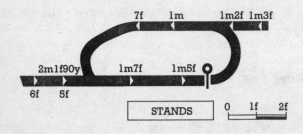

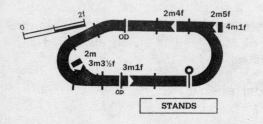

The flat, left-handed galloping track at Ayr is one of the fairest racetracks in Great Britain. In staying races, class horses and top weights excel; hard-luck stories are few and far between.

Jack Berry achieved a lifetime's ambition by winning the Ayr Gold Cup in 1988 with So Careful; overall his stable has an outstanding record here. Linda Perratt trains next door to the track. She is an able young trainer and any market moves for her runners are worth following. The marauders from Barry Hills and his protégé Peter Chapple-Hyam rarely leave empty-handed, while the first five runners Roger Charlton sent to the big Western meeting all won.

The highlight of the jumping fixtures held at Ayr is undoubtedly the Scottish Grand National. Traditionally run in April, participants have to negotiate four miles and 27 fences.

Gordon Richards has a fantastic record over jumps here and can be followed with absolute confidence year in and year out.

DRAW DATA: Five- and six-furlong dashes are run on the straight course. When the ground is fast, high numbers against the favoured stands rail are best. On soft or heavy ground this trend is reversed. Seven-furlong and mile races are run round the turn and low numbers have the call.

Statistics, 1990–94 (Flat)

TOP JOCKEYS: K. Darley 47, 22%; J. Carroll 20, 13%; K. Fallon 16, 12%; D. Holland 14, 28%; D. McKeown 14, 13%; J. Weaver 12, 15%.

TOP TRAINERS: J. Berry 29, 13%; B. Hills 19, 39%; M. H. Easterby 18, 18%; P. Chapple-Hyam 16, 40; Mrs M. Reveley 16, 20; Mrs J. Ramsden 14, 21.

FAVOURITES: 36.1%.

Statistics, 1989–94 (NH)

TOP JOCKEYS: N. Doughty 40, 28%; P. Niven 40, 27%; B. Storey 21, 11%; C. Grant 16, 11%; G. McCourt 15, 21%; M. Dwyer 12, 17%.

TOP TRAINERS: G. Richards 59, 22%; Mrs M. Reveley 34, 34%; G. M. Moore 18, 18%; Mrs S. Bradburne 16, 14%; J. O'Neill 15, 17%; M. Hammond 10, 15%.

FAVOURITES: 44.3%.

BANGOR
Class D (NH)

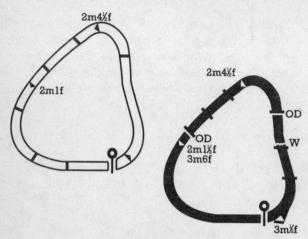

Bangor is a left-handed, sharp course with ridged undulations. Spectators watch the finishes head on from enclosures which do not boast a grandstand.

The hurdle course favours front-runners; the chase course clever jumpers. The fences are notoriously tricky – particularly the last – and do not necessarily suit bold-jumping horses.

The area is prone to wet weather in winter, often producing very heavy and testing ground. Martin Pipe does well with his super-fit charges, while Gordon Richards, a trainer who deals almost exclusively in big, strong chasing types, has the right sort of animal to deal with the testing conditions.

Statistics, 1989–94 (NH)

TOP JOCKEYS: N. Doughty 21, 30%; R. Dunwoody 18, 22%; G. McCourt 13, 18%; C. Grant 10, 22%; M. Dwyer 10, 20%; J. Lodder 10, 14%.

TOP TRAINERS: G. Richards 35, 26%; M. Pipe 22, 31%; N. Twiston-Davies 10, 23%; F. Jordan 10, 15%; J. White 9, 32%; J. O'Neill 8, 19%.

FAVOURITES: 39.4%.

BATH
Class C (Flat)

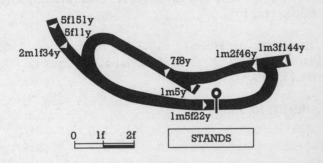

Bath is Britain's highest racecourse, 780 feet above sea level on Lansdown Hill. It has a kidney-shaped, left-handed circuit of just over a mile and a half, with a steadily rising run-in of four furlongs and an almost straight five-furlong 151 yards course starting from a spur.

It is exposed and therefore cool even on the warmest day. Because it doesn't boast a watering system, the ground at Bath rides fast in the summer but the lovely downland turf ensures there is no 'jar'. Positive jockeys thrive here, often poaching races early in the straight by hugging the rail on the inner. Another valuable half-length can be gained as the run-in kinks to the left around the furlong pole.

Bath is one of the few tracks where Richard Hannon has a respectable strike rate.

Don't get a plugged lie before racing; the car park doubles as a golf course.

DRAW DATA: A high draw in sprints need not be a disadvantage as long as the jockey makes a positive start.

Statistics, 1990–94 (Flat)

TOP JOCKEYS: Pat Eddery 33, 30%; J. Williams 26, 11%; J. Reid 23, 18%; T. Quinn 23, 16%; R. Cochrane 13, 16%; Paul Eddery 13, 16%.

TOP TRAINERS: B. Hills 18, 19%; I. Balding 18, 15%; R. Hannon 17, 12%; P. Cole 16, 13%; R. Hodges 15, 9%; J. Berry 13, 22%.

FAVOURITES: 36.5%.

BEVERLEY
Class C (Flat)

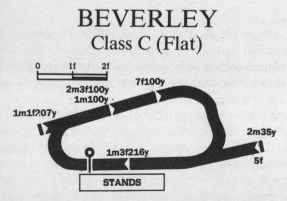

Beverley is a right-handed track built on the side of a hill. It drains well and rarely suffers from extremes of going. The unique contours mean middle-distance and staying horses must have the capability to gallop smoothly downhill on the back straight, negotiate the difficult bottom bend, and then tackle the severe two-and-a-half furlong climb to the winning post.

Not surprisingly, Beverley fosters course specialists, none more popular or successful than Rapid Lad, victorious on no fewer than 14 occasions.

There is often plenty of scrimmaging in the home straight and good jockeyship is essential. Northern aces Kevin Darley and Mark Birch both ride the course with rare cunning; beware of inexperienced apprentice jockeys.

Local trainer Mick Easterby is a dab hand at producing a 'springer' to win one of the numerous selling races run here; he has some big hitters among his owners which sometimes leads to fun and games in the betting ring.

DRAW DATA: High numbers have a big advantage on the slightly dog-legged five-furlong straight course, and on the round course up to one mile one furlong, especially in large fields or when the going is soft.

Statistics, 1990–94 (Flat)

TOP JOCKEYS: K. Darley 50, 19%; M. Birch 20, 10%; J. Lowe 20, 9%; W. Ryan 16, 18%; G. Duffield 16, 16%; J. Carroll 16, 13%.

TOP TRAINERS: M. H. Easterby 25, 13%; J. Berry 23, 14%; H. Cecil 15, 36%; I. Balding 15, 32%; Mrs M. Reveley 15, 15%; R. Whitaker 15, 12%.

FAVOURITES: 36.9%.

BRIGHTON
Class C (Flat)

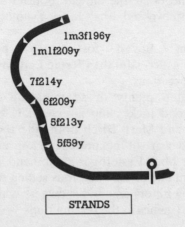

1m3f196y
1m1f209y

7f214y

6f209y

5f213y

5f59y

STANDS

The racecourse is situated high above the town overlooking Brighton Marina and Roedean Girls' School – that is if anything is visible on those days when there is a sea fret. Looking from the stands, it is a left-handed C-shaped circuit, about a mile and a half in length, the significant feature being the sharp descent from the four-furlong marker to the two-furlong pole.

Horses ill at ease on the gradients have little time to make up lost ground in the quarter-mile rise to the post, which is why course specialists like 1960s handicapper Operatic Society are able to build a sequence.

The course resembles Epsom and winners there do well here. The camber runs from the stands side to the far rail and in wet weather the fields tack over to take advantage of faster ground under the stands rail. It is a bad course for light weights and apprentices.

The razor gangs of Graham Greene's *Brighton Rock* are thankfully a thing of the past.

DRAW DATA: In sprints, those drawn low are favoured, but only if they have early speed and can act on the track.

Statistics, 1990–94 (Flat)

TOP JOCKEYS: T. Quinn 46, 18%; W. Carson 44, 27%; M. Roberts 31, 22%; J. Reid 28, 13%; Pat Eddery 27, 25%; L. Dettori 26, 24%.

TOP TRAINERS: R. Hannon 39, 18%; L. Cumani 27, 42%; R. Akehurst 23, 22%; Sir M. Prescott 19, 25%; P. Cole 19, 14%; R. Hodges 17, 13%.

FAVOURITES: 38.2%.

CARLISLE
Class D (Flat)   Class C (NH)

The right-handed, pear-shaped Carlisle course, set astride a huge hill, is not one for the faint-hearted. The stands boast a summer view second to none, but on a wet winter's day, spectators have to take the full force of wind and rain, while the leg-weary runners clamber up the mountainous three-furlong home straight.

Flat racing is of poor quality. When southern raiders – the likes of Stoute, Cumani and Dunlop – come looking for easy pickings, stick with their superior ammunition. The same applies to the Tompkins–Robinson combo. A weak betting market means attractively priced favourites are rare; it often pays to step in early.

National Hunt racing is generally of a better standard. The clay-based subsoil often generates gluepot conditions, giving

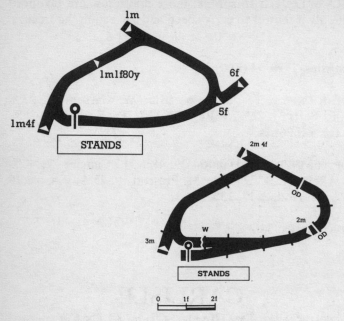

the slower, staying types a much better chance of success. For these reasons, under either code, lightly weighted animals warrant close inspection.

Up-and-coming trainer Micky Hammond knows what is required to win here; local heroes Gordon Richards and Neale Doughty are very successful but smaller outfits also hold their own.

DRAW DATA: High numbers are best up to a one mile.

Statistics, 1990–94 (Flat)

TOP JOCKEYS: G. Duffield 24, 22%; D. McKeown 23, 18%; K. Darley 21, 16%; J. Carroll 18, 16%; P. Robinson 13, 38%; K. Fallon 11, 12%.

TOP TRAINERS: J. Berry 27, 22%; Sir M. Prescott 16, 38%; M. Tompkins 13, 31%; Mrs M. Reveley 13, 20%; Mrs J. Ramsden 11, 24%; M. Johnston 10, 18%.

FAVOURITES: 32.5%.

Statistics, 1989–94 (NH)

TOP JOCKEYS: N. Doughty 28, 26%; P. Niven 26, 26%; B. Storey 23, 13%; M. Dwyer 18, 21%; C. Grant 11, 10%; L. Wyer 8, 18%.

TOP TRAINERS: G. Richards 34, 18%; J. O'Neill 17, 14%; M. Hammond 16, 18%; Mrs M. Reveley 15, 27%; G. M. Moore 15, 21%; C. Parker 14, 13%.

FAVOURITES: 40.3%.

CARTMEL
Class D (NH)

Set in the heart of the Lake District, Cartmel's tight, left-handed one-mile circuit provides plenty of drama for the large Bank Holiday crowds. The course undulates violently, suiting small, nippy types who can scuttle round the bends at breakneck speed. There is a half-mile run-in on the chase course which sometimes leads to unexpected turnarounds among the leaders.

Over recent seasons favourites have an almost 50 per cent strike rate.

Cartmel's unusual topography often rekindles the enthusiasm of stale or ungenuine horses; in no sense could this

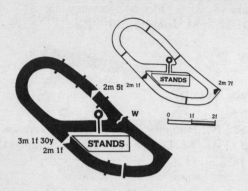

course ever be described as boring. Southern trainer John
White successfully raids virtually every meeting nowadays.
Local top dogs include Gordon Richards and Dudley
Moffatt.

As Jonjo O'Neill says: 'You haven't been racing if you
haven't been to Cartmel.'

Statistics, 1989–94 (NH)

TOP JOCKEYS: N. Doughty 10, 39%; D. Moffatt 8, 24%;
G. McCourt 7, 32%; C. Grant 7, 20%; W. Worthington 7,
16%; P. Niven 6, 24%.

TOP TRAINERS: G. Richards 19, 37%; M. Chapman 12,
17%; J. White 9, 16%; G. M. Moore 8, 31%; D. Moffatt 8,
24%; M. Pipe 7, 29%.

FAVOURITES: 45.7%.

CATTERICK
Class D (Flat)   Class D (NH)

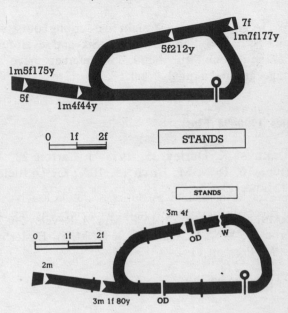

Catterick is a very sharp left-handed oval course, nine furlongs in circumference. The easy nature of the track places little demand on stamina. Because the home straight is so short, front-runners and top weights thrive; long-striding and staying types are best avoided.

A positive jockey like John Carroll has mastered the art of hustling a horse out of the stalls to gain a good early position; pin your faith on his lightning-fast starts and you are sure to back a winner or two.

There have been a number of track specialists in recent years, notably the trail-blazing Gods Solution, with eight course wins to his credit.

The soft fences on the National Hunt course rarely cause

problems. Local trainers Micky Hammond and George Moore can be followed with confidence when fielding ex-Flat racers in novice hurdle company.

DRAW DATA: There is a straight five-furlong course where low numbers have a slight advantage. Six- and seven-furlong heats are run round the bend; low numbers have a big advantage, granted a quick break.

Statistics, 1990–94 (Flat)

TOP JOCKEYS: K. Darley 35, 19%; J. Carroll 28, 18%; J. Fortune 16, 16%; M. Birch 15, 10%; G. Duffield 14, 14%; J. Lowe 13, 9%.

TOP TRAINERS: J. Berry 32, 15%; Mrs M. Reveley 20, 23%; T. Barron 20, 19%; B. Hills 18, 36%; M. H. Easterby 12, 7%; Sir M. Prescott 11, 24%.

FAVOURITES: 40.0%.

Statistics, 1989–94 (NH)

TOP JOCKEYS: M. Dwyer 24, 26%; P. Niven 18, 18%; B. Storey 13, 11%; R. Garrity 12, 12%; L. Wyer 12, 11%; C. Grant 11, 10%.

TOP TRAINERS: Mrs M. Reveley 24, 24%; J. FitzGerald 16, 19%; G. Richards 12, 14%; N. Tinkler 11, 25%; M. Hammond 11, 16%; G. M. Moore 11, 14%.

FAVOURITES: 33.8%.

CHELTENHAM
Class A (NH)

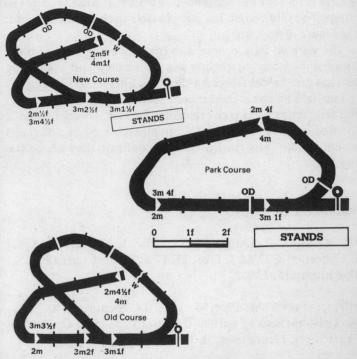

The controversy over the stiff Cheltenham fences first sur-
faced in 1932. The course inspector lopped six inches off the
lot, yet 56 horses fell in the three days of the Festival
meeting. The problems of Cheltenham, spiritual home of
jumping, lie in the mind. Third-last fences here are no more
'bogeys' than elsewhere. This is where races begin and where
tired horses feel the strain.

Riders are revved up as they go out into the country for the
last time and the fence to get across at all costs is the first
ditch. A mistake here often puts the horse on the ropes; the

second ditch two fences later can finish the job.

The left-handed Old and New courses, used for races like the Gold Cup and Champion Hurdle at the Festival, will always represent the supreme test with that final gradient to climb. The Old course has one obstacle in the home straight; the New course, two.

The watered Park course, also left-handed and used for the October meetings, is slightly less demanding and undulating and has four fences (three hurdles) in a long finishing straight.

Ian Balding has a good record because he is selective with the few jumpers he converts from the Flat. Charlie Swan is the first choice of the Irish to continue the long line of giants in the saddle. His record already confirms they chose the right man.

Statistics, 1989–94 (NH)

TOP JOCKEYS: R. Dunwoody 55, 22%; A. Maguire 20, 15%; J. Osborne 18, 13%; J. Frost 15, 17%; G. McCourt 15, 14%; D. Murphy 15, 13%.

TOP TRAINERS: M. Pipe 54, 18%; D. Nicholson 40, 23%; N. Twiston-Davies 26, 19%; J. Gifford 24, 15%; G. Balding 21, 16%; N. Henderson 20, 17%.

FAVOURITES: 38.1%.

CHEPSTOW
Class C (Flat)   Class B (NH)

A left-handed oval course in picturesque surroundings on the Welsh side of the Severn Bridge, it is almost two miles

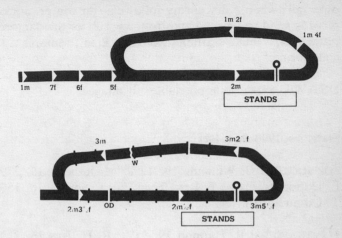

in circumference with a five-furlong run-in and a straight mile course. Despite major undulations up the straight – parts of the races are invisible from the stands – it is a fair course.

Frankie Dettori clinched his first century of winners here – there is now a race named in his honour – and he retains a strong following. Tom Jones's Newmarket raiders are worth a look.

Locally-trained Persian War, which won three Champion Hurdles, and course clerk the late John Hughes, put Chepstow on the map as a major jumping venue.

It needs a great galloper to take on this tough track. So those who accused Carvill's Hill of chickening out of his Cheltenham Gold Cup challenge should be shown replays of his Welsh National triumph here.

Chepstow's wide-open spaces and five fences in the home straight allow a jockey to ride a race, but even the most experienced are faced with getting their horses back on their hocks to jump the last two fences, flat out downhill.

The track can be quite rough for the later meetings,

especially when a dry spring follows a wet winter. Jockey records need to be rewritten following Peter Scudamore's retirement, but trainer Martin Pipe remains all-conquering.

DRAW DATA: No appreciable advantage.

Statistics, 1990–94 (Flat)

TOP JOCKEYS: J. Williams 19, 12%; M. Roberts 15, 37%; L. Dettori 14, 24%; J. Reid 12, 13%; T. Sprake 10, 15%; T. Quinn 9, 10%.

TOP TRAINERS: R. Hannon 19, 13%; R. Hodges 13, 11%; H. Cecil 11, 33%; L. Cumani 9, 45%; H. Candy 9, 20%; B. Hills 8, 20%.

FAVOURITES: 35.9%.

STATISTICS, 1989–94 (NH)

TOP JOCKEYS: R. Dunwoody 25, 25%; J. Lower 13, 24%; A. Maguire 10, 17%; C. Llewellyn 10, 10%; B. Powell 9, 11%; Richard Guest 8, 17%.

TOP TRAINERS: M. Pipe 67, 27%; Mrs J. Pitman 16, 17%; D. Nicholson 15, 38%; N. Twiston-Davies 13, 20%; G. Balding 12, 13%; D. Barons 11, 15%.

FAVOURITES: 43.1%.

CHESTER
Class B (Flat)

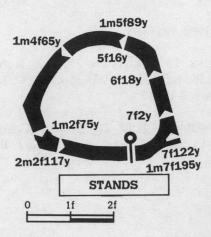

The racecourse at Chester is unique. Its egg-shaped circuit turns constantly left round the small one-mile perimeter. Most definitely a front-runners' track; at the very least contenders must be positively ridden near the pace. The short home straight allows little time to make up any early lost ground. Big, long-striding animals are generally ill at ease.

Despite the iniquities of the course there is still some top-class racing. Millionaire owner Robert Sangster's roots are in this part of the world. Until recently most of his horses have been trained by Barry Hills, and both have an excellent record at the course.

The nearby village of Tarporley is home for trainer Alan Bailey. He is a shrewd judge known for making inroads into the local bookmakers' satchels.

Favourites in handicaps have a poor record. A course for specialists, but even their chances can be thwarted by a poor draw in races up to seven furlongs.

DRAW DATA: Low numbers have a big advantage up to seven furlongs. This advantage is almost immediately negated by a sluggish start.

Statistics, 1990–94 (Flat)

TOP JOCKEYS: Pat Eddery 26, 27%; M. Roberts 17, 19%; A. Munro 16, 16%; W. Swinburn 13, 19%; D. Holland 12, 17%; J. Carroll 12, 13%.

TOP TRAINERS: B. Hills 21, 27%; J. Gosden 17, 28%; M. Stoute 16, 25%; R. Hannon 15, 22%; J. Berry 15, 12%; H. Cecil 12, 29%.

FAVOURITES: 38.0%.

DONCASTER
Class B (Flat)   Class B (NH)

Home to the St Leger, Doncaster is a wide-open galloping track. The long and searching five-furlong stretch to the winning post, occasionally subject to strong headwinds, requires plenty of courage from man and beast.

The sandy subsoil of Town Moor drains well and the ground is good or fast virtually all year round. The powerful Stoute, Cecil and Gosden yards in Newmarket all show a decent level-stake profit with their choicely bred, strong galloping types.

Follow Pat Eddery and you will not go far wrong; he has a near one-in-four strike rate here.

The jump track also stages competitive racing, and there is money to be made following Jimmy FitzGerald's yard,

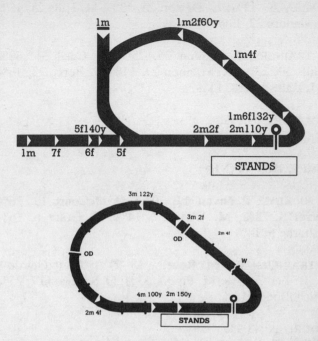

notably when the stable money is down and classy Mark Dwyer is on board. The hurdles track is excellent and very fair; the soft, portable fences on the chase course encourage horses to take liberties, and a race can easily be lost thanks to one horrendous mistake.

DRAW DATA: In sprints on the straight mile, high numbers have the advantage of the stands rail. In fields of more than 15, opportunistic riders drawn low can switch to the faster strip of ground on the far rail.

Statistics, 1990–94 (Flat)

TOP JOCKEYS: Pat Eddery 46, 21%; W. Carson 31, 13%;

K. Darley 29, 12%; L. Dettori 25, 13%; M. Hills 23, 15%; W. Swinburn 22, 13%.

TOP TRAINERS: J. Gosden 36, 25%; H. Cecil 31, 30%; B. Hills 30, 23%; R. Hannon 27, 11%; J. Berry 22, 16%; Mrs J. Ramsden 20, 11%.

FAVOURITES: 33.0%.

Statistics, 1989–94 (NH)

TOP JOCKEYS: P. Niven 17, 30%; G. McCourt 10, 26%; L. Wyer 8, 22%; M. Dwyer 7, 14%; C. Grant 6, 16%; J. Osborne 6, 14%.

TOP TRAINERS: Mrs M. Reveley 13, 21%; J. FitzGerald 9, 15%; R. Lee 7, 41%; M. Pipe 7, 33%; O. Sherwood 7, 25%; D. Nicholson 7, 18%.

FAVOURITES: 43.9%.

EDINBURGH
Class D (Flat)   Class D (NH)

Edinburgh is a flat, oval, ten-furlong, right-handed course. The home bend is extremely sharp; horses thrown wide or unable to handle the turn lose many lengths and often drop out of contention.

Newmarket handler Mark Prescott has seized on the poor racing and poached many races in recent seasons, normally accompanied by George Duffield who rides this tight track with supreme tactical awareness.

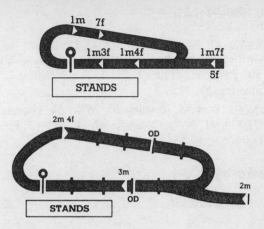

The fences on the National Hunt course are tricky. The hurdle course is slick and suits front-runners. Micky Hammond and Mary Reveley line up numerous winners. Few ride the track better than Peter Niven.

DRAW DATA: Over five furlongs, low numbers are best when the stalls are on the stands side. The reverse applies when the stalls are placed on the far rail. High numbers have the call over seven furlongs and a mile.

Statistics, 1990–94 (Flat)

TOP JOCKEYS: K. Darley 35, 21%; J. Carroll 30, 19%; J. Weaver 28, 30%; G. Duffield 24, 20%; K. Fallon 15, 11%; D. McKeown 13, 11%.

TOP TRAINERS: J. Berry 39, 21%; M. Johnston 15, 18%; M. Naughton 15, 16%; M. Tompkins 11, 42%; Sir M. Prescott 11, 23%; M. H. Easterby 9, 18%.

FAVOURITES: 43.1%.

Statistics, 1989–94 (NH)

TOP JOCKEYS: G. McCourt 18, 28%; C. Grant 18, 21%; B. Storey 17, 15%; M. Dwyer 14, 25%; P. Niven 13, 17%; T. Reed 13, 17%.

TOP TRAINERS: Mrs M. Reveley 16, 28%; M. Hammond 16, 23%; N. Tinkler 11, 36%; Denys Smith 11, 18%; J. FitzGerald 9, 20%; J. Johnson 8, 15%.

FAVOURITES: 46.3%.

EPSOM
Class B (Flat)

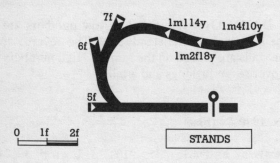

Epsom is a left-handed course, a mile and a half in length and home of the world's most famous Flat race, the Derby. For its first six furlongs the Derby, which starts almost opposite the stands, is run predominantly uphill, but then the course takes a tumbling, turning descent to Tattenham Corner and the three-and-a-half furlong home straight. This continues downhill until 150 yards from home, when it rises quite sharply. The ultimate test for Classic middle-distance three-year-olds is perceived as unfair in some quarters, but the influence of Derby winners down the years suggests otherwise.

The straight five-furlong track is the fastest in the world. Ground forfeited in the early stages of sprints – be it from a slow start or an inability to act on the gradients – is rarely wholly made up. Top weights do well; apprentices less so. But the intricacies of the camber, which throws runners towards the far rail, can embarrass even the most senior jockeys.

In soft ground, fields often swing over to the stands rail. That's also the best place to be in five-furlong sprints when the stalls are positioned on the stands side rail.

Considering he rides this difficult track so infrequently, French-based Cash Asmussen has a remarkable success rate. Jack Berry's well-drilled sprinters come down the hill here to some effect.

DRAW DATA: High numbers are best over five furlongs, especially in the wet.

Statistics, 1990–94 (Flat)

TOP JOCKEYS: M. Roberts 24, 18%; Pat Eddery 21, 16%; J. Reid 16, 16%; W. Carson 14, 16%; L. Dettori 11, 14%; R. Cochrane 10, 15%.

TOP TRAINERS: R. Hannon 15, 12%; J. Berry 12, 26%; D. Elsworth 10, 18%; R. Akehurst 10, 15%; Lord Huntingdon 8, 40%; C. Brittain 8, 14%.

FAVOURITES: 29.9%.

EXETER
Class C (NH)

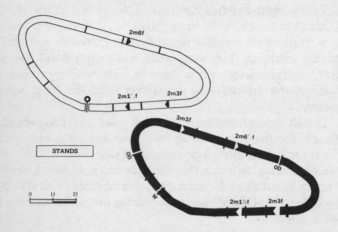

The biggest (acreage-wise) track in the country, and it has no watering system. Some say Exeter should do away with the early meetings, when the ground is invariably firm, but research has confirmed that watered ground produces more injuries than going that has been left to its own devices.

Horses know the time of day when they have been round Exeter's long bends, up and down its undulations and taken on the stiff but fair fences of the two-mile, right-handed circuit.

Desert Orchid and Barnbrook Again began their chase careers here; Noddys Ryde sadly ended his, but the fact that Gordon Richards would bring his best horse all the way from Cumbria underlines the quality of the track for chasers. The same cannot be said for the hurdle course on the inside of the chase course (summer) or stands side (winter), but then the prize money for hurdlers is nowhere near as good.

Trainer Josh Gifford is not far behind Martin Pipe in

percentage terms and obviously picks and chooses his moments in the West Country.

Statistics, 1989–94 (NH)

TOP JOCKEYS: J. Frost 21, 16%; Peter Hobbs 19, 23%; R. Dunwoody 19, 20%; M. Fitzgerald 14, 16%; M. Foster 12, 27%; J. Lower 11, 29%.

TOP TRAINERS: M. Pipe 101, 36%; P. Hobbs 30, 24%; G. Balding 13, 19%; Mrs J. Retter 12, 16%; R. Frost 9, 8%; Mrs A. Knight 8, 8%.

FAVOURITES: 44.6%.

FAKENHAM
Class D (NH)

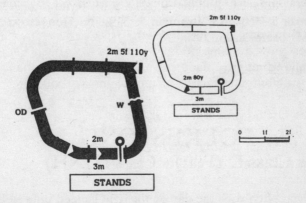

A Square mile with undulations may seem an unpromising site for a jumping course, especially one 22 miles from the nearest railway station. But good ground and the fact that the right horses are sent here – people rarely go out of their way to furthest East Anglia – means the form of the regulars holds up. Sharp horses that can 'rail', horses transported from Newmarket where they were brought up to run and go on the Flat, are just the right sorts, over hurdles at least. Chase fields are small and comprise either the local hunting types or the slower ex-Flat horses.

One 'interloper' in recent years has been Charlie Brooks who, with pleasant memories of his amateur riding days here, has a tremendous record as a trainer. Kim Bailey is the other Lambourn trainer beginning to make regular, successful sorties.

Statistics: 1989–94 (NH)

TOP JOCKEYS: D. Murphy 7, 24%; R. Dunwoody 6, 26%; A. Maguire 6, 23%; Mr M. Armytage 5, 50; M. Brennan 5, 22%; Mr G. Oxley 4, 27%.

TOP TRAINERS: J. Jenkins 9, 21%; M. Ryan 7, 29%; C. Brooks 5, 46%; O. Brennan 5, 33%; N. Henderson 5, 33%; M. Tompkins 5, 23%.

FAVOURITES: 39.5%.

FOLKESTONE
Class D (Flat)   Class D (NH)

Jockeyship often wins the day on the right-handed mile-and-a quarter round course at Folkestone. It is a sharp track and the momentum gained by a bold forward move on the approach to the short two-and-a-half furlong straight is usually vital.

Horses who can race close to the pace and react quickly are favoured. The straight six furlongs is undulating and a position hard against the stands rail seems to confer at least a couple of lengths' advantage.

Poor prizes and trappy fences off tight bends do not give jumps trainers from far afield much incentive to take on the M25, leaving Folkestone out on a limb.

Only one jockey, Declan Murphy, has got into double figures here in the last five years; likewise just two trainers, Josh Gifford and Gardie Grissell. Even then Josh's strike rate is only 20 per cent, a reflection of the quality of horses he sends.

DRAW DATA: The lower the better in sprints.

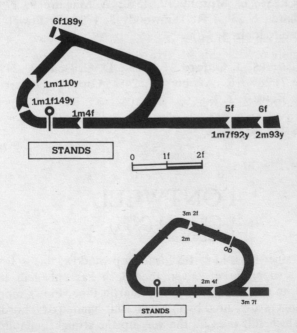

Statistics, 1990–94 (Flat)

TOP JOCKEYS: R. Cochrane 28, 21%; Pat Eddery 27, 30%; T. Quinn 25, 15%; B. Rouse 16, 9%; G. Duffield 15, 15% Paul Eddery 15, 13%.

TOP TRAINERS: R. Hannon 23, 16%; G. Harwood 21, 34%; R. Akehurst 17, 17%; P. Cole 14, 19%; J. Berry 10, 26%; J. Pearce 10, 24%.

FAVOURITES: 39.0%.

Statistics, 1989–94 (NH)

TOP JOCKEYS: D. Murphy 10, 15%; A. Maguire 9, 17%; M. Richards 7, 23%; R. Dunwoody 7, 17%; B. Powell 6, 15%; Peter Hobbs 5, 17%.

TOP TRAINERS: J. Gifford 17, 20%; D. Grissell 12, 24%; M. Pipe 7, 28%; R. Akehurst 7, 24%; Capt. T. Forster 7, 21%; R. Rowe 7, 21%.

FAVOURITES: 41.0%.

FONTWELL
Class D (NH)

Every trainer must have his local shop window; this is Josh Gifford's supermarket. Even then Josh has only half the winners, in percentage terms, of Martin Pipe. Pipe's nippy front-runners are suited by this tight, left-handed oval hurdle track, which still rises all the way up the straight, enabling

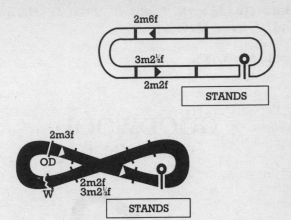

that extra steel that Pipe puts into his charges to come into play.

Round the hourglass-shaped chase course, which has a particularly useless water jump – grandstand spectators get a rear view – and a first fence down the far side taken downhill, a true course specialist is thrown up every generation. Usually it is a front-runner and the most recent darling of Fontwell punters is St Athans Lad. He is best on fast ground; when it was soft, Ryan Price used to send his hurdlers right round the outside, covering a furlong further than the rest of the field, and usually finishing a long way in front; the ground is that much better under the stands rail.

Statistics, 1989–94 (NH)

TOP JOCKEYS: J. Frost 21, 27%; M. Perrett 21, 22%; D. Morris 20, 21%; A. Maguire 20, 17%; Peter Hobbs 19, 22%; D. Murphy 13, 16%.

TOP TRAINERS: J. Gifford 33, 20%; M. Pipe 32, 35%;

P. Hobbs 19, 33%; R. Curtis 16, 20%; G. Harwood 15, 43%; D. Grissell 14, 19%.

FAVOURITES: 47.3%.

GOODWOOD
Class A (Flat)

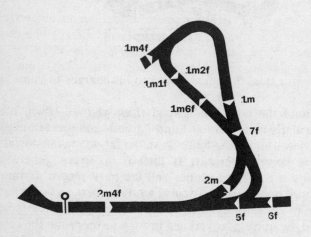

The five-day Glorious Goodwood meeting is one of the racing highlights of the year; always a favourite with P. G. Wodehouse's Bertie Wooster, don't you know, until he lost a packet on a horse called Ocean Breeze.

The Stewards' Cup is run over the straight six-furlong course, the start for which is out of sight from the stands. In that race they climb for a furlong but the last five furlongs is one of the fastest in the country and its headlong rush downhill is not to the liking of every horse.

Races over two and a half miles start in front of the

stands and proceed back up the course, swinging left-handed at the two-mile start, taking a right-handed loop about a mile and a quarter from home, and then joining the straight again with a right-handed turn five furlongs from home. All other races, bar those over a mile and a quarter, pick up the straight three and a half furlongs from the finish.

It is a regular occurrence on the round course to hear a hard luck story or two after the runners have jostled for position inside the last two furlongs. In soft ground, fields cut across to the stands' rail.

The big names dominate here; Eddery and Carson clearly outstrip their jockey rivals, while Henry Cecil's one-in-four strike rate – better still with his two-year-olds – is very commendable given that this is one of the most competitive meetings in the country.

DRAW DATA: Little discernible advantage.

Statistics, 1990–94 (Flat)

TOP JOCKEYS: W. Carson 50, 17%; Pat Eddery 46, 19%; J. Reid 42, 18%; L. Dettori 30, 15%; R. Cochrane 28, 13%; M. Roberts 26, 13%.

TOP TRAINERS: R. Hannon 39, 11%; I. Balding 27, 20%; J. Gosden 26, 21%; J. Dunlop 26, 15%; H. Cecil 22, 26%; M. Stoute 19, 16%.

FAVOURITES: 32.1%.

HAMILTON
Class D (Flat)

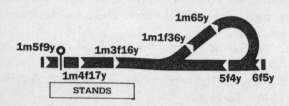

Close to Glasgow, Hamilton Park is a right-handed course laid out in the shape of a tennis racket. From the one-mile-one-furlong start it loops uphill, then sharply downhill, and finally climbs again for the final furlong.

The notorious dip in the home straight often gets boggy, so mudlarks are in their element. Shouldering big weights in these conditions is difficult and it often pays to side with useful young claiming jockeys, especially as the stiff finish can reduce tired horses to a virtual standstill.

The standard of racing is weak and Newmarket raiders regularly make the 720-mile round trip in search of soft races. Northern trainers Jack Berry and Mary Reveley both have excellent strike rates.

DRAW DATA: High numbers have a big advantage on the straight five- and six-furlong courses; the effect is more pronounced when the going is soft.

Statistics, 1990–94 (Flat)

TOP JOCKEYS: J. Carroll 51, 21%; K. Darley 49, 19%; D. McKeown 30, 16%; J. Weaver 26, 24%; G. Duffield 20, 15%; J. Lowe 20, 9%.

TOP TRAINERS: J. Berry 57, 20%; Mrs M. Reveley 31, 22%;
M. Johnston 28, 16%; P. Haslam 19, 18%; M. Tompkins 17,
26%; B. Hanbury 13, 36%.

FAVOURITES: 39.7%.

HAYDOCK
Class B (Flat)   Class A (NH)

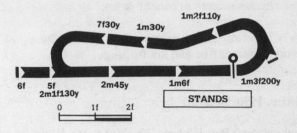

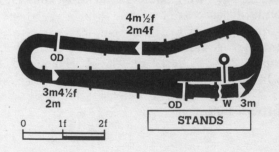

Haydock is a flat, left-handed track with superb new facilities. The long home straight suits waiting tactics in staying
races, though there is often plenty of scrimmaging; it is
unusual to see horses make all the running.

Prize money is good and all the leading trainers are regular visitors. John Gosden, in particular, seems to have the knack of producing decent-priced winners for his principal owner Sheik Mohammed.

It never just rains, it pours in the Manchester area and the going often becomes testing. Under these conditions top weights can flounder. Shop around for decent apprentices.

The winter sport here is a joy. The stiff drop fences produce all sorts of drama; sloppy jumpers rarely prevail. That grand old Gordon Richards-trained chaser Twin Oaks gained his last eight wins here. Martin Pipe's training methods, focusing on superior fitness and stamina, have brought him enormous success in recent years.

DRAW DATA: Those drawn high against the stands' rail have the call over five and six furlongs.

Statistics, 1990–94 (Flat)

TOP JOCKEYS: Pat Eddery 32, 30%; W. Ryan 26, 19%; L. Dettori 23, 18%; M. Roberts 21, 19%; R. Hills 19, 17%; J. Carroll 19, 10%.

TOP TRAINERS: J. Gosden 27, 29%; H. Cecil 21, 37%; J. Dunlop 20, 21%; J. Berry 19, 9%; R. Hannon 15, 15%; B. Hills 14, 18%.

FAVOURITES: 31.0%.

Statistics, 1989–94 (NH)

TOP JOCKEYS: N. Doughty 34, 35%; G. McCourt 19, 21%; M. Dwyer 19, 16%; G. Bradley 13, 24%; R. Dunwoody 13, 22%; P. Niven 8, 16%.

TOP TRAINERS: M. Pipe 42, 33%; G. Richards 40, 33%;
J. FitzGerald 12, 21%; C. Brooks 11, 30%; D. McCain 9,
12%; M. H. Easterby 8, 20%.

FAVOURITES: 45.6%.

HEREFORD
Class D (NH)

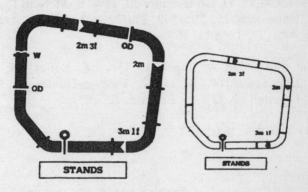

Since Harry Brown backed himself to catch the biggest
salmon of the season on the nearby Wye and ride a winner in
the same hour, donkeys' years ago – he netted the fish but
fell when clear in a chase – this square, right-handed track
has been unlucky for punters. It is plenty long enough (a mile
and a half) for gallopers, but with the last two obstacles on
both tracks met downhill, it produces fallers.

   One day in 1985 an accumulator on the six races would
have produced odds of 47 million to one: nobody collected.
Ten years previously, racing commenced for the evening
meeting at 1.30: 14 races and 219 runners later, the last
weighed-in was announced! It cannot have been a thrill a

minute; the quality of runners here is invariably ordinary.

This is the course where a four-timer from the amateur rider Mr R. Dunwoody made the racing world sit up and take notice. Of the up-and-coming brigade David Bridgwater has a good record; Simon McNeill for the more 'mature' generation. Martin Pipe's position remains unchallenged – even by the likes of Kim Bailey, John Edwards and David Nicholson.

Statistics, 1989–94 (NH)

TOP JOCKEYS: D. Bridgewater 20, 21%; S. McNeill 15, 21%; R. Dunwoody 15, 20%; D. Burchell 13, 28%; J. Osborne 12, 40%; D. Tegg 11, 16%.

TOP TRAINERS: M. Pipe 41, 33%; K. Bailey 16, 21%; N. Henderson 14, 47%; N. Twiston-Davies 14, 29%; D. Burchell 12, 22%; J. Edwards 12, 19%.

FAVOURITES: 38.0%.

HEXHAM
Class C (NH)

The crushing uphill home bend at Hexham separates the men from the boys at this undulating mile-and-a-half Northumberland track. Set on the side of a deep valley, the course forms a natural amphitheatre and is without question one of the best viewing tracks in the land.

The subsoil is clay, producing extremes of going from hard to heavy. When the going gets tough, the tough get going. Ex-Flat racers have a poor record; stick with the more robust staying types to get results.

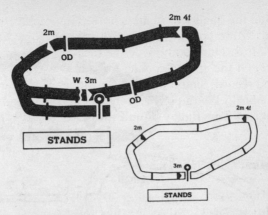

Statistics, 1989–94 (NH)

TOP JOCKEYS: C. Grant 32, 23%; T. Reed 24, 20%; P. Niven 23, 21%; B. Storey 18, 12%; M. Dwyer 17, 26%; N. Doughty 15, 24%.

TOP TRAINERS: G. Richards 28, 24%; G. M. Moore 24, 24%; Mrs M. Reveley 18, 24%; M. Hammond 18, 18%; P. Monteith 16, 31%; L. Lungo 12, 30%.

FAVOURITES: 39.9%.

HUNTINGDON
Class C (NH)

Oliver Cromwell's family have a close association with this track; there is still a Lord Protector Hurdle. Of more real significance is the Gifford connection. Josh was born in a farmhouse overlooking the course and his runners are always to be respected. Yet he comes just a respectable second in

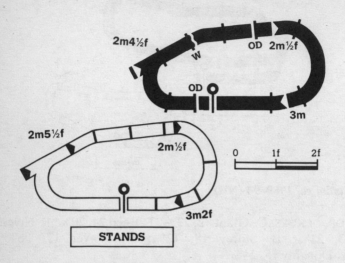

the lists to Ferdie Murphy, most of whose winners here came when he trained for owner Geoff Hubbard. This is one course where you should not back Martin Pipe's runners blindly.

The pancake flat, right-handed circuit rides fast and tends to have competitive fields because of its proximity to good road connections.

It has a black reputation for novice-chase fallers. The fences are stiff and there is much grief.

Statistics, 1989–94 (NH)

TOP JOCKEYS: R. Dunwoody 24, 18%; A. Maguire 20, 20%; D. Murphy 19, 18%; J. Railton 11, 24%; J. Ryan 10, 25%; G. McCourt 9, 18%.

TOP TRAINERS: F. Murphy 24, 17%; D. Nicholson 19, 29%; Mrs J. Pitman 15, 33%; J. Gifford 15, 19%; K. Bailey 12, 36%; J. Upson 10, 18%.

FAVOURITES: 39.4%.

KELSO
Class C (NH)

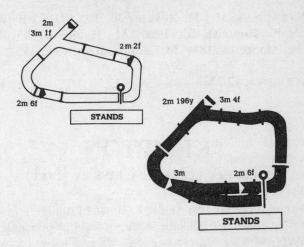

Kelso is an up hill, down dale course, left-handed and quite sharp until the 500-yard run-in, which is one of the longest and toughest in the country.

The rebuilt fences are now among the stiffest around; the four in the back straight are all downhill and need to be taken steadily. Not the ideal track to bring inexperienced novice chasers, and backers should steer well clear of this type of race.

Staying chases often provide thrilling finishes in the final gruelling slog to the line. Market signals for the bumper races run here are normally spot-on. Mary Reveley hot-pots oblige just about every time of asking, albeit at short prices.

Statistics, 1989–94 (NH)

TOP JOCKEYS: P. Niven 43, 34%; N. Doughty 26, 27%; B. Storey 23, 13%; C. Grant 21, 15%; M. Moloney 13, 21%; A. Dobbin 13, 18%.

TOP TRAINERS: Mrs M. Reveley 36, 32%; G. Richards 34, 21%; P. Monteith 20, 19%; M. Hammond 15, 18%; G. M. Moore 14, 18%; Mrs J. Goodfellow 10, 24%.

FAVOURITES: 42.2%.

KEMPTON
Class A (Flat)   Class A (NH)

Kempton is the nearest course to central London, a feature-less right-handed triangular course of about one mile five furlongs, with an unprepossessing water-filled gravel pit in the middle. The course is diagonally dissected by a straight six-furlong track. The mile-and-a-quarter Jubilee course starts on an extension to the round course. It is virtually flat throughout and a very fair test.

Although the run-in is under three furlongs, rarely do you see the pacemakers lasting home. In soft ground the fields fan out into the straight and the horse taking the spot nearest the stands rail has pole position.

Pat Eddery has ridden almost double the number of

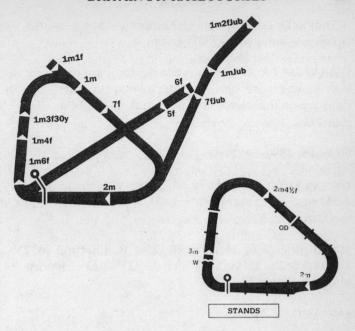

winners of his nearest rival. David Elsworth has a good record here on the Flat and over jumps.

Kempton isn't universally popular, though it's hard to see any objections to a course made for the quicksilver jumper, whose turn of foot can usually be guaranteed good ground. This is why the French horses, Nupsala and The Fellow have done so well here and why in the 1980s all roads on Boxing Day led to Sunbury to see Desert Orchid strut his stuff.

But Kempton is competitive. Arkle ended his career here, battling on to finish a length behind Dormant (receiving 21 pounds) in the 1966 King George VI Chase despite fracturing a pedal bone in his off-fore hoof, and Dessie's career concluded with a fall in the same race 25 years later. This is a great course for sharpening up hurdlers, too, but even over timber, the last flight is gratefully cleared; Night Nurse was just one notable to come a cropper.

They take no prisoners at Kempton – not since the war anyway, when it was a POW camp.

DRAW DATA: In sprints, when the stalls are on the far side high numbers are best, considerably so on soft; when the stalls are on the stands side, low numbers are best.

Statistics, 1990–94 (Flat)

TOP JOCKEYS: Pat Eddery 50, 21%; W. Carson 31, 14%; A. Munro 21, 15%; M. Roberts 20, 10%; T. Quinn 19, 10%; L. Dettori 19, 9%.

TOP TRAINERS: R. Hannon 33, 11%; R. Charlton 16, 23%; J. Dunlop 16, 12%; J. Gosden 15, 15%; D. Elsworth 14, 11%; M. Stoute 12, 14%.

FAVOURITES: 28.6%.

Statistics, 1989–94 (NH)

TOP JOCKEYS: R. Dunwoody 33, 24%; J. Osborne 25, 20%; G. McCourt 14, 20%; D. Murphy 12, 11%; M. Perrett 9, 13%; A. Maguire 8, 14%.

TOP TRAINERS: N. Henderson 19, 23%; M. Pipe 18, 25%; O. Sherwood 14, 23%; J. Gifford 14, 11%; D. Nicholson 11, 17%; D. Elsworth 10, 15%.

FAVOURITES: 39.3%.

LEICESTER
Class C (Flat)   Class C (NH)

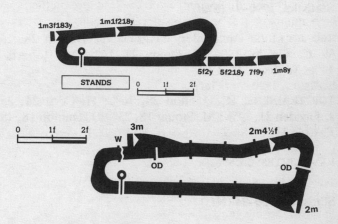

A right-handed track of one mile six furlongs, galloping in nature. All races up to a mile are run on the straight course. From the seven-furlong start the course swings downhill quite sharply until picking up the round course four and a half furlongs from home, and is therefore not ideal for a horse that needs time to find its stride. The course then climbs uphill before levelling off near the finish.

It's quite a severe test and there are plenty of surprises in two-year-old races, particularly in the early part of the season.

Stoute and Swinburn can never be overlooked when they get together at Leicester.

A combination of taxing clay and limestone soil, and an uphill haul to the finish can upset the loftiest reputation.

Leicester is a good place to give a novice an introduction – it's where Golden Miller won his first race – and it will tell you all you need to know.

Jenny Pitman and Martin Pipe have been nose-to-nose here over the years.

DRAW DATA: Inconclusive, but in fields of 20 or more runners, a high draw seems an advantage.

Statistics, 1990–94 (Flat)

TOP JOCKEYS: Pat Eddery 31, 23%; L. Dettori 28, 16%; W. Carson 26, 18%; T. Quinn 24, 16%; M. Roberts 24, 14%; W. Ryan 22, 12%.

TOP TRAINERS: R. Hannon 28, 16%; H. Cecil 24, 25%; J. Gosden 21, 24%; M. Stoute 18, 23%; J. Dunlop 18, 18%; P. Cole 13, 14%.

FAVOURITES: 33.5%.

Statistics 1989–94 (NH)

TOP JOCKEYS: R. Dunwoody 13, 18%; S. Smith Eccles 12, 25%; C. Llewellyn 9, 19%; J. Osborne 9, 18%; M. Richards 7, 24%; N. Williamson 6, 16%.

TOP TRAINERS: M. Pipe 27, 36%; Mrs J. Pitman 20, 27%; O. Sherwood 9, 39%; D. Nicholson 9, 17%; J. Mackie 6, 22%; S. Mellor 6, 14%.

FAVOURITES: 39.3%.

LINGFIELD (Turf)
Class B (Flat)   Class B (NH)

A cigarette advert used to pronounce that leafy Lingfield had 'style'. Now it has Derby and Oaks trials because of its

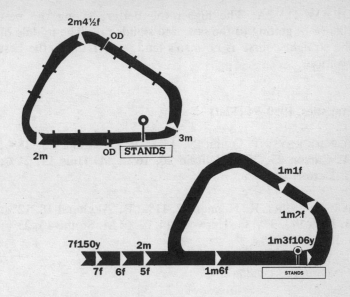

similarities to Epsom, racing on sand, trotting, and plenty of enterprise.

The triangular mile-and-a-half turf course has an uphill climb to its furthest point from the stands. The drift down from there helps horses conserve energy and unless the going is heavy this is not a stayers' track. The turn into the home straight nearly four furlongs out is very sharp and tends to throw horses out wide; it is badly sited and unfair and many races are lost at this point. Be wary of first-time visitors because of that bend.

The straight course of seven furlongs 140 yards is one of the easiest in the country, being predominantly downhill the whole way.

South coast trainer Guy Harwood likes to run his quality two-year-olds here.

Lingfield's fences can be trappy and races are often won by the positive jockey who makes his move first in the home straight.

DRAW DATA: The higher the better, giving the best chance of getting to the favoured stands rail. The middle of the straight course is no man's land; either rail is the best position.

Statistics, 1990–94 (Flat)

TOP JOCKEYS: T. Quinn 29, 15%; R. Cochrane 28, 18%; W. Carson 25, 26%; J. Reid 20, 16%; M. Hills 19, 21%; L. Dettori 19, 19%.

TOP TRAINERS: R. Hannon 22, 11%; R. Akehurst 18, 12%; B. Hills 14, 33%; G. Harwood 14, 23%; M. Stoute 13, 23%; J. Berry 13, 21%.

FAVOURITES: 33.8%.

Statistics, 1989–94 (NH)

TOP JOCKEYS: A. Dicken 22, 36%; A. Maguire 20, 23%; D. Gallagher 14, 13%; J. Osborne 13, 28%; D. O'Sullivan 13, 12%; M. Ahern 11, 17%.

TOP TRAINERS: Miss B. Sanders 32, 33%; J. Jenkins 20, 16%; S. Dow 19, 31%; R. Akehurst 18, 31%; T. Thomson Jones 16, 28%; D. Grissell 16, 24%.

FAVOURITES: 47.2%.

LINGFIELD (All-Weather)
Class D (Flat)

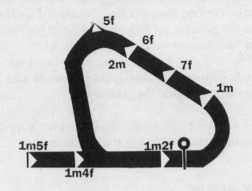

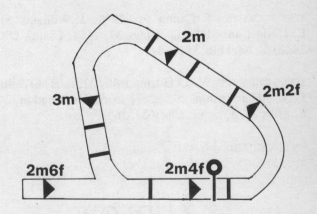

The ability to quicken off a high cruising speed is a character-istic which is rewarded at Lingfield's all-weather track. Only a mile and a quarter in circumference, it lies within the turf track. The races are run at a breakneck pace and it is vital to have taken up a good position by the second last turn, four furlongs from home, because by the time the field swings into

the short two-furlong straight the outcome is often a fore-
gone conclusion.

The Equitrack surface is less dense than Southwell's Fibresand, flies up higher and is more stingy; races are less likely to
be won by horses coming from off the pace here. Equitrack is
the surface for the popular Al Bahathri gallop at Newmarket,
whose trainers have a good strike-rate at Lingfield.

Michael Hills is very good at going to the front and
dictating the pace to suit his needs; Billy Newnes and John
Williams are others who ride the course well.

DRAW DATA: With relatively small fields, a positive
jockey is more important than any stall position.

Statistics, 1990–94 (Flat)

TOP JOCKEYS: T. Quinn 61, 19%; J. Williams 51, 13%;
L. Dettori 48, 31%; D. Biggs 39, 11%; Emma O'Gorman
38, 23%; M. Hills 31, 16%.

TOP TRAINERS: W. O'Gorman 36, 22%; R. O'Sullivan 34,
17%; M. Johnston 29, 22%; Lord Huntingdon 24, 23%;
B. Hills 23, 33%; C. Elsey 23, 16%.

FAVOURITES: 33.5%.

LUDLOW
Class D (NH)

Lowly Ludlow teaches us the moral that there is no hard and
fast rule to finding winners. Ludlow is a quick, right-handed
course, yet not against gallopers; it's flat and often firm, not

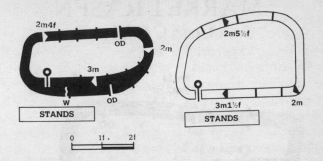

least on the four road crossings. The horses aren't always good enough to maintain the inevitable fast pace.

Messrs Pipe, Nicholson and Bailey harvest most of the winners, as do jockeys Dunwoody, Llewellyn and Williamson.

Ludlow is reputed to be the oldest jump course, dating back to 1729: the stands seem older, though they are in fact Edwardian. They should be in a museum, soon.

Statistics, 1989–94 (NH)

TOP JOCKEYS: R. Dunwoody 17, 25%; N. Williamson 13, 16%; B. Powell 10, 35%; J. Osborne 8, 21%; C. Llewellyn 8, 12%; A. Maguire 7, 15%.

TOP TRAINERS: D. Nicholson 19, 24%; M. Pipe 18, 23%; J. Edwards 15, 21%; K. Bailey 11, 21%; R. Lee 11, 15%; N. Henderson 8, 29%.

FAVOURITES: 39.9%.

MARKET RASEN
Class C (NH)

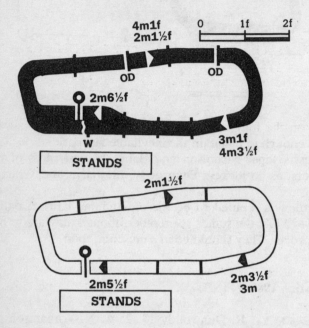

Market Rasen's easy mile-and-a-quarter, right-handed oval course is ideal for the handy, nippy type, placing little demand on staying power. The fences are not difficult until, it seems, the third last, which, despite being modified in recent seasons, still causes more than its fair share of casualties.

Trainer Nigel Tinkler enjoys plenty of success, especially with hurdlers, but they are invariably backed off the boards. Much better to side with the local father–son combination of Owen and Martin Brennan, who have a superb record rewarding supporters with a healthy level-stake profit.

Cast your net no further than Peter Easterby or Chris Thornton in 'bumper' events; both enjoy considerable success in this type of heat. A good meeting for the big stables.

Statistics, 1989–94 (NH)

TOP JOCKEYS: P. Niven 26, 27%; G. McCourt 26, 27%; L. Wyer 21, 23%; M. Brennan 21, 14%; M. Dwyer 19, 21%; D. Byrne 17, 19%.

TOP TRAINERS: J. FitzGerald 30, 27%; Mrs M. Reveley 26, 36%; M. H. Easterby 26, 34%; N. Tinkler 24, 27%; O. Brennan 20, 14%; M. Pipe 18, 36%.

FAVOURITES: 36.9%.

NEWBURY
Class A (Flat)   Class A (NH)

One of the fairest tracks in the country with few, if any, idiosyncrasies. It now boasts a superb, if rather compact, new stand which has replaced the course's focal point, the bar under the old stand. That's where you met anyone who was anyone in jump racing, providing you could find your way through a fog of cigar smoke and condensation.

The left-handed oval course extends to almost two miles and is galloping in nature; there is also a straight mile. The racing is fiercely competitive and the form tends to work out well; particularly informative are the large fields of maidens in the autumn which often mark the introduction of Classic candidates for the following year.

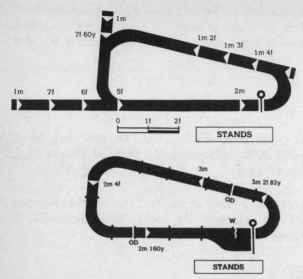

Peter Chapple-Hyam, from nearby Manton, is rapidly becoming the dominant force at his local track.

Newbury is at least as popular with jumping's participants as Cheltenham. Good horses can show their jumping skills and jockeys their race-riding art; the cross fence, taken slightly downhill, adds a touch of spice.

This is Lambourn territory, though the days of Winter–Walwyn supremacy are gone and not even Pipe has wrested dominance. Two trainers to watch for are Nigel Twiston-Davies and Mark Tompkins.

DRAW DATA: No appreciable advantage.

Statistics, 1990–94 (Flat)

TOP JOCKEYS: Pat Eddery 51, 18%; W. Carson 41, 16%; L. Dettori 35, 16%; J. Reid 35, 15%; M. Roberts 34, 13%; W. Swinburn 25, 13%.

TOP TRAINERS: R. Hannon 42, 9%; P. Chapple-Hyam 30, 33%; J. Gosden 29, 23%; H. Cecil 23, 24%; R. Charlton 19, 16%; J. Dunlop 17, 10%.

FAVOURITES: 35.0%.

Statistics, 1989–94 (NH)

TOP JOCKEYS: R. Dunwoody 54, 27%; J. Osborne 28, 22%; P. Holley 15, 23%; J. Frost 14, 17%; A. Maguire 14, 17%; G. McCourt 11, 15%.

TOP TRAINERS: M. Pipe 28, 28%; N. Henderson 28, 22%; D. Nicholson 25, 23%; O. Sherwood 24, 25%; D. Elsworth 20, 20%; Mrs J. Pitman 12, 14%.

FAVOURITES: 41.4%.

NEWCASTLE
Class B (Flat)   Class B (NH)

The two-mile, left-handed galloping track at Newcastle represents one of the fairest courses in the country. The valuable Northumberland Plate, otherwise known as the Pitmen's Derby, invariably attracts some of the best staying handicappers in training.

Top weights can struggle since the four-furlong home straight rises steadily all the way to the line.

Peter Easterby and stable jockey Mark Birch have a good record. Level-stake backers of the Maurice Camacho–Nicky Connorton combination are quids in over recent seasons. Willie Carson rode a six-timer here in June 1990 and two

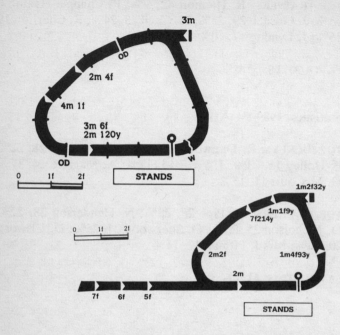

years later Pat Eddery, having ridden a treble at Newmarket in the afternoon, travelled on to ride four further winners at Gosforth Park. Needless to say, both have a strong affection for this track.

The Fighting Fifth and Ekbalco Hurdles attract top-class timber merchants to the course, and together with the four-mile Eider Chase provide memorable jump action every season. The fences are stiff and unforgiving; the hurdle course a true test. No single stable dominates, but good form achieved at Newcastle holds up well, and often points to profitable betting opportunities at other tracks.

DRAW DATA: Over five, six and seven furlongs, high numbers are favoured unless the ground is soft, when the trend is reversed.

Statistics, 1990–94 (Flat)

TOP JOCKEYS: K. Darley 27, 14%; J. Carroll 22, 15%; W. Carson 20, 36%; D. McKeown 18, 14%; M. Birch 16, 11%; G. Duffield 15, 18%.

TOP TRAINERS: J. Berry 25, 16%; Mrs M. Reveley 19, 13%; M. Stoute 18, 29%; H. Cecil 13, 34%; Mrs J. Ramsden 13, 13%; J. Watts 12, 16%.

FAVOURITES: 37.4%.

Statistics, 1989–94 (NH)

TOP JOCKEYS: C. Grant 35, 22%; P. Niven 22, 18%; T. Reed 18, 16%; B. Storey 17, 12%; G. McCourt 14, 25%; L. Wyer 14, 17%.

TOP TRAINERS: G. M. Moore 17, 27%; J. Johnson 17, 18%; Mrs M. Reveley 16, 21%; M. H. Easterby 13, 19%; G. Richards 12, 15%; M. Hammond 12, 15%.

FAVOURITES: 43.0%.

NEWMARKET
Class A (Flat)

No longer the official headquarters of racing, since the Jockey Club/British Horseracing Board moved to Portman Square, but still home to Britain's largest single horse population. The wide open expanse of Newmarket Heath, with hardly a tree in sight, is not to everyone's taste but

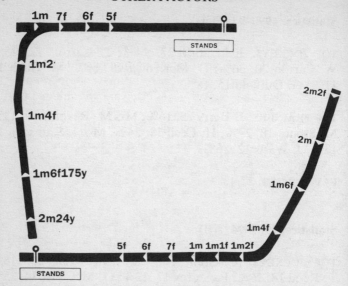

throughout the year it puts on the most strongly contested
racing anywhere in the country, dominated by the local
trainers.

It is hellishly difficult to back winners at Newmarket, but
punters can at least console themselves with the fact that the
races there conceal a stack of future winners. The back-end
maidens, for example, require a performance of Listed race
quality to triumph. The course extends past the Cesarewitch
start, two and a quarter miles from home, and there is a
right-hand bend leading to a daunting mile-and-a-quarter
straight run home. It is a wide open, galloping track, very
much exposed to the wind. Excellent judgement of pace is
required and the ability to time the finishing challenge to
perfection, as the track goes sharply downhill from the
two-furlong pole into the Dip and then climbs all the way to
the line. Because of the difficulties, few apprentices shine
here. The course drains well and rarely rides soft.

Pat Eddery is the first jockey to go through the 100 barrier
for Newmarket winners in the last six years; Henry Cecil

won't be far behind among the trainers. Look out for relative new boys Chapple-Hyam and Charlton, who hold their own against the Newmarket hordes.

The July Course used in the summer months has similar characteristics but a rather more intimate atmosphere – the pre-parade ring even has trees. Beware the midges in summer, though.

DRAW DATA: No advantage on either course.

Statistics, 1990–94 (Rowley Mile)

TOP JOCKEYS: Pat Eddery 69, 20%; W. Swinburn 43, 16%; W. Carson 41, 11%; L. Dettori 39, 11%; M. Roberts 37, 10%; M. Hills 21, 10%.

TOP TRAINERS: H. Cecil 39, 18%; J. Gosden 35, 17%; M. Stoute 32, 14%; L. Cumani 30, 13%; B. Hills 29, 12%; R. Hannon 25, 7%.

FAVOURITES: 31.4%.

Statistics, 1990–94 (July Course)

TOP JOCKEYS: L. Dettori 37, 17%; Pat Eddery 35, 17%; W. Carson 34, 18%; M. Roberts 32, 16%; W. Swinburn 30, 17%; B. Raymond 16, 12%.

TOP TRAINERS: R. Hannon 32, 15%; H. Cecil 24, 23%; J. Gosden 21, 18%; L. Cumani 20, 17%; M. Stoute 20, 17%; P. Cole 15, 27%.

FAVOURITES: 36.0%.

NEWTON ABBOT
Class D (NH)

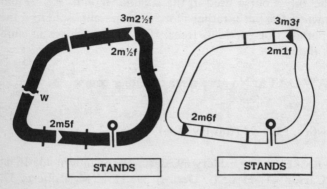

Newton Abbot suffers from extremes of going, too often on the same day. The watering system, on what is reclaimed marshland adjacent to the River Teign, sometimes makes it appear the Teign has claimed parts of the course back. The bends at one meeting early in the 1993/4 season were squelchy, the straight like a road and the official going 'good to firm'.

Yet, though only one mile round, left-handed Newton Abbot is a fair track . . . apart from some eccentric starting. Horses can win ridden from behind or from the front.

The Pipe–Scudamore domination was as marked here as anywhere, Pipe having had over 100 winners more than his nearest rival, Philip Hobbs. The challenge to Pipe's dynasty may now be left to John White, the coming man, and not only way down west.

Statistics, 1989–94 (NH)

TOP JOCKEYS: R. Dunwoody 34, 26%; Peter Hobbs 16, 17%; M. Fitzgerald 16, 13%; G. McCourt 13, 30%; J. Frost 13, 8%; G. Bradley 12, 30%.

TOP TRAINERS: M. Pipe 113, 31%; P. Hobbs 26, 23%;
R. Hodges 17, 13%; D. Barons 15, 12%; Mrs J. Retter 14,
15%; P. Nicholls 12, 25%.

FAVOURITES: 40.2%.

NOTTINGHAM
Class C (Flat)   Class C (NH)

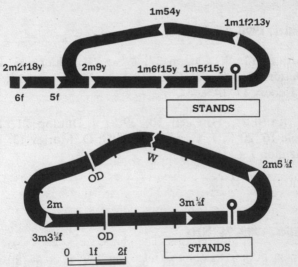

The Nottingham round course is left-handed and nondescript,
extending to about a mile and a half with a run-in of over four
furlongs; there is also a six-furlong straight course. It puts on
typical Midlands fare with the emphasis on quantity rather than
quality. It's a flat course and provides a fair test.

The feature of the jumping track, with its emphasis on
speed, is the long run-in: don't count your winnings too soon.
The prize money doesn't take too much counting either, so it

rarely attracts top horses. In February, though, there is the Champion Hurdle Trial and a Grade 2 chase on the same day. Royal Gait won the hurdle before going on to take the Champion two years ago.

North meets south here and Graham McCourt (principally for Nigel Tinkler) and Peter Niven (mainly for Mrs Reveley) rival the totals of Pipe's riders and the yards of Henderson and Nicholson.

DRAW DATA: High numbers have a definite advantage over five and six furlongs.

Statistics, 1990–94 (Flat)

TOP JOCKEYS: W. Carson 37, 19%; Pat Eddery 33, 26%; L. Dettori 29, 19%; W. Ryan 21, 13%; M. Roberts 18, 11%; Paul Eddery 17, 14%.

TOP TRAINERS: H. Cecil 30, 39%; J. Dunlop 21, 19%; P. Cole 16, 20%; J. Gosden 13, 31%; D. Morley 13, 16%; R. Hannon 13, 11%.

FAVOURITES: 37.1%.

Statistics, 1989–94 (NH)

TOP JOCKEYS: G. McCourt 16, 22%; M. Dwyer 14, 16%; J. Osborne 13, 22%; R. Dunwoody 13, 17%; P. Niven 10, 21%; R. Beggan 7, 18%.

TOP TRAINERS: M. Pipe 11, 23%; D. Nicholson 10, 19%; J. FitzGerald 10, 18%; N. Henderson 9, 27%; Mrs M. Reveley 7, 19%; J. Mackie 7, 18%.

FAVOURITES: 38.7%.

PERTH
Class C (NH)

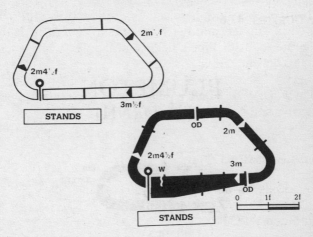

Perth is a tight but perfectly level right-handed course with sharp bends and relatively easy fences: speed rather than stamina is required. The track's highly efficient watering system means the going rarely gets firm, thus attracting runners from the length and breadth of the land.

In big fields many lengths can be saved by sticking to the inner; front-runners do exceptionally well.

Favourites have an outstanding record, particularly over hurdles. Level-stake backers of Scottish trainer Peter Monteith, known for producing trail-blazers, are showing a healthy profit over recent seasons.

Statistics, 1989–94 (NH)

TOP JOCKEYS: P. Niven 24, 30%; M. Dwyer 21, 23%; N. Doughty 19, 20%; C. Grant 18, 18%; G. McCourt 16, 24%; L. O'Hara 12, 19%.

TOP TRAINERS: G. Richards 32, 18%; Mrs M. Reveley 18, 43%; M. Hammond 17, 27%; P. Monteith 14, 18%; K. Bailey 11, 46%; Miss L. Perratt 10, 23%.

FAVOURITES: 47.6%.

PLUMPTON
Class D (NH)

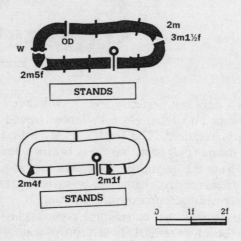

This track has a strong local following. It is also a wide boys' course – they spill off the train from London in droves.

The left-handed circuit, little more than a mile round, is not popular with jockeys, though; down the far side it can be like riding the wall of death. But the fence at the top of the hill has been moved 25 yards and the one at the bottom also, reducing fallers by 25 per cent.

It is a track which favours quick, handy jumpers and

always on the job here is recent course specialist Manhattan Boy.

But, oh dear, those tight turns and the cloying clay underfoot that dries out to brickwork. Joe Guest and Ray Goldstein didn't get their reputation as the iron men of racing the easy way – it came from hitting the deck at Plumpton.

Statistics, 1989–94 (NH)

TOP JOCKEYS: A. Maguire 35, 28%; R. Dunwoody 30, 24%; M. Perrett 14, 20%; J. Osborne 10, 23%; D. Murphy 9, 22%; D. Skyrme 9, 15%.

TOP TRAINERS: J. White 36, 27%; J. Ffitch-Heyes 16, 9%; R. Akehurst 15, 31%; J. Jenkins 15, 19%; A. Moore 15, 8%; D. Grissell 13, 19%.

FAVOURITES: 44.3%.

PONTEFRACT
Class C (Flat)

Pontefract is a left-handed course; the final six furlongs are uphill with a very sharp bend leading into the short two-furlong home straight. The inevitable bunching gives rise to more hard-luck stories and stewards' inquiries than on any other course I can think of. For this reason steer well clear of apprentices and inexperienced jockeys. Help yourself to stay in profit by siding with Yorkshire-based strongman Kieran Fallon, who can mix it with the best round here.

Newmarket yards raid regularly. Henry Cecil has only a handful of runners per season, but maintains a near-50 per

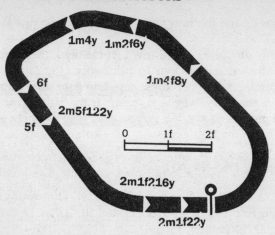

cent strike rate. Mark Tompkins also considers this well-run track one of his lucky venues. Millionaire owner Jack Ramsden has rattled the bookmakers in these parts for some time. Any springers in the market trained by his wife Lynda are normally worth a decent investment.

DRAW DATA: Over five and six furlongs, low numbers are best; the advantage is enhanced considerably given a fast start, and lost totally if slowly away.

Statistics, 1990–94 (Flat)

TOP JOCKEYS: K. Darley 25, 13%; M. Roberts 22, 23%; L. Dettori 19, 18%; W. Ryan 18, 20%; K. Fallon 18, 13%; A. Munro 16, 16%.

TOP TRAINERS: R. Hollinshead 25, 13%; H. Cecil 18, 49%; Mrs M. Reveley 17, 17%; J. Berry 17, 12%; Mrs J. Ramsden 17, 11%; M. Tompkins 13, 14%.

FAVOURITES: 39.2%.

REDCAR
Class C (Flat)

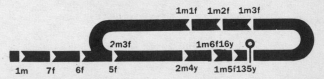

The left-handed, perfectly level galloping track at Redcar has a very fair five-furlong home straight. The sandy subsoil drains quickly, often making the ground unsuitably firm. There is also a straight mile.

Patience is a virtue in staying races. With plenty of time to make up lost ground, hitting the front too soon at Redcar can have dire consequences.

Mary Reveley trains nearby and her runners, particularly those owned by Peter Savill and partnered by his retained jockey Kevin Darley, always command immense respect. The wealthy Savill has handed out a big beating to rails bookmakers in recent seasons, so much so that the majority have closed his betting accounts.

Trainer Tom Jones and jockey Richard Hills are among the best of the Newmarket visitors. Regular Lambourn raider John Hills also makes his presence felt. Favourites in all bar two-year-old races have a good record.

DRAW DATA: In races up to a mile, high numbers are best. In fields of 15 or more, those drawn low switch to the faster far side rail and reverse this trend.

Statistics, 1990–94 (Flat)

TOP JOCKEYS: K. Darley 50, 19%; M. Birch 24, 12%; Paul Eddery 20, 22%; G. Duffield 20, 15%; K. Fallon 18, 11%; R. Hills 17, 17%.

TOP TRAINERS: Mrs M. Reveley 50, 16%; M. H. Easterby 22, 10%; J. Berry 21, 12%; Sir M. Prescott 13, 30%; J. Gosden 13, 19%; H. Thomson Jones 12, 25%.

FAVOURITES: 36.8%.

RIPON
Class C (Flat)

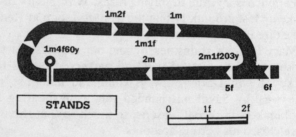

Ripon is a right-handed, oval galloping track. The home straight measures five furlongs, with a good covering of grass generally taking any jar out of the ground.

Although no particular pattern holds sway, Jack Berry's youngsters normally merit support. In three-year-old handicaps, Michael Stoute often finds the perfect opportunities for some of his lesser lights.

By and large not a front-runners' track. Good three-pound and five-pound claimers on top weights are the each-way value at this course.

DRAW DATA: Low numbers against the stands rail are best in medium or small fields. The trend is reversed in fields of 20 or more when high numbers head for the far rail.

Statistics, 1990–94 (Flat)

TOP JOCKEYS: K. Darley 28, 16%; M. Birch 19, 11%; W. Ryan 17, 19%; D. McKeown 17, 12%; J. Carroll 15, 13%; N. Connorton 13, 12%.

TOP TRAINERS: J. Berry 23, 16%; H. Cecil 22, 49%; M. H. Easterby 18, 9%; M. Stoute 14, 26%; M. Johnston 12, 15%; J. Gosden 11, 27%.

FAVOURITES: 37.2%.

SALISBURY
Class B (Flat)

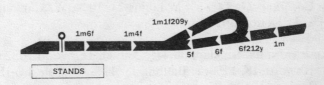

TWO world famous Americans – Steve Cauthen and Mill Reef – made their British debuts at Salisbury. Cauthen started on a very inhospitable day and in similar filthy, wet conditions races are decided by who gets to the favoured stands rail first. In the dry, it is a fair track.

As at Lord March's Goodwood, the long-distance races at Salisbury start in front of the stands and the fields travel back up the course before swinging away left-handed at a point about a mile and a quarter from home, and then round a right-handed loop until the dog-legged straight mile course is rejoined some seven furlongs from the finish. The ground climbs steadily for the last four furlongs and is galloping in nature.

Local trainer Richard Hannon, whose horses have to vacate their Salisbury Plain gallops in time for the army tank manoeuvres to begin, is not surprisingly the leading trainer numerically. But because of his modest strike rate, punters would be better looking to Newmarket raiders – Fanshawe, Stoute and Gosden – for their bets. Walter Swinburn is another to make the most of his visits from Suffolk.

DRAW DATA: No appreciable advantage in sprints until the ground becomes soft, then low numbers have the best chance of getting to the stand rail.

Statistics, 1990–94 (Flat)

TOP JOCKEYS: J. Reid 27, 16%; Pat Eddery 25, 20%; R. Cochrane 24, 14%; J. Williams 23, 10%; W. Carson 20, 13%; L. Dettori 19, 17%.

TOP TRAINERS: R. Hannon 44, 13%; G. Harwood 20, 23%; D. Elsworth 18, 11%; I. Balding 15, 11%; P. Cole 14, 15%; J. Dunlop 14, 12%.

FAVOURITES: 32.2%.

SANDOWN
Class A (Flat)   Class A (NH)

Jumping was first shown on television (in the 1947/8 season) from Sandown and it was a good choice. Nowhere do you

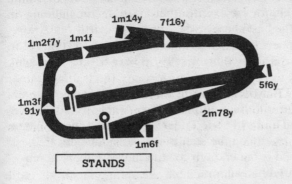

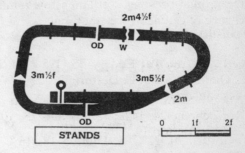

feel remote from the action. Even the Members' Lawn gives a commanding view of the racing.

Despite the testing nature of the four-furlong uphill home straight, this is the front-runners' track par excellence. The horse that has to come from behind here is carrying a three-pound penalty and only those with a good turn of foot overcome it. Even over jumps, trail-blazers like Tingle Creek and Kilbrittain Castle built up big followings here.

The course, a right-handed oval, measures one mile five furlongs; the straight five furlongs which dissects it is one of the stiffest in the country and the draw plays a significant role. No jockey can imagine himself invincible here.

Jump races can be won and lost over the three close-coupled 'Railway' fences in the back straight. But more often those fences are just the appetizer; the stiff uphill climb comes to its climax on a run-in that has been the undoing of virtually all the best chasers and hurdlers, apart from Arkle.

Northern trainers have a good record – someone like Peter Easterby knows he need bring only his very best to Sandown.

DRAW DATA: When the stalls for five-furlong races are set against the far rail, high numbers have a massive advantage in soft ground and a big one under any circumstances. When the stalls are placed on the stands side, low numbers are best unless the field is big enough for the high numbers to make for the favoured far rail.

Statistics, 1990–94 (Flat)

TOP JOCKEYS: Pat Eddery 55, 19%; M. Roberts 42, 16%; T. Quinn 34, 16%; L. Dettori 32, 17%; W. Carson 30, 12%; W. Swinburn 29, 16%.

TOP TRAINERS: R. Hannon 40, 13%; M. Stoute 24, 15%; J. Gosden 20, 22%; J. Dunlop 18, 16%; R. Akehurst 17, 13%; P. Cole 16, 14%.

FAVOURITES: 32.9%.

Statistics, 1989–94 (NH)

TOP JOCKEYS: R. Dunwoody 31, 24%; D. Murphy 18, 23%; J. Osborne 17, 17%; A. Maguire 12, 20%; M. Perrett 9, 17%; Mr C. Ward Thomas 8, 40%.

TOP TRAINERS: J. Gifford 27, 18%; D. Nicholson 23, 30%; M. Pipe 17, 21%; C. Brooks 12, 22%; Capt. T. Forster 9, 21%; O. Sherwood 9, 16%.

FAVOURITES: 39.9%.

SEDGEFIELD
Class D (NH)

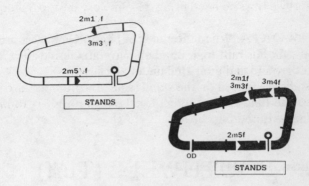

Sedgefield is a tight, left-handed undulating course covering ten furlongs. Although the racing is nowhere near top-class and the track is very exposed to the weather, it is popular on account of the regular thrilling finishes.

Good jockeyship is essential as each race draws to a conclusion. Contenders in both hurdle races and chases gallop full pelt downhill for three furlongs praying they will take the final obstacle in their stride, before battling it out on the short but stiff uphill run-in. Over the years, Chris Grant has made an art form of riding this tricky track.

Mary Reveley has established a wonderful strike rate here: nowadays virtually one in every three of her runners wins. Stable jockey Peter Niven partners the majority of the stable's fancies. Back them and you will still have some money left in your pocket come the end of the season.

The cross fence adjacent to the stands causes more drama than most and must be negotiated three times in staying events. Not all horses act on this trappy circuit and course specialists are always worth bearing in mind.

Statistics, 1989–94 (NH)

TOP JOCKEYS: P. Niven 61, 28%; C. Grant 46, 20%;
L. Wyer 30, 25%; M. Dwyer 30, 22%; J. Callaghan 20, 17%;
R. Hodge 12, 21%.

TOP TRAINERS: Mrs M. Reveley 69, 32%; G. M. Moore 30,
20%; M. H. Easterby 26, 28%; J. FitzGerald 19, 30%;
J. Johnson 15, 11%; J. Hellens 14, 25%.

FAVOURITES: 42.5%.

SOUTHWELL (Turf)
Class D (NH)

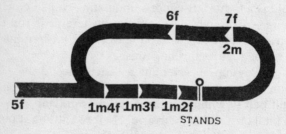

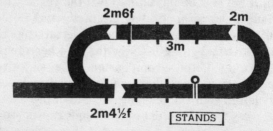

The turf course at Southwell is where Phil Tuck equalled the
late Johnnie Gilbert's record (10) for the most consecutive

winning rides over jumps, aboard Doronicum on 3 September 1986.

Neither of them would recognize the place now.

The turf track lies inside the all-weather one and is very sharp, especially for chasers. The ability to jump quickly is paramount.

DRAW DATA: No appreciable advantage.

Statistics, 1989–94 (NH)

JOCKEYS: S. Wynne 25, 20%; Gary Lyons 22, 18%; S. Smith Eccles 21, 25%; P. Niven 19, 20%; Diane Clay 18, 30%; R. Dunwoody 18, 27%.

TOP TRAINERS: R. Hollinshead 38, 26%; M. Pipe 22, 32%; W. Clay 30, 17%; J. Harris 30, 16%; B. Preece 18, 15%; Mrs M. Reveley 16, 29%.

FAVOURITES: 40.6%.

SOUTHWELL (All-Weather)
Class D (Flat)

Southwell stages year-round all-weather Flat racing on the custom-built ten-furlong oval circuit. The course is sharp and left-handed. The surface used is Fibresand, which leads to slower times than at Lingfield's Equitrack. In the wet, the going can become deep and testing.

It is a track that favours handy types with a high cruising speed – they go like the clappers. Because of the three-furlong run-in, races can be won from off the pace as a challenge is thrown down in the middle of the track, out of the 'kickback'.

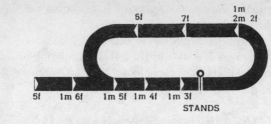

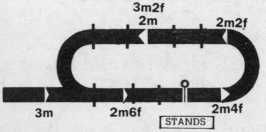

Overall the standard is poor . . . but it will get better.

The all-weather surface is a bonanza for course specialists. Reg Hollinshead's now-retired Suluk won 18 races, while David Chapman's Flat racer Tempering is already well into double figures.

David Barron retains his dominance in the trainers' table, backers achieving a small level-stake profit on all runners. Alex Greaves ('Queen of the Sand') and George Duffield are the leading jockeys. Diane Clay has a superb strike rate on the all-weather hurdle course.

The market is notoriously weak, especially in winter when the crowds are small.

DRAW DATA: No advantage, even on the straight five-furlong course.

Statistics, 1990–94 (Flat)

TOP JOCKEYS: Alex Greaves 57, 21%; G. Duffield 42, 16%;

J. Quinn 38, 8%; D. McKeown 37, 11%; S. Wood 36, 9%;
Emma O'Gorman 35, 16%.

TOP TRAINERS: T. Barron 63, 20%; D. Chapman 50, 10%;
W. O'Gorman 44, 20%; J. Berry 40, 16%; S. Norton 34,
20%; R. Hollinshead 30, 8%.

FAVOURITES: 35.1%.

STRATFORD
Class C (NH)

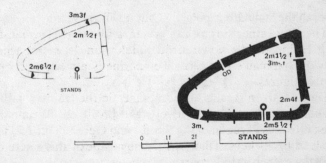

If the MCC want to know how to prepare a perfect Test
match wicket they could do worse than come to Stratford,
where the level, left-handed track is turned out in better trim
than anywhere else.

Traditions die hard but Stratford has given up the water
jump without any sit-ins and this is a good place for a handy
novice. The siting of another fence in the straight, to
compensate for the loss of the water, has not been a success;
there have been a fair few fallers there already.

Carl Llewellyn has thrust himself towards the forefront of

Stratford jockeys and one of his stables, Tim Forster's, pushes Martin Pipe hard. Mark Dwyer and Jimmy FitzGerald feel the ground is worth venturing south for and they have good success rates.

Statistics, 1989–94 (NH)

TOP JOCKEYS: R. Dunwoody 22, 20%; C. Llewellyn 17, 25%; A. Maguire 16, 21%; Peter Hobbs 10, 23%; J. Osborne 10, 20%; G. McCourt 10, 18%.

TOP TRAINERS: M. Pipe 25, 25%; Capt. T. Forster 16, 26%; G. Richards 11, 31%; P. Hobbs 11, 18%; Mrs J. Pitman 11, 17%; D. Nicholson 10, 15%.

FAVOURITES: 36.4%.

TAUNTON
Class D (NH)

Some of the progress that has caught up with this sausage-shaped, right-handed track, has been for the best. The cambered bends have saved meetings that were once abandoned as the first drop of rain turned the course into a skidpan.

Talk of this being an easy course is lost on jockeys who have to ride the quality of novice chaser attracted here. The number who have hit the deck at the first fence in the straight is growing by the meeting; sometimes there aren't many left when the field gets back to this fence, the third last, on the final lap. Oddly, the first of the two hurdles in the straight here claims more than its share of victims, too.

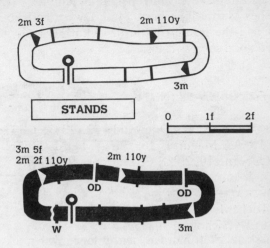

Martin Pipe is streets ahead of Philip Hobbs and Ron Hodges in his accumulation of winners in what amounts to his own backyard. Mick Fitzgerald will be glad he has seen the back of the now-retired Peter Scudamore who dominated so comprehensively.

Personally I'd like to see the back of the jet trainers that regularly scream overhead *en route* to RAF Crewkerne.

Statistics, 1989–94 (NH)

TOP JOCKEYS: M. Fitzgerald 13, 13%; J. Lower 11, 25%; M. Richards 10, 24%; S. Burrough 10, 14%; N. Mann 9, 20%; J. Frost 9, 10%.

TOP TRAINERS: M. Pipe 53, 28%; R. Hodges 21, 11%; P. Hobbs 9, 11%; C. Popham 8, 8%; S. Mellor 6, 35%; J. Old 6, 35%.

FAVOURITES: 37.5%.

THIRSK
Class C (Flat)

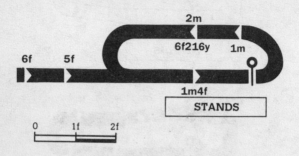

Thirsk is a left-handed, ten-furlong oval track. The home bend is quite sharp but the four-furlong home straight gives adequate compensation. The ground dries quickly and the going can get very fast.

This course is the venue for success after success for one of Yorkshire's greatest ever trainers, Peter Easterby. Peter is not one to part easily with his money, so stable fancies, partnered by Mark Birch or Steve Maloney, can usually be relied upon to do the business.

Mark Johnston is starting to pick off races with ever-increasing frequency and watch for the Billy Newnes–Peter Calver combination. But in truth the locals have a tough time fending off the Newmarket raiders.

DRAW DATA: High numbers have a major advantage over five and six furlongs.

Statistics, 1990–94 (Flat)

TOP JOCKEYS: G. Duffield 28, 26%; M. Birch 21, 12%;

D. McKeown 14, 11%; J. Weaver 13, 21%; J. Carroll 13, 11%; J. Fortune 13, 11%.

TOP TRAINERS: M. H. Easterby 18, 11%; R. Whitaker 15, 12%; J. Dunlop 13, 41%; T. Barron 13, 10%; J. Berry 13, 10%; H. Cecil 12, 43%.

FAVOURITES: 34.5%.

TOWCESTER
Class C (NH)

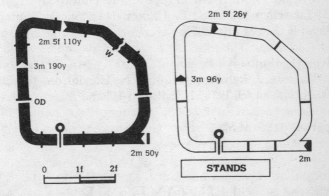

Turn up in tweeds and brogues and you wouldn't look out of place on Lord Hesketh's racecourse, which occupies part of his estates; this is National Hunt at its most enthusiastic.

It is a lazy cliché to say the course suits only sloggers. True, it's on the side of a hill and on clay; but, as with so many tracks, it's the way it's ridden and the suitability of the horse that count most. Larksmore won two chases here in 1991 and 1993, at 33–1 and 50–1, and has hardly been sighted anywhere else. M. I. Babe has won six times round here, though her rider, Ronnie Beggan, says she doesn't really stay. In her two-mile chases, after settling down over the first three and passing the stands, she turns right and can coast downhill for almost the next mile, conserving finishing speed for the thrust uphill over the final five furlongs.

The Brennans, father Owen (trainer) and son Martin (jockey) are top dogs. Look out, too, for expensive novice hardware from Jenny Pitman. Towcester is one of the worst tracks for Pipe raiders.

Statistics, 1989–94 (NH)

TOP JOCKEYS: M. Brennan 25, 35%; R. Dunwoody 21, 16%; C. Llewellyn 13, 13%; L. Harvey 11, 11%; J. White 10, 23%; R. Beggan 10, 20%.

TOP TRAINERS: O. Brennan 26, 32%; Mrs I. McKie 15, 20%; Mrs J. Pitman 14, 26%; N. Henderson 10, 20%; D. Nicholson 10, 19%; J. Gifford 10, 12%.

FAVOURITES: 36.9%.

UTTOXETER
Class B (NH)

Uttoxeter's owner Stan Clarke chooses Martin Pipe to train his horses, like Rolling Ball and Lord Relic. Clarke's talent-spotting isn't limited to trainers: in clerk of the course David McAllister and commercial manager Gordon Brown, he has a first-class back-up team. Uttoxeter is one of the few success stories among British racetracks with sponsors for virtually

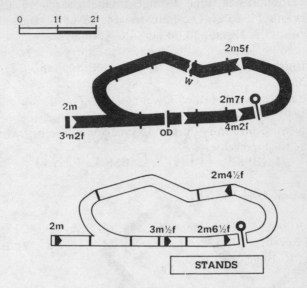

every race, vastly increased prize money and improved TV patronage.

The ten-furlong course has easy left-handed turns but the back straight undulates and bends this way and that, causing the careless jumper to lose concentration. In long-distance novice chases, there can be plenty of carnage.

The Tetley Bitter Midlands Grand National, run between the twin peaks of Cheltenham and Aintree, is the feature race of the year. As you would expect, Stan Clarke's trainer Martin Pipe dominates the figures. It is also a track where Tim Forster and veteran John Webber run some of their best horses.

Statistics, 1989–94 (NH)

TOP JOCKEYS: R. Dunwoody 35, 24%; J. Osborne 24, 25%; N. Williamson 21, 17%; G. McCourt 16, 18%; A. Maguire 15, 16%; N. Doughty 13, 23%.

TOP TRAINERS: M. Pipe 43, 31%; G. Richards 17, 19%; J. Edwards 15, 15%; O. Sherwood 14, 25%; K. Bailey 14, 23%; Capt. T. Forster 13, 31%.

FAVOURITES: 39.4%.

WARWICK
Class C (Flat)   Class C (NH)

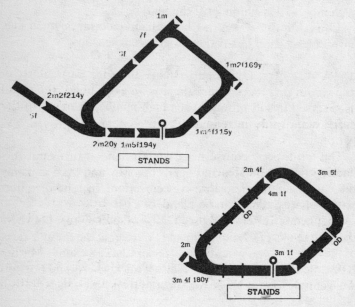

The Warwick course is left-handed and over a mile and three-quarters in circumference. The dog-legged five-furlong course joins the round course at about half-way. Braziers in the enclosures look as if they may have come in a job lot from Warwick Castle, whose tower overlooks the track. In long-distance races, the fields disappear from view for what seems like an age at a point furthest from the stands.

Surprisingly, Jack Berry tops the trainers' list by some way, even though it is so far from his home base. But expect Peter Chapple-Hyam to close the gap in years to come.

Crudwell, an old Warwick favourite, holds the chase record of 39 wins, many of them round here. Apart from doing away with the water jump, which nobody misses, Crudwell would find the NH course much the same. It takes some jumping, especially the five fences in the back straight. A well-schooled novice will take to Warwick and the short straight is still long enough to give a horse with a turn of foot a chance, if it is running off the final bend.

Look out for the pre-Cheltenham meeting, which has given many good Festival clues in recent seasons.

DRAW DATA: Low numbers have the edge particularly in the six-furlong races where there is an early bend; the trend is reversed in soft ground when high numbers can get to the faster stands side more quickly.

Statistics, 1990–94 (Flat)

TOP JOCKEYS: W. Carson 23, 24%; Pat Eddery 19, 29%; A. Munro 16, 17%; J. Reid 15, 19%; Paul Eddery 15, 15%; J. Williams 15, 10%.

TOP TRAINERS: J. Berry 21, 18%; H. Cecil 13, 33%; P. Chapple-Hyam 11, 26%; J. Dunlop 10, 19%; R. Charlton 9, 32%; M. Bell 9, 23%.

FAVOURITES: 33.2%.

Statistics, 1989–94 (NH)

TOP JOCKEYS: R. Dunwoody 39, 29%; J. Osborne 12, 14%; A. Maguire 10, 17%; G. McCourt 8, 17%; C. Llewellyn 8, 11%; M. Perrett 7, 22%.

TOP TRAINERS: M. Pipe 37, 26%; D. Nicholson 21, 22%; Mrs J. Pitman 16, 18%; N. Gaselee 12, 31%; N. Henderson 12, 21%; G. Balding 12, 15%.

FAVOURITES: 38.5%.

WETHERBY
Class A (NH)

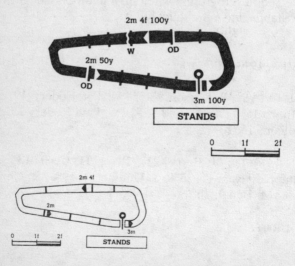

Wetherby is one of our finest National Hunt courses. Stiff fences and a steady climb to the finish put the accent on jumping ability and stamina. Racing is top-class and many Cheltenham Festival contenders are on show.

Horsemanship rather than brute strength in the saddle is required and I have seen some classic riding performances from Mark Dywer and Neale Doughty here. Both like to let their horses lob along on a long rein, see a stride, and then ask for a mighty leap.

Jimmy FitzGerald and Gordon Richards deal in big, strapping chasing types – ideal for Wetherby's stern test. Peter Easterby and Lorcan Wyer are the combination to follow over the much sharper hurdle track.

The betting market is well supported; prices and value hold up well. A good place to have a wager.

Statistics, 1989–94 (NH)

TOP JOCKEYS: P. Niven 38, 22%; L. Wyer 30, 21%; M. Dwyer 30, 17%; C. Grant 27, 13%; G. McCourt 22, 19%; N. Doughty 21, 23%.

TOP TRAINERS: Mrs M. Reveley 37, 29%; G. Richards 30, 22%; M. H. Easterby 25, 18%; J. FitzGerald 22, 20%; M. Hammond 16, 14%; N. Tinkler 15, 16%.

FAVOURITES: 41.3%.

WINCANTON
Class C (NH)

Another course which fosters misconceptions. Wincanton is hardly 'galloping' because jockeys are forever having to haul their mounts round tight bends, especially sharp being the

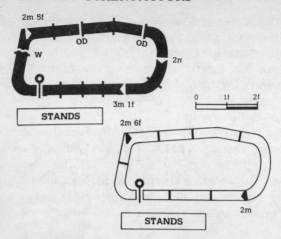

home turn – and that after one of the trickiest downhill fences there is.

Wincanton has acknowledged Cheltenham trials in the Kingwell Pattern Hurdle and the Jim Ford Chase, yet being right-handed it isn't even the same way round as Cheltenham!

But this track does sharpen up a horse and even the Dickinsons used to come down from their northern stronghold, with such as Silver Buck, before hitting the Festival. Wincanton may be 'West Country' but no course illustrates better how competitive the winter game has become. Desert Orchid was a regular here, over fences and hurdles.

Robert Alner has made a belated start to his professional racing career but expect this local trainer to make up for lost time. And watch, too, for Lady Herries who has a good record with her few runners.

Statistics, 1989–94 (NH)

TOP JOCKEYS: R. Dunwoody 34, 21%; B. Powell 16, 11%; J. Osborne 15, 23%; D. Murphy 11, 20%; P. Holley 11, 12%; J. Frost 11, 10%.

TOP TRAINERS: M. Pipe 37, 29%; Mrs J. Pitman 24, 34%; J. Gifford 15, 14%; D. Elsworth 14, 17%; P. Hobbs 14, 13%; R. Hodges 14, 7%.

FAVOURITES: 42.1%.

WINDSOR
Class C (Flat)   Class C (NH)

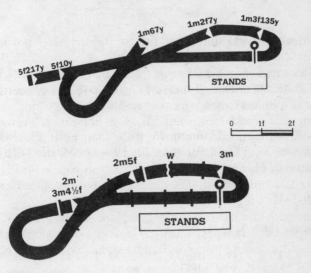

Quortina is one of a number of course specialists down the years that have thrived on this track's idiosyncrasies. The bends are sharp, but with an almost five-furlong straight there is plenty of time to make up lost ground.

Pat Eddery, with double the tally of his nearest rival, is an irresistible force around Windsor.

Moderate jumping horses travel like stink round here and

all kinds of grief results at the three fences in the straight, after they have crossed the intersection of the course.

The quality over hurdles is lifted by the New Year's Day Hurdle, which used to raise hopes for Cheltenham that were not fulfilled; it has sunk back to being a handicap. The Thames water table gives the going a sinking feeling – it's often on the soft side.

For all his accomplishments, Martin Pipe isn't among the leading trainers.

DRAW DATA: High numbers have a slight advantage at up to six furlongs.

Statistics, 1990–94 (Flat)

TOP JOCKEYS: Pat Eddery 53, 24%; L. Dettori 26, 18%; J. Reid 18, 11%; M. Roberts 17, 13%; R. Cochrane 16, 14%; T. Quinn 15, 10%.

TOP TRAINERS: R. Hannon 43, 18%; H. Cecil 13, 34%; L. Cumani 10, 30%; I. Balding 10, 19%; P. Makin 9, 21%; M. Jarvis 8, 24%.

FAVOURITES: 34.1%.

Statistics, 1989–94 (NH)

TOP JOCKEYS: J. Osborne 14, 19%; M. Richards 12, 15%; R. Dunwoody 9, 15%; P. Holley 8, 26%; N. Williamson 8, 13%; G. Moore 8, 10%.

TOP TRAINERS: P. Hobbs 12, 25%; R. Akehurst 10, 25%; N. Henderson 10, 23%; Mrs J. Pitman 10, 21%; D. Elsworth 9, 29%; P. Hedger 8, 24%.

FAVOURITES: 35.3%.

WOLVERHAMPTON
Class D (Flat)   Class C (NH)

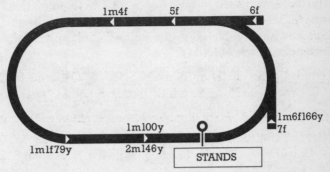

The Wolverhampton course used to be shrouded in smoke from three adjacent factory chimneys, the Three Sisters. But now there is light at the end of the tunnel, 24 hours a day if the present management is to be believed, for Wolverhampton is in the vanguard of floodlit racing on the country's newest all-weather track.

A plan of the course shows it to be very sharp. A left-handed oval, barely a mile in circumference, the track has a short two-furlong straight.

Comedy Of Errors and Gaye Brief used to tune up at Wolverhampton before their Champion Hurdle challenges, but it will be some time before horses of that calibre run here again. We will have to wait a couple of years before new trends emerge, but as the country's third all-weather circuit, it should soon become a friend to the punter.

Statistics, 1990–94 (Flat)

TOP JOCKEYS: J. Weaver 31, 29%; L. Dettori 14, 17%; K. Darley 12, 20%; J. Williams 10, 11%; A. Mackay 9, 11%; G. Duffield 8, 26%.

TOP TRAINERS: M. Johnston 17, 38%; J. Berry 15, 19%; P. Haslam 14, 24%; Lord Huntingdon 12, 27%; R. Hollinshead 11, 8%; Sir M. Prescott 9, 35%.

FAVOURITES: 38.2%.

Statistics, 1989–94 (NH)

TOP JOCKEYS: R. Dunwoody 26, 28%; J. Osborne 14, 23%; M. Lynch 10, 25%; S. Smith Eccles 8, 24%; N. Hawke 6, 50%; N. Mann 6, 19%.

TOP TRAINERS: D. Nicholson 19, 35%; M. Pipe 18, 30%; J. Edwards 9, 18%; R. Lee 9, 17%; Miss H. Knight 8, 25%; J. Chugg 7, 41%.

FAVOURITES: 37.9%.

WORCESTER
Class C (NH)

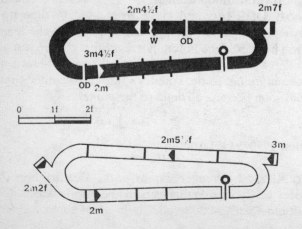

The Severn runs alongside Worcester's straight and when the river rises it can turn the course into a marina. Paradoxically, the going down the back straight would sometimes stop an exocet. Hopefully this won't dismay form students terminally; Worcester has a lot going for it, if not always the going.

As a lay-out, the left-handed one-mile-five-furlong circuit is very fair and a great place to school a novice chaser (and many are schooled). The long sweeping bend out of the equally long back straight allows jockeys to go where they want and ride a race.

Nigel Twiston-Davies is the coming man among trainers and Worcester will be his springboard . . . when the Severn hasn't overflowed, that is.

Statistics, 1989–94 (NH)

TOP JOCKEYS: R. Dunwoody 34, 14%; J. Osborne 29, 26%; A. Maguire 23, 19%; B. Powell 18, 13%; Peter Hobbs 15, 20%; N. Williamson 15, 15%.

TOP TRAINERS: M. Pipe 42, 30%; O. Sherwood 25, 34%; P. Hobbs 24, 22%; D. Nicholson 19, 17%; Miss H. Knight 14, 30%; K. Bailey 14, 17%.

FAVOURITES: 37.2%.

YARMOUTH
Class C (Flat)

Newmarket-by-the-sea and, of course, the local trainers do well. There must be something about the atmosphere amid the sand dunes and holiday chalets because when a horse

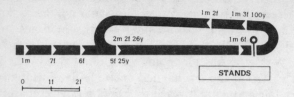

likes Yarmouth it can keep coming back for more. Eve, a bit of a Greta Garbo who liked to race alone, and Annabelle Royale are recent multiple winners over the track.

And yet it is a flat, featureless, left-handed oval circuit of some one mile five furlongs with a straight mile and none of the obvious eccentricities one associates with a specialists' track.

As you would expect, Newmarket's Henry Cecil is the man to follow here, scoring with three in every ten of his runners.

DRAW DATA: High numbers have the advantage on the straight course.

Statistics, 1990–94 (Flat)

TOP JOCKEYS: M. Roberts 39, 18%; L. Dettori 26, 16%; R. Hills 24, 18%; W. Ryan 23, 17%; G. Duffield 23, 17%; P. Robinson 19, 18%.

TOP TRAINERS: H. Cecil 30, 30%; J. Gosden 20, 20%; M. Tompkins 20, 13%; G. Wragg 19, 20%; M. Stoute 19, 18%; C. Brittain 19, 12%.

FAVOURITES: 36.8%.

YORK
Class A (Flat)

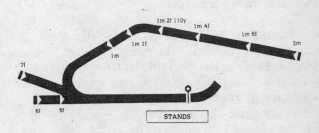

Voted Racecourse of the Year on numerous occasions, York's level two-mile, left-handed galloping track offers the best of British racing. Quality-laden international fields come in search of the huge prize money on offer; winner-finding is not easy and favourites have a poor record in non-handicap events.

Top trainers, top jockeys and leading owners dominate the action: Cecil, Stoute, Eddery and Roberts, to single out a few. And don't forget the young pretender, Manton's Peter Chapple-Hyam. Single-handedly he has put his patron Robert Sangster back in the big time after years of one-way Arab-owned traffic.

The recent watering policy has come in for fierce criticism. The ground does appear patchy, favouring those racing hard against the far rail – a path used by joggers every day – on a strip of much faster ground. In staying races this has given front-runners – those turning into the straight first – a big advantage.

DRAW DATA: Over the straight five and six furlongs, middle numbers are best. The seven-furlong course begins from a spur and low numbers have the call, especially if making a fast start.

Statistics, 1990–94 (Flat)

TOP JOCKEYS: Pat Eddery 49, 21%; W. Carson 39, 15%; M. Roberts 35, 14%; L. Dettori 34, 17%; W. Swinburn 23, 11%; A. Munro 17, 12%.

TOP TRAINERS: J. Gosden 34, 27%; H. Cecil 26, 23%; M. Stoute 26, 18%; R. Hannon 22, 12%; J. Dunlop 19, 21%; M. H. Easterby 17, 10%.

FAVOURITES: 33.6%.

Chapter Fifteen

Trainers and Jockeys

TRAINERS

A friend from Perth, Western Australia was over in England on holiday. A keen athlete and road racer, he was delighted at my offer to see how racehorses were trained and we spent a fascinating morning with one of Britain's top trainers.

Arriving as the horses pulled out for first lot, we watched them walk to the gallops, where they did two half-speed canters up the all-weather strip. Stopping only briefly for a pick of grass *en route* back to the stables, the horses were 'banged up' like inmates of a maximum security prison, little more than one hour after exercise had begun.

My friend, looking on incredulously, said: 'Is that it?'

Despite his demanding job in marketing, he was used to pounding the roads for 100 miles a week, with daily rounds of calisthenics and weight training on top . . . all for his strictly amateur career. Here were professional equine athletes locked away in their boxes for 23 of every 24 hours.

But racehorses have been trained this way for a century or more. It is impossible to tell a Thoroughbred to 'feel the burn' and push through the pain barrier. All its work has to be done 'on the bridle' with the horse enjoying the experience; you could say, being tricked into shape. The canny trainer knows he must not overface his charge at home or he will be left with nothing come race-day.

Of course, there have been some modern innovations. The automatic horse-walker is now a common piece of apparatus in a racing yard, perhaps to give some extra activity in the afternoon. So is the equine swimming pool, which helps the horse to exercise without putting undue strain on its legs, while successful horsemen like Martin Pipe and Michael Dickinson have experimented with interval training.

For the modern trainer, dealing with owners can be more problematic than looking after the stable inmates. The days when the majority of horses were owned by their wealthy breeders, who gave trainers *carte blanche*, are long gone. Nowadays, owing to the greatly increased cost of labour, food and equipment, as well as the poor prize money structure of racing, only a few lucky owners make it pay. And whereas in the past a top trainer might have had just 10 owners, in these days of syndicates he could have 100 and more.

Trainers feel the same financial pressures as their owners and, like them, many rely on at least the occasional coup to keep themselves solvent. But despite the obvious temptations, I'm confident that the vast majority of trainers give both their owners and the racing public a fair deal.

The successful backer must know the qualities not only of horses but also of their trainers. In particular, he should know which trainers are the most expert in placing their horses: that is, in entering for races they can win. Not all trainers have the raw material necessary to win the Classics or the great races over fences. All we can ask of them is that they do the best job possible with each horse in their care.

Michael Stoute, Paul Cole and Barry Hills have all become top-class trainers who number some of the world's richest men among their patrons – but it wasn't always like that. They all began with one thing in common: modest horses, and not many of them. Stoute was born in Barbados, son of the local Commissioner of Police, and had no racing background; for a number of years, Cole was known as a selling plate king; Hills set himself up as a trainer after backing Frankincense to win the 1968 Lincoln Handicap when he was still travelling head lad for the horse's trainer John Oxley. By expert skill they have gradually upgraded their tackle and now train some of the best Thoroughbreds in the world. The skill at placing horses, which initially earned them their reputations two decades ago, remains paramount.

The backer should also learn which market moves to follow. 'Springers' from some stables are far more successful than those from others, and this reflects the difference in the judgement of trainers. The reader should note both the successful and the unsuccessful springers, and will in time be able to know the trainers on whom he can rely with some confidence.

Many backers are keen to support horses from what they believe to be the biggest betting stables. They always think that the horse will be the vehicle for a gamble and is therefore worthy of support. Here they make two errors. In the first place, the horse may not necessarily be fancied at all. It may be the forecast favourite in the newspapers because the racing journalists know that if it is fancied by the stable a short price will be returned. It is also possible that when the betting opens on the course the bookies will be taking no chances about the horse and put it in at short odds. When later the horse eases in the market and loses, the punter is probably right in thinking that the horse did not have the confidence of the stable behind it.

The second mistake the punter makes is, in my view, equally serious. It is to back these horses at all. They note that horses often win when they are heavily supported in the market and they feel that they have shared in the gamble with connections. The point they fail to realize is that whereas the people directly concerned with the horse have taken the cream of the market, the punters are left only with the skimmed milk, that is to say with the starting price – perhaps less than half of the opening show.

Following trainers who, by common consent, are the best in their profession rarely offers the punter true value – but there are exceptions. Henry Cecil and Martin Pipe are the leading trainers respectively in the Flat and jumping worlds. Although coming from vastly different backgrounds, their approach is somewhat similar – rarely do you see a Cecil or a Pipe runner which is not 100 per cent ready to do itself justice, even on its first appearance in public, and however fancied it may be in the market.

The most striking thing about Pipe horses is how fit they are. They may not all be capable of winning beauty contests, but they are trained to the minute. Superior fitness allows them to score when their trademark front-running tactics are enforced. They set a true gallop and maintain it all the way to the line whereas superior horses, which are perhaps not as well conditioned, falter.

Pipe has survived the stigma of a scurrilous TV 'exposé' of his methods but anyone who still believes he is a wind-'em-up, break-'em-down trainer should have been at the 1993 Cheltenham Festival. I looked at every horse in the paddock over the three days and of the six animals that I considered were exceptionally fit and bursting with health and vitality, four of them were trained by Pipe.

Pipe's father David is a bookmaker and the set-up at Nicholashayne was originally funded by his money; the stable even runs a phone line for punters informing them about the chances of the horses. So it is all very betting-oriented; but they can't all be 'expected' and there is some money to be made backing the lesser-fancied Pipe horses – often when ridden by his conditional jockeys – because the punter can be confident the horse will turn up fit to do the job.

Our very own Scout of the *Daily Express*, John Garnsey, has exploited the skills of Henry Cecil down the years knowing that virtually every horse that leaves Warren Place for the racecourse is capable of winning. Cecil is unorthodox, eccentric even. He professes to look at the form book about once a month, and says: 'The form book can never really tell you how good your horses are. It may give clues to their ability but it doesn't tell you about their state of mind or attitude.' Cecil's touch with his own horses is ethereal but at least his dismissal of the form book explains why he is such a rotten tipster.

The fact that the Cecil yard is not a gambling stable is clear from the number of apparent second strings of his which win. Perhaps the most famous of all was in November 1989 when Belmez made his racecourse debut in a Newmarket maiden. Cecil also saddled the 2–1 chance Satin Wood but it was 50–1 outsider Belmez which was successful – and, I am credibly informed, he did not go unbacked by a number of shrewd insiders. The lesson was not learned, however. In the King George VI and Queen Elizabeth Diamond Stakes the following year, 15–2 shot Belmez, ridden by Michael Kinane, beat the Cecil number one Old Vic, ridden by Steve Cauthen.

Cecil and Pipe are so successful they cannot be ignored; but in general, the punter would be well advised to patronize more underrated handlers if they are looking for value and ultimately a profit from their betting. Look for those trainers who, though very able, have yet to be 'discovered' by punters and bookmakers.

My own favourite is Lady Herries, wife of former Test cricketer Colin Cowdrey. There was a general feeling that here is a wealthy woman – the Duchess of Norfolk's daughter – who is merely playing at the training of racehorses. This misconception was lessened by the exploits in 1994 of Celtic

Swing. She is a superb trainer – with one proviso: think twice before backing her horses first time out. In the 1993/4 National Hunt and 1994 Flat seasons she sent out 44 individual horses from her Angmering Park base near Littlehampton in Sussex and only seven of them obliged at the first time of asking. But a £10 level stake on all subsequent appearances of her horses would have netted a pre-tax profit of £340.

Let's now examine some trainer statistics. The first set of figures reproduced here are the basic championship tables for the 1993 and 1994 Flat as well as the 1992/3 and 1993/4 NH seasons, the sort published in the *Daily Express* every Monday.

The Trainers' Championships
1993 Flat

	Wins	Strike rate (%)	Win only prize money (£)
H. Cecil	94	23	1,245,395
R. Hannon	182	15	1,229,061
M. Stoute	65	15	1,072,279
J. Gosden	110	24	1,024,017
J. Dunlop	93	17	700,810
J. Berry	133	16	552,511
G. Wragg	35	17	428,485
C. Brittain	37	8	413,901
P. Chapple-Hyam	52	22	407,191
I. Balding	50	15	383,675

1994 Flat

	Wins	Strike rate (%)	Win only prize money (£)
M. Stoute	109	18	1,388,410
J. Dunlop	82	16	1,309,985
H. Cecil	76	23	1,046,674
J. Gosden	93	18	774,151
R. Hannon	112	10	640,815
M. Johnston	117	17	665,723
P. Cole	69	12	487,995
L. Cumani	47	18	456,740
J. Berry	131	14	494,113
I. Balding	51	13	407,795

1992/3 National Hunt

	Wins	Strike rate (%)	Win only prize money (£)
M. Pipe	194	25	808,006
D. Nicholson	100	27	492,438
N. Twiston-Davies	76	24	451,407
G. Richards	104	23	327,790
J. Gifford	49	16	285,913
J. FitzGerald	62	23	261,080
Mrs M. Reveley	90	26	250,587
N. Henderson	53	18	242,927
G. Balding	38	13	212,992
K. Bailey	57	19	170,195

1993/4 National Hunt

	Wins	Strike rate (%)	Win only prize money (£)
D. Nicholson	81	24	554,906
M. Pipe	127	22	570,281
N. Twiston-Davies	72	16	407,359
K. Bailey	87	23	339,615
J. Gifford	51	16	241,358
Mrs M. Reveley	103	26	313,186
N. Henderson	48	18	194,491
P. Hobbs	64	21	203,476
G. Richards	48	16	172,571
O. Sherwood	41	20	175,940

The other examples are tables that might just help in pinpointing some of those underrated trainers. In my youth I was told that a quick way of measuring the success or otherwise of a training establishment was to note how closely the tally of winners came to the number of individual horses representing the stable. Loosely, the thinking behind this is that it takes a skilful trainer to win a race with every horse in his yard. To establish an order of merit, simply divide the number of winners by the number of representatives; a figure above 1 indicates an extremely successful trainer.

In the sample listing here I have included only those trainers who have saddled at least 15 winners, as using much smaller yards can give a distorted picture.

1994 Flat		*1993/4 National Hunt*	
M. Johnston	1.21	C. Mann	1.67
T. Barron	1.03	Miss C. Saunders	1.58
Sir M. Prescott	0.98	Mrs M. Reveley	1.20
D. Loder	0.98	K. Bailey	1.14
P. Haslam	0.95	M. H. Easterby	1.07
J. Berry	0.92	M. Barnes	1.06
M. Channon	0.87	G. Harwood	1.06
Lady Herries	0.86	D. Nicholson	1.00
P. Walwyn	0.85	S. Dow	1.00
J. Pearce	0.83	P. Cheesbrough	0.96
Mrs M. Reveley	0.79	C. Egerton	0.96
G. Lewis	0.79	J. Edwards	0.95
W. Haggas	0.79	Mrs S. Bramall	0.91
H. Thomson Jones	0.77	P. Hobbs	0.89
Lord Huntingdon	0.76	O. Brennan	0.86
Mrs J. Ramsden	0.76	M. Pipe	0.85
T. Mills	0.76	N. Tinkler	0.85
M. Bell	0.75	L. Lungo	0.84
R. Charlton	0.75	R. Akehurst	0.77

Lady Herries, whom I have already praised, holds a very respectable eighth place in the Flat trainers' table. She does not appear in the National Hunt table because she had too few winners; but I can reveal that her eleven successes from eight individual horses over jumps would have given her a rating of 1.38 – better than many of the other principals.

Here are some comments about other names who appear in the table.

MARK JOHNSTON: A former vet, Johnston has built himself up from nothing into one of the country's leading handlers and has put the training centre of Middleham back on the map. He hit the big-time in 1994 with 2000 Guineas

winner Mister Baileys, and the patronage of Sheik Mohammed will be an ongoing boost. Although more than capable
of holding his own on the major tracks, the biggest profits
from Johnston runners in 1994 came from Class C and D
courses.

SIR MARK PRESCOTT: Prescott has long been adept at
placing horses to run up winning sequences in non-handicaps
on minor courses, but he has not yet had the chance to prove
himself with a really top-class horse. Headline-grabbing wins
in 1994 from stable standard-bearers Hasten To Add and
Wizard King may now persuade owners to give him the
opportunity to put that right.

DAVID LODER: Few trainers have made their mark as
quickly as David Loder. After only two and a half seasons
with a licence, Loder is not yet able to mount a numerical
challenge to the big battalions but is firmly established as one
of the most capable trainers around. He takes great pride in
his strike rate – a healthy 26.4 per cent in 1994. This season's
planned link-up with Jason Weaver can only aid Loder's
progress.

LYNDA RAMSDEN: With husband Jack helping to plot
the campaigns, the Ramsden team is among the shrewdest
in the business. They usually manage to win with the
majority of their horses, but don't expect wins to be
repeated – in 1994, out of 29 individual winners, not one
managed to score more than twice. This is a yard that
warrants close scrutiny, as you have to catch the Ramsden
runners on the right day.

ROGER CHARLTON: Since sending out three Derby
winners in his first season with a licence, Roger Charlton's
Beckhampton yard has been hitting the target more quietly
but no less effectively. Charlton never over-faces his horses

or runs them without a chance, which is reflected in a generally admirable strike rate. His horses usually begin to hit form in earnest in early summer.

CHARLIE MANN: Lambourn-based Mann just squeaks into the table with 15 winners, but it may pay to take his high placing with a pinch of salt as seven of those were provided by one horse, Sheer Ability. Without that one in the statistics, Mann scored eight wins from eight other horses, recording a figure of 1 – commendable but less dramatic than the chart-topping 1.67.

CAROLINE SAUNDERS: Miss Saunders trains only hunter chasers, but she does remarkably well with them. She recorded 19 wins from 45 runs in 1993/4, a phenomenal strike rate of 42.2 per cent. What's more, the wins were spread fairly evenly between her seven individual winners, and despite the average starting price of her horses being little over 7–4 she clocked up a healthy level stakes profit. Think carefully before opposing one of her horses in a hunter chase.

DAVID NICHOLSON: The Duke's horses seem to have benefited from moving to their new base at Jackdaw's Castle in 1992. He recorded his first century of winners in 1992/3 and became Champion Trainer in 1993/4. Dual Champion Chase winner Viking Flagship has kept Nicholson in the Cheltenham Festival limelight, but a commendable strike rate and level stakes profit with both his hurdlers and chasers are testament to his ability to produce the goods throughout the season.

CHARLIE EGERTON: Eton-educated son of a Jockey Club member he may be, but Egerton has risen through the training ranks purely on ability. Widely congratulated for his handling of Mysilv in the 1994/5 season, Egerton may have another star on his hands if Seekin Cash comes back fit in 1995/6. His 22.2 per cent strike rate with runners first time out is one of the best around.

OWEN BRENNAN: The father and son team of Owen and Martin Brennan is one of jumping's quiet success stories. Towcester is their home ground, with a superb record of ten winners from 30 runners in 1993/4 showing a level stakes profit of nearly £30. Brennan is capable of producing the goods at other courses, as he showed in 1994/5 with the decent novice chaser Strath Royal. A yard to note.

Ability to train winners first time out is a significant factor which is not addressed in either of my groups of tables, and the reader should make a note of those conditioners who have the ability to tune up their charges for the first run. Over jumps the big three of Pipe, Nicholson and Reveley are unsurpassed in this department, while on the Flat three names which regularly crop up are Roger Charlton, Peter Chapple-Hyam and Bill O'Gorman. This is not the only time that the careers of the young tyros, Charlton and Chapple-Hyam, have overlapped – they both gained Classic success at the beginning of their careers and they both do well with their raiders to Newmarket, a sure sign of training excellence.

Another group to monitor are those trainers who appear to run into form at different times of the year. Jack Berry has always been a quick starter while Luca Cumani builds up momentum in the second half of the season; Martin Pipe and John White don't let the grass grow under their feet in the early weeks of the jumping season, while former dual champion Nicky Henderson doesn't start firing his salvoes until the winter ground has truly arrived.

There is also some profit to be made concentrating on

those yards which do particularly well over fences. It hardly needs saying that such stables are the most successful when it comes to schooling their horses at home.

The phenomenal success of the operation spearheaded by Michael Dickinson during the early 1980s was founded on the superb jockey talent he had at his disposal. With Graham Bradley, Robert Earnshaw, Ronnie Beggan, 'Sooty' White, Dermot Browne and Chris Pimlott to conduct the schooling, is it any wonder that the Dickinson chasers were well-nigh invincible?

No one stable now dominates quite like the Dickinsons did in that era, but the strength in depth among jockeys working for Mary Reveley and Jimmy FitzGerald makes their chasers worth noting. It is no surprise, either, that Andy Turnell, no mean pilot himself, has a cracking record with his chasers.

You may have formed your own lists – which trainers place their horses most adroitly, whose springers can be backed with confidence, which underrated trainers offer the best chance of obtaining value and who specializes in a certain type of horse or at a specific time of the year – but all trainers, from the best to the worst, are susceptible to losses of form. There will be times when even the best-run outfits are going through such a poor run of fortune, whether due to sickness or something less tangible, that they are not sure when the next winner will come. Equally, there will be periods when for no accountable reason every runner sent out by the yard runs out of its skin.

I would certainly not dissuade the reader if he were to have a bet only when the particular trainer was 'on a roll'. If the run is spotted in time, and selective methods are used, some rewarding bets can be landed, because in-form trainers can win races with the most unlikely material. Look especially for their horses which are coming back after a break; perhaps they last ran when the stable was out of sorts.

Before placing any bet, it's advisable to check on the current well-being of the stable in question. The *Racing Post*'s 'Today's Trainers' feature is ideal for this purpose. It details the exploits of each trainer's runners in the previous fortnight, including how many days it is since the last winner was registered under either code. Of course, like all statistics, it doesn't tell the whole story – the expert backer may have formed the impression that an individual trainer's horses were running into form before it came to light in the bald facts – but as a general guide it will do. I suggest, though, that the reader concentrates his focus on those yards which are regularly among the winners and not just those who are going through a successful burst which may never be repeated.

Finally, there are three particular areas that the serious punter will profit from studying: transfers; travellers; and those trainers whose policy is to attack the same prizes each year.

Horses sometimes improve beyond all recognition after switching stables. This is not simply a case of moving from a luckless yard to a thriving one; often a change of surroundings is all that is required to rekindle a horse's enthusiasm. I hold no trainer in higher esteem than Mary Reveley, but after Sarawat was taken out of her yard following a run of four successive defeats the gelding landed a monster gamble in the Tote Ebor on its first outing for Reg Akehurst. It was by no means the first time that Akehurst had quickly been able to improve on the work of a colleague. He's also done well with horses transferred from Albert Davison, including Satin Lover and Millsolin.

Martin Pipe is another handler who has been able to profit from the misfortune of others, notably in the case of Bonanza Boy, formerly with Philip Hobbs, and the horses which owner Brian Kilpatrick once had with David Murray-Smith, like Aquilifer and Sabin Du Loir. The 'miraculous' improvement wrought when they moved to Pipe is in some part explained by the fact that each horse had plummeted in the handicap while running moderately for an out-of-form trainer; the Wellington wizard inherited not only talented horses but well-handicapped ones.

Punters who back horses running at their local tracks are flying in the face of statistics. Trainers use courses nearby for convenience and, if the figures are to be believed, often as part of the schooling process. The notable exceptions to this rule are Mary Reveley and Peter Chapple-Hyam, who have wonderful records at Redcar and Newbury respectively.

The reader would do better to look at those horses which have travelled more than 200 miles to contest a race. The abolition of travel allowances some years ago means that such trips are expensive and a waste of money for all concerned unless the horse can return with some prize money. Jack Berry is without doubt a brilliant trainer, but his strike rate with horses sent south is even better than that around his local haunts. For a similar reason, runners coming from abroad bear the closest inspection, especially those of France's top trainer André Fabre and Ireland's top duo Dermot Weld and Jim Bolger.

In Chapter 14, 'Britain's 59 Racecourses', I have dealt with trainers who have eye-catching records at specific tracks. Some also specialize in particular races. Soon after he started training, Barry Hills gained one of his first successes in the 1970 Dee Stakes at Chester with Golden Monad. It is a contest Hills patently loves to win: in 1990 Blue Stag became his ninth success in the race when taking the scalp of subsequent Arc de Triomphe hero Saumarez.

Blues Traveller, Hills's representative in the 1993 Dee Stakes, could finish only second, but he did go on to take third spot in the Derby at 150–1!

JOCKEYS

Over 40 years ago Alex Bird, one of the most successful professional punters of all time, adopted a system for backing the mounts of the talented Irish jockey Martin Molony when he visited England. Bird explained: 'I developed a staking method on his mounts. I backed the first horse to win £500. If that lost, I backed him to win £500 next time, plus what I had lost on his previous ride. I continued backing this way until he rode a winner, then I reverted to my original stake. In all, I won about £60,000 backing Molony.'

Four decades later, there is some scope for adopting a similar system using three of the best riders in Europe (none of whom rides in England on a regular basis): Mick Kinane, Charlie Swan and Cash Asmussen. Not even Sheik Mohammed's mighty petrodollar could permanently lure Kinane away from Ireland and his job with Dermot Weld. But on his rare forays across the Irish Sea he rarely leaves empty-handed. Tirol (Two Thousand Guineas), Belmez (King George VI and Queen Elizabeth Diamond Stakes), Commander In Chief (Derby) and Opera House (Coral-Eclipse) are recent examples of his success in Group 1 company over here when he has been called upon as a supersub.

Swan, too, has so far resisted overtures to bring him to England full-time. The talents of the current record-breaking Irish jumps champion were never better displayed than at the 1993 and 1994 Cheltenham Festivals, when he won the Ritz Club Trophy as top jockey.

Also much in demand are the services of the intense and highly articulate French-based, South Dakota-born Cash Asmussen, whose link-up with owner Stavros Niarchos and trainer François Boutin in 1993 brought him a clutch of major European races including the first three French Classics of the season on Kingmambo, Madeleine's Dream and Hernando.

Kinane, Swan and Asmussen highlight the cosmopolitan nature of a top jockey's job nowadays and the lavish lifestyle which can come with success. The jockey's week can now be a seven-day slog: early-morning gallops, afternoon and sometimes evening racing in the summer and, at a time when they might want to recharge their batteries for the coming week, globe-trotting on Sunday looking to ride more lucrative winners in France, Germany, Italy or even the States.

To the punter, of course, the study of the jockey should come a poor second behind that of the horse and its trainer. But the man in the saddle remains a vital element in the equation. He has, after all, the responsibility for ensuring the horse has a safe and uninterrupted passage and, on the Flat at least, for making split-second decisions – whether to go for a narrow gap on the rails or switch to the outside – which could mean the difference between winning and losing.

The brave men who ride over the sticks for a living have the unenviable task of keeping the potentially lethal cocktail of an unskilled novice chaser and an unforgiving steeplechase fence from bringing their relatively short sporting career to a premature halt.

The risk of injury and the constant dieting notwithstanding, I have met few ex-jockeys who would not give up training in a trice if they could turn the clock back and become jockeys again. For them the irresistible draw would still be the exhilaration of riding in a race and the knowledge that once they had slipped out of the saddle their responsibility was over. As trainers they have to live with their horses 24 hours a day, and no one has yet come up with a way of softening the blow when a trainer has to ring an owner to say their favourite horse has broken down on the gallops and will never race again.

The Jockeys' Championships

1993 Flat			1994 Flat		
	Wins	Strike rate (%)		Wins	Strike rate (%)
Pat Eddery	169	21	L. Dettori	233	18
L. Dettori	149	17	J. Weaver	200	18
K. Darley	143	17	Pat Eddery	154	19
T. Quinn	123	14	K. Darley	154	16
G. Duffield	116	15	T. Quinn	115	12
W. Carson	115	14	J. Reid	98	14
M. Roberts	114	16	M. Hills	89	14
J. Reid	108	14	W. Carson	87	13
W. Ryan	96	14	J. Carroll	83	13
J. Carroll	94	15	Paul Eddery	83	11

The Jockeys' Championships

1992/3 National Hunt			1993/4 National Hunt		
	Wins	Strike rate (%)		Wins	Strike rate (%)
R. Dunwoody	173	23	R. Dunwoody	198	22
P. Scudamore	129	31	A. Maguire	194	21
A. Maguire	125	17	J. Osborne	105	21
P. Niven	108	28	N. Williamson	104	18
J. Osborne	102	20	P. Niven	89	22
G. McCourt	70	16	M. Fitzgerald	68	12
N. Doughty	69	26	G. McCourt	65	16
C. Llewellyn	68	17	D. Murphy	58	16
M. Dwyer	61	19	D. Bridgewater	58	15
C. Grant	58	14	L. Wyer	48	18

The championship tables reproduced here show the top ten Flat jockeys in 1993 and 1994 as well as the top ten jump jockeys in the corresponding seasons. As can be seen, the same names appear year after year.

Here are some remarks about several of the principal protagonists.

FRANKIE DETTORI: Racing's hottest property, the effervescent and highly talented Dettori smashed the two hundred winner barrier in 1994 and captivated the racing public with his victory celebrations on Lochsong and Barathea. Again taking advantage of the all-weather to put winners on the board in the early months of 1995, Dettori should be at the top of the tree for many years to come.

JASON WEAVER: Like Dettori, a product of the Luca Cumani school. Weaver made the most of his association with Mark Johnston in 1994, capturing his first classic on board Mister Baileys. He will no longer have to commute between Middleham and Newmarket, as this season he takes up a new position at headquarters with David Loder. Weaver is another to make full use of the all-weather in deciding the title race.

PAT EDDERY: For many years the dominant jockey, Eddery has now been overtaken by the young turks Dettori and Weaver. In 1994 Eddery rode over 150 winners for the tenth season in a row, but his total of 154 left him some way behind the top two. 1994 also brought the news that Eddery had lost his position as retained jockey to Khalid Abdulla. It remains to be seen how he will cope as a freelance, but his strong self-belief and will to win should stand him in good stead.

KEVIN DARLEY: Darley became the first northern jockey for years to mount a serious bid for the jockeys' title when third in 1993, a position he shared with Pat Eddery in 1994. Darley will again have the backing of the numerically strong Mary Reveley yard around the

northern tracks, and will be smacking his lips in anticipation of his link-up with Peter Savill's Celtic Swing. Darley
can show great strength in a finish without needing
recourse to his whip.

WILLIE CARSON: The galloping grandfather failed to
break a century of winners in 1994 for only the second time in
23 years – and the first was because of five weeks off with
injury. Carson is hustling less for outside mounts than he
used to, but still enjoys one of racing's plum jobs as retained
jockey to Hamdan Al Maktoum. He is no back number, as
he showed when producing Erhaab fast and late to win the
1994 Derby.

RICHARD DUNWOODY: For years in the shadow of
Peter Scudamore, Dunwoody looked set to rule the roost
when taking over the retired Scu's job with Martin Pipe at
the start of the 1993/4 season. However, he found he was
challenged for top position by his replacement as David
Nicholson's stable jockey, Adrian Maguire. Dunwoody held
on to win a thrilling jockeys' championship race by four in
1993/4, and Miinnehoma provided him with a second Grand
National winner. He should have a good few years at the top
of his profession yet if he wants to carry on.

ADRIAN MAGUIRE: The young Irishman made a tremendous impact on his first season with David Nicholson,
winning the King George on Barton Bank and Champion
Chase on Viking Flagship, and coming within an ace of the
jockeys' title. Maguire is fearless at his fences and strong in a
finish, but has been in trouble more than once for over-
enthusiasm with the whip, notably on Ramstar in January
1994.

JAMIE OSBORNE: Long tipped as a future champion, the
stylish and articulate Osborne scored a century of winners in

1993/4 to add to his breakthrough in 1992/3. He still has a long way to go, though, before he can mount a numerical challenge to Maguire and Dunwoody.

NORMAN WILLIAMSON: Williamson has come of age since linking up with Kim Bailey. He finished fourth in the jockeys' title in 1993/4 with 104 winners, and together with Bailey completed the remarkable Champion Hurdle–Gold Cup double in 1995 with Alderbrook and Master Oats. Increasingly assured in the saddle, with strength in a finish, and enjoying a job with the trainer of the moment, Williamson could easily develop into a serious title challenger.

PETER NIVEN: Few who knew Niven during his 'wild man' days as an amateur rider with David Nicholson could have imagined his development into a genuinely top class jockey. He has forged a remarkable partnership with trainer Mary Reveley in an unlikely setting near the Cleveland coast and despite riding more than 100 winners in two of the last three seasons he remains a most underrated pilot.

GRAHAM McCOURT: McCourt is a most underrated jockey who has a fine record in the midlands and the north. He needs only the National to complete his set of the big three jumps races, having won the Champion on Royal Gait and the Gold Cup on Norton's Coin.

I am happy when I am able to fancy a horse ridden by any of these experts, although I fear that I must generally accept a shorter price in consequence. This is not always the case, though, and one should be vigilant and note when one of these men has taken over from an inexperienced or lesser-known jockey. The in-form jockey riding with confidence is not afraid to go for a narrow gap or have a cut at the last two fences when others delay just long enough for the winning chance to disappear.

This brings us to the vexed question of the allowances claimed by apprentice and conditional riders. Apprentices are entitled to claim the following allowances in Flat races:

seven pounds until they have won 20 races; thereafter
five pounds until they have won 50 races; thereafter
three pounds until they have won 95 races.

The exceptions are races confined to apprentices, rated stakes handicaps which have Listed race status and non-handicaps with guaranteed prize money of at least £8,000.

In chases, hurdles and National Hunt Flat races, conditional jockeys under the age of 25 are entitled to claim the following allowances:

seven pounds until they have won 15 races; thereafter
five pounds until they have won 30 races; thereafter
three pounds until they have won 55 races.

The exceptions are races confined to conditional jockeys, the Grand National and all non-handicaps with guaranteed prize money of £5,000.

To what extent, if at all, should the backer take these allowances into account? Certainly in a race at Beverley, Kevin Darley is usually worth more than seven pounds against a young apprentice; likewise Neale Doughty compared with an inexperienced conditional at Bangor. Nevertheless, on certain uncomplicated courses – the straight ones on the Flat where horses to a large extent run their own races – and in contests which are certain to be truly run and not develop into tactical affairs, the allowance is of great significance. I incline to the view that one should ignore the allowance claimed by unknown riders, but that one should respect it when taken by those who have proved their ability.

Two experienced amateurs who have now joined the claiming conditional ranks and are likely to hold their own against senior professionals are Tom Jenks and Andrew Thornton.

The definitive example of an apprentice being extremely good value for his allowance came in the career of Nagwa, the most successful two-year-old filly this century with 13 wins for trainer Barry Hills in 1975. Her last nine victories were gained in the hands of the then seven-pound-claiming apprentice Ray Cochrane and in at least three of those races the narrowness of the verdict was such that the claim really counted.

In amateur races on the Flat and over the jumps there is often such a wide divergence of ability on display that it is as well to start by studying the jockeys rather than the horses. The same is true in the four-month hunter-chase season which begins at the end of January. I know several professionals who specialize in these amateur events over jumps. Certainly an effective team of a fast-rising rider and a proven horse can often run up a sequence of half a dozen wins, though the prices about them are often far from generous.

Chapter Sixteen

Golden Rules

I want to stress seven Golden Rules for backers which summarize a great deal of the advice previously given. The reader who adheres strictly to them should win every year; the reader who ignores them is likely to pay a heavy price.

Never bet unless you have a good reason and it is based solely on considerations of form.
This rule is fundamental. If the reader is able to discipline himself so that he can decide on some days not to have a bet at all, he has taken the first step to success. Believe what you see, not what you hear; never back a two-year-old first time out no matter how strong the whisper. 'Considerations of form' also cover the going; bet only when the form recorded was on ground similar to the prevailing ground.

Always bet to a level stake.
This will prevent the reader from backing winners to a £10 stake and losers to a £100 stake. By all means increase the *level* of your stakes during a good run; equally, reduce them or stop altogether during a bad run. Each bet should represent approximately one-fortieth of your 'bank'. I like to keep the bets small enough never to detract from the enjoyment; that way the anxiety level is kept to a minimum.

Never rely on starting price.
No horse can be considered a bet whatever the price. Don't risk disappointment by leaving a bet with your bookmaker in the

hope of a favourable starting price. Decide on the odds you are prepared to accept; if they are available and you can say to yourself, 'Win or lose, that's a bet,' then step in.

If you missed the wedding, don't go to the funeral.
Consistent form in a racehorse is a precious commodity for the punter. If a horse has won at 12–1 or longer, don't accept less than 5–2 the next time it runs – in many cases its chance will be no better and it is often carrying a penalty for victory. Forgive a horse one or two bad runs if the rest of its record is consistent.

Never bet in handicaps unless the horse has very recent form.
It is possible for the expert to win on this type of bet but I would remind the novice backer that they must rely on form since the publication of the weights. In addition, I would suggest that even then they should refrain from a wager if the horse starts favourite. 'Never back a favourite in a handicap' has always been a sound maxim.

Specialize.
Even the most dedicated professional punter finds it hard to keep tabs on our fast-expanding racing programme. It would pay the amateur to break down the fixture list to a manageable size by specializing in one or more of the following groups: (a) all-weather racing; (b) two-year-old events; (c) your local tracks; (d) juvenile hurdlers.

Never back a horse that hasn't run for 50 days.
Unless the ground has been unsuitable for the horse, such an absence usually indicates an injury problem and there can be no guarantee it is fully fit. The exception to the rule – for skilled backers only – is when the horse represents a talented trainer whose team is in particularly good form.

These seven principles are tried, tested and successful. Remain faithful to them until the ever-changing character of racing renders them obsolete.

I hope the indulgent reader will profit from the advice in this book and that he will keep it constantly with him for reference.

I wish him great success.

PART FIVE

RESULTS SECTION AND TABLES

Chapter Seventeen

Principal Races

Trainers are creatures of habit. Year in and year out they prepare similar horses for the same programme of events. This section aims to help the reader profit from a study not only of trainers' methods but also of the other key recurring elements among winners of our most important races.

For each race I have included details of the last six winners – ten for the Classics and major championship races – but the pool of data from which conclusions are drawn goes back more than 20 years. In addition to monitoring which trainers 'farm' certain valuable prizes, I have looked for the key prep races, important trends concerning age and weight, and whether the market had any significance. Only when there were firm conclusions to be drawn have I drawn them.

In a race where the draw may have proved important, I have put the winning stalls position after the winner's name.

All Group 1 and 2 Pattern Races on the Flat have been included in this survey, as well the major early-closing handicaps for which an ante-post market was formed.

Over jumps, all Grade 1 championship races are tabulated, as well as those prestigious handicaps which have achieved Grade 3 status.

The Flat

William Hill Lincoln Handicap 1m Doncaster March

	FORM	WINNER	AGE/WEIGHT	TRAINER	JOCKEY	SP
1994	003211-	Our Rita (6)	5 8-5	Dr J. Scargill	D. Holland	16-1
1993	000-	High Premium (5)	5 8-8	Mrs J. Ramsden	K. Fallon	16-1
1992	123012-	High Low (17)	4 8-0	W. Haggas	J. Quinn	16-1
1991	1-01111	Amenable (23)	6 8-4 (7ex)	T. Barron	Alex Greaves	22-1
1990	13-120	Evichstar (14)	6 8-0	J. FitzGerald	A. Munro	33-1
1989	02231-	Fact Finder (6)	5 7-9	R. Akehurst	T. Williams	20-1

● First leg of the Spring Double and a bookies' benefit – only one winning favourite (Cataldi, 1985) in the last 15 years. Overall draw pattern is low, particularly on soft, but the evidence is not conclusive. Hurdlers have a poor recent record but 2 of the last 3 sharpened up on the new all-weather tracks. Twelve of the last 13 winners carried 8st 9lb or less.

European Free Handicap 7f Newmarket April

	FORM	WINNER	AGE/WEIGHT		TRAINER	JOCKEY	SP
1994	13302-3	Bluegrass Prince	3	8-13	R. Hannon	L. Dettori	10–1
1993	122-	So Factual	3	9-6	G. Harwood	Pat Eddery	8–1
1992	314-	Pursuit Of Love	3	9-1	H. Cecil	Pat Eddery	11–4
1991	213-	Mystiko	3	9-2	C. Brittain	M. Roberts	11–1
1990	01123-	Anshan	3	9-7	J. Gosden	Pat Eddery	9–2
1989	210-	Danehill	3	9-1	J. Tree	Pat Eddery	6–1

● High weights have not been a drawback because 7 of the last 12 winners ran in top company as 2-year-olds. All of the last 4 winners have gone on to win or make the frame in the Two Thousand Guineas. During the same period, Pat Eddery has won the race 4 times.

Gardner Merchant Mile (Group 2) 1m Sandown April

	FORM	WINNER	AGE/WEIGHT	TRAINER	JOCKEY	SP
1994	21211-0	Penny Drops	5 8-11	Lord Huntingdon	D. Harrison	8–1
1993	404312-	Alhijaz	4 9-6	J. Dunlop	W. Carson	6–1
1992	13314-1	Rudimentary	4 9-0	H. Cecil	S. Cauthen	2–1F
1991	141301-	In The Groove	4 9-3	D. Elsworth	S. Cauthen	15–8
1990	41323-	Markofdistinction	4 9-0	L. Cumani	L. Dettori	9–2
1989	21-1	Reprimand	4 9-0	H. Cecil	S. Cauthen	7–4JF

● Formerly the Trusthouse Forte Mile and first run in 1985. The biggest priced winners were 8–1 chance Vertige (1987), the first of 2 French-trained winners, and Penny Drops. Fancied runners from the major stables dominate.

Madagans One Thousand Guineas (Group 1) 1m Newmarket April

	FORM	WINNER	AGE/WEIGHT	TRAINER	JOCKEY	SP
1994	2-	Las Meninas	3 9-0	T. Stack (Ire)	J. Reid	12–1
1993	2111-3	Sayyedati	3 9-0	C. Brittain	W.R. Swinburn	4–1
1992	122-2	Hatoof	3 9-0	Mrs C. Head (Fr)	W.R. Swinburn	5–1
1991	111-1	Shadayid	3 9-0	J. Dunlop	W. Carson	4–6F
1990	121-1	Salsabil	3 9-0	J. Dunlop	W. Carson	6–4F
1989	11-	Musical Bliss	3 9-0	M. Stoute	W.R. Swinburn	7–2
1988	111-1	Ravinella	3 9-0	Mrs C. Head (Fr)	G. Moore	4–5F
1987	1311-1	Miesque	3 9-0	F. Boutin (Fr)	F. Head	15–8F
1986	2111-	Midway Lady	3 9-0	B. Hanbury	R. Cochrane	10–1
1985	111-1	Oh So Sharp	3 9-0	H. Cecil	S. Cauthen	2–1F

● The last shock winner was On The House (33–1) in 1982. Nine of the 12 winners since have been no bigger than 5–1. Newmarket's Nell Gwyn is no longer the most important trial – no winner of that race has done the double since Oh So Sharp in 1985. Nine of the last 12 winners had a prep run including the four French-trained heroines.

Jockey Club Stakes (Group 2) 1m 4f Newmarket April

	FORM	WINNER	AGE/WEIGHT	TRAINER	JOCKEY	SP
1994	4000-2	Silver Wisp	5 8-9	D. Nicholson	M. Hills	20–1
1993	13-	Zinaad	4 8-9	M. Stoute	W.R. Swinburn	3–1F
1992	0000-	Sapience	6 8-12	D. Elsworth	R. Cochrane	40–1
1991	21-1	Rock Hopper	4 8-7	M. Stoute	Pat Eddery	8–11F
1990	32113-	Roseate Tern	4 8-9	L. Cumani	L. Dettori	17–2
1989	10124-1	Unfuwain	4 8-10	W. Hern	W. Carson	5–6F

● Roseate Tern was the only winning filly since Shebeen in 1975. Michael Stoute has the best trainers' record, winning 3 times in the last 12. During the same period, 8 of the winners were unpenalized. After a rough time during the 1980s, favourites have won 3 of the last 6, but shocks are not uncommon.

Two Thousand Guineas (Group 1) 1m Newmarket May

	FORM	WINNER	AGE/WEIGHT	TRAINER	JOCKEY	SP
1994	13101-	Mister Baileys	3 9-0	M. Johnston	J. Weaver	16–1
1993	1111-2	Zafonic	3 9-0	A. Fabre (Fr)	Pat Eddery	5–6F
1992	11111-4	Rodrigo De Triano	3 9-0	P. Chapple-Hyam	L. Piggott	6–1
1991	213-1	Mystiko	3 9-0	C. Brittain	M. Roberts	13–2
1990	3211-1	Tirol	3 9-0	R. Hannon	M. Kinane	9–1
1989	11-	Nashwan	3 9-0	W. Hern	W. Carson	3–1F
1988	1-1	Doyoun	3 9-0	M. Stoute	W.R. Swinburn	4–5F
1987	4111-2	Don't Forget Me	3 9-0	R. Hannon	W. Carson	9–1
1986	11-1	Dancing Brave	3 9-0	G. Harwood	G. Starkey	15–8F
1985	31-1	Shadeed	3 9-0	M. Stoute	L. Piggott	4–5F

● Few surprises – Mister Baileys was the first SP longer than 9–1 since Known Fact won in 1980. Zafonic was only the 3rd French horse to win the race in the last 27 years. In recent seasons only Dick Hern has trained the winner without having a prep race (Nashwan and Brigadier Gerard). Henry Cecil has not won it for 18 years.

Tote Dante Stakes (Group 2) 1m 2f 85y York May

	FORM	WINNER	AGE/WEIGHT	TRAINER	JOCKEY	SP
1994	01123-2	Erhaab	3 9-0	J. Dunlop	W. Carson	11–2
1993	111-1	Tenby	3 9-0	H. Cecil	Pat Eddery	1–3F
1992	213-10	Alnasr Alwasheek	3 9-0	M. Stoute	S. Cauthen	7–2
1991	01-30	Environment Friend	3 9-0	J. Fanshawe	G. Duffield	20–1
1990	2-12	Sanglamore	3 9-0	R. Charlton	Pat Eddery	11–2
1989	2-1	Torjoun	3 9-0	L. Cumani	R. Cochrane	6–1

● 1987 winner Reference Point is unique on 2 counts – he is the only one of Henry Cecil's 7 winners of this race to go on and win the Derby and the only one in the last 14 years who didn't need at least one prep run before winning here.

Polo Mints Yorkshire Cup (Group 2) 1m 6f York May

	FORM	WINNER	AGE/WEIGHT		TRAINER	JOCKEY	SP
1994	1423-40	Key To My Heart	4	8-9	D. Moffatt	J. Reid	16–1
1993	3031-42	Assessor	4	9-0	R. Hannon	T. Quinn	9–1
1992	21320-0	Rock Hopper	5	8-13	M. Stoute	Pat Eddery	100–30JF
1991	112101-	Arzanni	4	8-9	L. Cumani	L. Dettori	5–1
1990	21110-1	Braashee	4	8-9	A. Stewart	M. Roberts	11–8F
1989	001-41	Mountain Kingdom	5	8-9	C. Brittain	S. Cauthen	2–1F

● Shocks are rare – apart from Line Slinger at 33–1 in 1983, only two other winners in the last 14 years have started longer than 5–1 and in that time there have been 8 winning favourites. The well-represented 6-year-old and older group has now lost for 13 straight years.

Juddmonte Lockinge Stakes (Group 2) 1m Newbury May

	FCRM	WINNER	AGE/WEIGHT	TRAINER	JOCKEY	SP
1994	02320-4	Emperor Jones	4 9-0	J. Gosden	L. Dettori	11–2
1993	0331-01	Swing Low	4 9-0	R. Hannon	L. Piggott	12–1
1992	3411-	Selkirk	4 9-5	I. Balding	R. Cochrane	5–2
1991	432-1	Polar Falcon	4 9-0	J. Hammond (Fr)	L. Piggott	3–1
1990	11-01	Safawan	4 9-0	M. Stoute	W.R. Swinburn	5–1
1989	3C30-3	Most Welcome	5 9-1	G. Wragg	Paul Eddery	9–1

● It's 13 years since the favourite won. The Gardner Merchant (ex Forte) Mile is the best trial – recent winners Safawan, Most Welcome and Scottish Reel were all beaten in it. Prismatic, in 1985, was a rare 3-year-old winner.

UB Group Temple Stakes (Group 2) 5f Sandown May

	FORM	WINNER	AGE/WEIGHT		TRAINER	JOCKEY	SP
1994	11131-1	Lochsong	6	9-7	I. Balding	L. Dettori	4-9F
1993	00000-1	Paris House	4	9-7	J. Berry	J. Carroll	9-2
1992	1401-00	Snaadee	5	9-3	M. Stoute	Pat Eddery	14-1
1991	1110-21	Elbio	4	9-3	P. Makin	W.R. Swinburn	11-8F
1990	12-012	Dayjur	3	8-8	W. Hern	W. Carson	11-2
1989	123-01	Dancing Dissident	3	8-8	M. Stoute	W.R. Swinburn	3-1

● Michael Stoute has won this race 3 times in the last decade with Snaadee, Dancing Dissident and the dead-heater Petorius in 1984. The small Marlborough stable of Peter Makin was responsible for both Elbio (1991) and Treasure Kay (1987). It is essential to have had at least 1 prep race.

Ever Ready Derby (Group 1)   1m 4f   Epsom   June

	FORM	WINNER	AGE/WEIGHT	TRAINER	JOCKEY	SP
1994	1123-21	Erhaab	3 9-0	J. Dunlop	W. Carson	7-2F
1993	-111	Commander In Chief	3 9-0	H. Cecil	M. Kinane	15-2
1992	1121-20	Dr Devious	3 9-0	P. Chapple-Hyam	J. Reid	8-1
1991	23011-4	Generous	3 9-0	P. Cole	A. Munro	9-1
1990	2-12	Quest For Fame	3 9-0	R. Charlton	Pat Eddery	7-1
1989	11-1	Nashwan	3 9-0	W. Hern	W. Carson	5-4F
1988	1-11	Kahyasi	3 9-0	L. Cumani	R. Cochrane	11-1
1987	311-1	Reference Point	3 9-0	H. Cecil	S. Cauthen	6-4F
1986	21-11	Shahrastani	3 9-0	M. Stoute	W.R. Swinburn	11-2
1985	31-311	Slip Anchor	3 9-0	H. Cecil	S. Cauthen	9-4F

● The race suits late developers proven over a mile as 2-year-olds, but not at top level. An unbeaten sequence as a 3-year-old is important. Before Commander In Chief, Cecil's 3rd winner in the last decade, only Morston (1973) had been unraced as a 2-year-old. Only 2 SPs above 10-1 in the last 20 years. Home-breds have won 9 of the last 12 runnings.

Ever Ready Coronation Cup (Group 1) 1m 4f Epsom June

	FORM	WINNER	AGE/WEIGHT	TRAINER	JOCKEY	SP
1994	3210-42	Apple Tree	5 9-0	A. Fabre (Fr)	T. Jarnet	12–1
1993	10231-2	Opera House	5 9-0	M. Stoute	M. Roberts	9–4JF
1992	0220-11	Saddlers' Hall	4 9-0	M. Stoute	W.R. Swinburn	5–4F
1991	1301-12	In The Groove	4 8-11	D. Elsworth	S. Cauthen	7–2
1990	11/10-2	In The Wings	4 9-0	A. Fabre (Fr)	C. Asmussen	15–8F
1989	20113-4	Sheriff's Star	4 9-0	Lady Herries	R. Cochrane	11–4F

• A prep race is essential, preferably in the Prix Ganay, source of 5 of the last 9 winners (4 of them French-trained; Subotica was unlucky not to make it 6 out of 9 in 1992). Favourites have a great record. Triptych (1987–8) was a rare back-to-back winner.

Energizer Oaks (Group 1) 1m 4f Epsom June

	FORM	WINNER	AGE/WEIGHT	TRAINER	JOCKEY	SP
1994	11-2	Balanchine	3 9-0	H. Ibrahim	L. Dettori	6-1
1993	1-11	Intrepidity	3 9-0	A. Fabre (Fr)	M. Roberts	5-1
1992	-11	User Friendly	3 9-0	C. Brittain	G. Duffield	5-1
1991	1310-14	Jet Ski Lady	3 9-0	J. Bolger (Ire)	C. Roche	50-1
1990	121-11	Salsabil	3 9-0	J. Dunlop	W. Carson	2-1F
1989	11-01	*Snow Bride	3 9-0	H. Cecil	S. Cauthen	13-2
1988	111-231	Diminuendo	3 9-0	H. Cecil	S. Cauthen	7-4F
1987	1-1	Unite	3 9-0	M. Stoute	W.R. Swinburn	11-1
1986	2111-1	Midway Lady	3 9-0	B. Hanbury	R. Cochrane	15-8F
1985	313-1	Circus Plume	3 9-0	J. Dunlop	L. Piggott	4-1

● Intrepidity stopped the rot for the French going back to Pawneese (1976). Three of the last 9 winners ran in the Prix Marcel Boussac as 2-year-olds. A win last time is almost essential. Only 5 fillies since 1970 have done the One Thousand Guineas—Oaks double.

* The winner Aliysa was disqualified and placed last after failing a dope test.

William Hill Golden Spurs Trophy Handicap 6f York June

	FORM	WINNER	AGE/WEIGHT	TRAINER	JOCKEY	SP
1994	23-142	Encore M'Lady (14)	3 7-11	F. Lee	N. Carlisle	20–1
1993	0-44300	Aradanza (6)	3 9-2	M. Channon	Paul Eddery	25–1
1992	23-0010	Orthorhombus (1)	3 9-2	G. Lewis	Paul Eddery	15–2
1991	0-12	Sheikh Albadou (1)	3 9-3	A. Scott	Pat Eddery	9–4F
1990	222-131	Katzakeena (1)	3 8-10 (7ex)	P. Makin	B. Raymond	7–2F
1989	3130-32	Sure Gold (11)	3 8-11	P. Walwyn	G. Baxter	15–1

● Two of the best sprinters of their crop, Sheikh Albadou and Cadeaux Genereux, safely managed to justify favouritism before going on to much greater things. A low draw seems virtually essential. The Eddery brothers, Pat and Paul, have won 4 of the last 7 between them.

Queen Anne Stakes (Group 2) 1m Royal Ascot June

	FORM	WINNER	AGE/WEIGHT	TRAINER	JOCKEY	SP
1994	100420-	Barathea	4 9-8	L. Cumani	M. Kinane	3–1
1993	243-241	Alflora	4 9-2	C. Brittain	M. Kinane	20–1
1992	21-02	Lahib	4 9-2	J. Dunlop	W. Carson	100–30F
1991	31-2410	Sikeston	5 9-8	C. Brittain	M. Roberts	9–1
1990	1323-14	Markofdistinction	4 9-5	L. Cumani	L. Dettori	7–1
1989	11210-2	Warning	4 9-8	G. Harwood	Pat Eddery	2–5F

• Four trainers have won 11 of the last 14 runnings: Cecil (4 in a row before the race was upgraded in 1985), Cumani (3), Harwood (2) and Brittain (2). The Lockinge Stakes is the key race, pinpointing 7 of the last 14 winners. A bad race for 3-year-olds.

Prince of Wales's Stakes (Group 2) 1m 2f Royal Ascot June

	FORM	WINNER	AGE/WEIGHT	TRAINER	JOCKEY	SP
1994	1110-12	Muhtarram	5 9-7	J. Gosden	W. Carson	6-4F
1993	1-120	Placerville	3 8-4	H. Cecil	Pat Eddery	11-2
1992	1/131-4	*Perpendicular	4 9-3	H. Cecil	W. Ryan	20-1
1991	2/311-1	Stagecraft	4 9-3	M. Stoute	S. Cauthen	6-4F
1990	03-131	Batshoof	4 9-5	B. Hanbury	Pat Eddery	2-1F
1989	2-411	Two Timing	3 8-4	J. Tree	Pat Eddery	5-1

● Since the race was reopened to them in the late 1960s, only 2 3-year-olds have won, but both were in the last 6 seasons and both ridden by dominant jockey Pat Eddery. A win last time is almost essential, as is form over 1m 2f (rather than 1m) in the current year.

* Kooyonga finished 1st but was disqualified and placed 3rd.

St James's Palace Stakes (Group 1) 1m Royal Ascot June

	FORM	WINNER	AGE/WEIGHT	TRAINER	JOCKEY	SP
1994	311-024	Grand Lodge	3 9-0	W. Jarvis	M. Kinane	6-1
1993	2022-11	Kingmambo	3 9-0	F. Boutin (Fr)	C. Asmussen	2-5F
1992	1-2131	Brief Truce	3 9-0	D. Weld (Ire)	M. Kinane	25-1
1991	1-1 2	Marju	3 9-0	J. Dunlop	W. Carson	7-4F
1990	21-34	Shavian	3 9-0	H. Cecil	S. Cauthen	11-1
1989	11-101	Shaadi	3 9-0	M. Stoute	W.R. Swinburn	6-4F

● Guineas winners have a chequered record – only Shaadi and Kingmambo winning in the last 12 years. Wins for small stables and shocks are not uncommon.

King Edward VII Stakes (Group 2) 1m 4f Royal Ascot June

	FORM	WINNER	AGE/WEIGHT	TRAINER	JOCKEY	SP
1994	31U	Foyer	3 8-8	M. Stoute	M. Kinane	7–2
1993	11-1212	Beneficial	3 8-8	G. Wragg	M. Hills	11–4
1992	103-144	Beyton	3 8-8	R. Hannon	M. Kinane	12–1
1991	0-12	Saddlers' Hall	3 8-8	M. Stoute	L. Piggott	7–1
1990	-101	Private Tender	3 8-8	H. Cecil	S. Cauthen	11–4F
1989	3-113	Cacoethes	3 8-8	G. Harwood	Pat Eddery	8–13F

● Five Derby also-rans have won recently but many more fail to make an impression. Henry Cecil has had 3 winners and a 2nd from his last 8 attempts.

Coronation Stakes (Group 1)   1m   Royal Ascot   June

	FORM	WINNER	AGE/WEIGHT	TRAINER	JOCKEY	SP
1994	12300-1	Kissing Cousin	3 9-0	H. Cecil	M. Kinane	13–2
1993	241-23	Gold Splash	3 9-0	Mrs C. Head (Fr)	G. Mosse	100–30
1992	1111-21	Marling	3 9-0	G. Wragg	W.R. Swinburn	8–11F
1991	121-121	Kooyonga	3 9-0	M. Kauntze (Ire)	W. O'Connor	3–1
1990	11113-4	Chimes Of Freedom	3 9-0	H. Cecil	S. Cauthen	11–2
1989	-131	Golden Opinion	3 9-0	A. Fabre (Fr)	C. Asmussen	7–2F

● Win or placed form in a Guineas is a virtual must – the winner of the Irish One Thousand has gone on to win this race 5 times in the last 11 years. Shocks are rare.

Royal Hunt Cup Handicap 1m Royal Ascot June

	FORM	WINNER	AGE/WEIGHT	TRAINER	JOCKEY	SP
1994	2004-01	Face North (30)	6 8-3	R. Akehurst	A. Munro	25-1
1993	110-10	Imperial Ballet (19)	4 8-12	H. Cecil	Pat Eddery	20-1
1992	001300-	Colour Sergeant (11)	4 7-13	Lord Huntingdon	D. Harrison	20-1
1991	14100-0	Eurolink The Lad (4)	4 8-9	J. Dunlop	J. Reid	25-1
1990	00-10	Pontenuovo (6)	5 7-7	D. Elsworth	G. Bardwell	50-1
1989	242-01	True Panache (5)	4 9-4	J. Tree	Pat Eddery	5-1F

• Look at the prices of the winners and then wonder why punters bother. True Panache is the only winning favourite in the last 18 years. Four-year-olds have won 15 of the last 18. Key races: York's Hambleton Handicap, Sandown's Whitsun Cup and Kempton's Jubilee Handicap. On firm ground, a low draw is favoured.

Gold Cup (Group 1) 2m 4f Royal Ascot June

	FORM	WINNER	AGE/WEIGHT	TRAINER	JOCKEY	SP
1994	0300-30	Arcadian Heights	6 9-2	G. Wragg	M. Hills	20–1
1993	11232-1	Drum Taps	7 9-2	Lord Huntingdon	L. Dettori	13–2
1992	1120-11	Drum Taps	6 9-2	Lord Huntingdon	L. Dettori	7–4F
1991	30_-203	Indian Queen	6 8-13	Lord Huntingdon	W.R. Swinburn	25–1
1990	21_1-21	Ashal	4 9-0	H. Thomson Jones	R. Hills	14–1
1989	10210-1	Sadeem	6 9-0	G. Harwood	W. Carson	8–11F

• Five Gold Cup winners in the last 16 years have returned to repeat the feat. Winners generally come from the first 2 in the betting.

Ribblesdale Stakes (Group 2)   1m 4f   Royal Ascot   June

	FORM	WINNER	AGE/WEIGHT	TRAINER	JOCKEY	SP
1994	0-1	Bolas	3 8-8	B. Hills	Pat Eddery	3–1F
1993	011-4	Thawakib	3 8-8	J. Dunlop	W. Carson	5–2F
1992	02-2232	Armarama	3 8-8	C. Brittain	M. Roberts	5–2F
1991	10-0	Third Watch	3 8-8	J. Dunlop	J. Reid	20–1
1990	4-1	Hellenic	3 8-8	M. Stoute	W. R. Swinburn	6–1
1989	-31	Alydaress	3 8-9	H. Cecil	S. Cauthen	4–1

● John Dunlop dominates with 4 wins and 3 places from his last 8 runners. Favourites had a losing run of 11 before the last 3 obliged. One prep race often seems enough; no penalty has been successfully carried since 1980. Up-and-comers rather than Oaks fillies are favoured.

Hardwicke Stakes (Group 2)   1m 4f   Royal Ascot   June

	FORM	WINNER	AGE/WEIGHT	TRAINER	JOCKEY	SP
1994	22(00-33	Bobzao	5 8-9	T. Mills	J. Reid	11–1
1993	2012-33	Jeune	4 8-9	G. Wragg	R. Cochrane	7–2
1992	320-012	Rock Hopper	5 8-12	M. Stoute	Pat Eddery	8–15F
1991	21-113	*Rock Hopper	4 8-12	M. Stoute	Pat Eddery	5–6F
1990	12:10-4	Assatis	5 9-0	G. Harwood	R. Cochrane	50–1
1989	12:-	Assatis	4 8-9	G. Harwood	Pat Eddery	4–11F

● Winners inevitably come from the front-runners in the betting. Newmarket's Jockey Club Stakes has been the source race for 5 of the last 10 scorers.

* Topanoora finished 1st but was disqualified and placed 2nd.

Wokingham Handicap 6f Royal Ascot June

	FORM	WINNER	AGE/WEIGHT	TRAINER	JOCKEY	SP
1994	00032-0	Venture Capitalist (30)	5 8-12	R. Hannon	J. Reid	20-1
1993	0320-03	Nagida (4)	4 8-10	J. Toller	J. Weaver (3)	11-1
1992	0-00433	Red Rosein (29)	6 8-1	J. Wilson	G. Carter	33-1
1991	10-001	Amigo Menor (4)	5 8-7	D. Murray-Smith	C. Rutter	14-1
1990	0-04241	Knight Of Mercy (17)	4 8-6 (7ex)	R. Hannon	Pat Eddery	16-1
1989	10-2034	Mac's Fighter (7)	4 9-12	W. O'Gorman	C. Asmussen	16-1

● The winners' prices reflect the difficulties. Stick with in-form sprinters who have won over 6f in handicap company. On fast ground the race can be won from any berth, but single-figure draws have a definite advantage when the ground is riding soft.

King's Stand Stakes (Group 2) 5f Royal Ascot June

	FORM	WINNER	AGE/WEIGHT	TRAINER	JOCKEY	SP
1994	1131-11	Lochsong	6 9-0	I. Balding	L. Dettori	1-3F
1993	404130-	Elbio	6 9-3	P. Makin	W.R. Swinburn	12-1
1992	141221-	Sheikh Albadou	4 9-3	A. Scott	W.R. Swinburn	7-2F
1991	110-211	Elbio	4 9-3	P. Makin	S. Cauthen	13-8F
1990	12-0121	Dayjur	3 8-10	W. Hern	W. Carson	11-2
1989	1000-1	Indian Ridge	4 9-3	D. Elsworth	S. Cauthen	9-4F

● Sandown's Temple Stakes (5 recent winners) is a much more significant guide than either the Duke Of York or Palace House Stakes. Six of the last 11 winners needed one prep race or less. Three-year-olds have won 7 of the last 15 runnings.

Newcastle 'Brown Ale' Northumberland Plate
Handicap   2m   Newcastle   June

	FORM	WINNER	AGE/WEIGHT		TRAINER	JOCKEY	SP
1994	321-000	Quick Ransom	6	8-8	M. Johnston	J. Weaver	25–1
1993	00-0011	Highflying	7	7-11 (3ex)	G.M. Moore	J. Fanning	7–1
1992	31110-2	Witness Box	5	9-9	J. Gosden	G. Duffield	6–1
1991	22000-2	Tamarpour	4	7-7	M. Pipe	E. Johnson	10–1
1990	0121-01	Al Maheb	4	8-11 (3ex)	A. Stewart	W. Carson	9–2
1989	010-1	Orpheus	3	7-7	G. Harwood	R. Fox	4–1JF

● Quick Ransom was only the 3rd winner for the north in the last 22 years. Orpheus (1989) was a rare 3-year-old runner, never mind winner. The tough finish ensures that mature stayers (5+) have the best record. Winners are lightly raced in the current season but in-form and penalized horses do well. Look out for Royal Ascot also-rans.

Royal Hong Kong Jockey Club Handicap 1m 2f Sandown July

	FORM	WINNER	AGE/WEIGHT	TRAINER	JOCKEY	SP
1994	2100-02	Knowth	5 7-8	R. Akehurst	J. Quinn	13-2F
1993	-211121	Smarginato	3 8-10 (4ex)	J. Dunlop	G. Carter	12-1
1992	04-0322	Fire Top	7 8-9	R. Akehurst	T. Quinn	14-1
1991	410001	You Know The Rules	4 7-12 (4ex)	M. Channon	C. Rutter	14-1
1990	140-012	Bold Fox	4 9-5 (4ex)	G. Harwood	R. Cochrane	12-1
1989	03400-1	Unknown Quantity	4 8-12	W. Hastings-Bass	B. Raymond	10-1

• An open and competitive handicap in which recent good handicap form is essential. There have been 3 penalized winners in the last 5, all of them at least 12-1 chances.

Coral-Eclipse Stakes (Group 1)   1m 2f   Sandown   July

	FORM	WINNER	AGE/WEIGHT	TRAINER	JOCKEY	SP
1994	020-032	Ezzoud	5 9-7	M. Stoute	W. Swinburn	5–1
1993	0232-21	Opera House	5 9-7	M. Stoute	M. Kinane	9–2
1992	1120-03	Kooyonga	4 9-4	M. Kauntze (Ire)	W. O'Connor	7–2F
1991	01-3010	Environment Friend	3 8-10	J. Fanshawe	G. Duffield	28–1
1990	11-1023	Elmaamul	3 8-10	W. Hern	W. Carson	13–2
1989	11-11	Nashwan	3 8-8	W. Hern	W. Carson	2–5F

• The last 12 winners have won over at least 1m 2f. Eight outright favourites have won in the last 16 years. Only 2 fillies have won in the race's 108-year history, Pebbles and Kooyonga. One prep race is not enough, 2 or 3 high-class winning runs are normal. Three-year-olds have the best record, winning 6 of the last 12.

Princess of Wales's Stakes (Group 2) 1m 4f Newmarket July

	FORM	WINNER	AGE/WEIGHT	TRAINER	JOCKEY	SP
1994	2102-23	Wagon Master	4 9-0	A. Stewart	R. Hills	7-1
1993	12-2300	Desert Team	3 8-1	J. Bolger (Ire)	W. Carson	10-1
1992	220-111	Saddlers' Hall	4 9-5	M. Stoute	Pat Eddery	4-7F
1991	1-11312	Rock Hopper	4 9-3	M. Stoute	Pat Eddery	4-6F
1990	1220-22	Sapience	4 9-0	J. FitzGerald	Pat Eddery	11-2
1989	1134-33	Carroll House	4 9-5	M. Jarvis	W.R. Swinburn	10-1

● Dick Hern (5) and Michael Stoute (3) have won 8 of the last 16 between them – Stoute's trio of 4-year-olds had all run well in the Coronation Cup. The last 6 winning 3-year-olds ran in either the English, Irish or French Derbys but none of them was in the 1st 3. Recent winning form not essential. Henry Cecil has a poor record. No shocks.

Falmouth Stakes (Group 2) 1m Newmarket July

	FORM	WINNER	AGE/WEIGHT	TRAINER	JOCKEY	SP
1994	11113-4	Lemon Souffle	3 8-6	R. Hannon	L. Piggott	6-5F
1993	4310-12	Niche	3 8-6	R. Hannon	L. Piggott	13-8F
1992	340-000	Gussy Marlowe	4 9-1	C. Brittain	M. Roberts	7-1
1991	00-0000	Only Yours	3 8-6	R. Hannon	M. Roberts	10-1
1990	1113-41	Chimes Of Freedom	3 8-12	H. Cecil	S. Cauthen	4-6F
1989	20-012	Magic Gleam	3 8-6	A. Scott	Pat Eddery	15-8

● The winner has usually won or been placed in the English or Irish One Thousand Guineas, or the Coronation Stakes; but, remember, winners of these races are vulnerable because of their penalties. Richard Hannon has won with his last 3 runners.

July Cup (Group 1) 6f Newmarket July

	FORM	WINNER	AGE/WEIGHT	TRAINER	JOCKEY	SP
1994	112-011	Owington	3 8-13	G. Wragg	Paul Eddery	3–1
1993	01-0100	Hamas	4 9-6	P. Walwyn	W. Carson	33–1
1992	102-122	Mr Brooks	5 9-6	R. Hannon	L. Piggott	16–1
1991	210-11	Polish Patriot	3 8-13	G. Harwood	R. Cochrane	6–1
1990	10-12	Royal Academy	3 8-13	V. O'Brien (Ire)	J. Reid	7–1
1989	2011-30	Cadeaux Genereux	4 9-6	A. Scott	Paul Eddery	10–1

● Three-year-olds have a good record, winning 9 of the last 15, and all but two of them were switching back to sprinting after making the frame in one of the Guineas races. So top milers do make top sprinters. Only 1 Kings Stand winner in the last decade, Never So Bold (1985), has followed up here.

John Smith's Magnet Cup Handicap 1m 2f 85y York July

	FORM	WINNER	AGE/WEIGHT		TRAINER	JOCKEY	SP
1994	0012-4	Cezanne	5	9-12	H. Ibrahim	G. Hind	9-2
1993	33-212	Baron Ferdinand	3	8-9	R. Charlton	R. Cochrane	4-1JF
1992	434-111	Mr Confusion	4	8-10	S. Norton	O. Pears	8-1
1991	01-3424	Halkopous	5	7-8	M. Tompkins	F. Norton	7-2JF
1990	020-111	Eradicate	5	9-4	P. Calver	W. Newnes	15-2
1989	2-12310	Icona	3	9-8	M. Stoute	T. Ives	12-1

● Despite the competitive nature of the race, it's one for form horses – 4 recent winners have extended unbeaten records in the current season. Five favourites have won in the last 12 years and during that time there has been no SP longer than 14–1. Lightly raced 3-year-olds dominate. Not a good race for penalized horses.

King George VI and Queen Elizabeth Diamond Stakes (Group 1) 1m 4f
Ascot July

	FORM	WINNER	AGE/WEIGHT	TRAINER	JOCKEY	SP
1994	1-10422	King's Theatre	3 8-9	H. Cecil	M. Kinane	12–1
1993	231-211	Opera House	5 9-7	M. Stoute	M. Roberts	8–1
1992	14-4121	St Jovite	3 8-9	J. Bolger (Ire)	S. Craine	4–5F
1991	011-411	Generous	3 8-9	P. Cole	A. Munro	4–6F
1990	1-113	Belmez	3 8-9	H. Cecil	M. Kinane	15–2
1989	11–111	Nashwan	3 8-8	W. Herm	W. Carson	2–9F

● Two key prep races – the Derby and the Eclipse. Three-year-olds have won 8 of the last 10 runnings and 7 had run in the Derby, 3 winning, while of the 4 beaten at Epsom, 3 (St Jovite, Dancing Brave and Petoski) won a Group race next time out and King's Theatre finished runner up in one. Four of the last 9 winners had won the Eclipse. Nine of the last 16 were completing a hat-trick at least.

Sussex Stakes (Group 1) 1m Goodwood July

	FORM	WINNER	AGE/WEIGHT	TRAINER	JOCKEY	SP
1994	2012	Distant View	3 8-9	H. Cecil	Pat Eddery	4–1
1993	2-11222	Bigstone	3 8-13	E. Lellouche (Fr)	D. Boeuf	14–1
1992	111-211	Marling	3 8-10	G. Wragg	Pat Eddery	11–10F
1991	-112	Second Set	3 8-13	L. Cumani	L. Dettori	5–1
1990	131-232	Distant Relative	4 9-7	B. Hills	W. Carson	4–1
1989	-111	Zilzal	3 8-10	M. Stoute	W.R. Swinburn	5–2

● Three-year-olds have dominated in the last 11 years, winning 9 times. During that period all winners were either 1st or 2nd on their previous start and only French-trained Bigstone started at a bigger price than 5–1. Not since Wollow (1976) has a Two Thousand Guineas winner won this race. Zilzal (1989) broke a 25-year jinx for Jersey Stakes winners.

Richmond Stakes (Group 2)   6f   Goodwood   July

	FORM	WINNER	AGE/WEIGHT	TRAINER	JOCKEY	SP
1994	2111	Sri Pekan	2 8-11	P. Cole	T. Quinn	9-4
1993	-111	First Trump	2 8-11	G. Wragg	M. Hills	100-30
1992	-0111	Son Pardo	2 8-11	R. Hannon	J. Reid	7-1
1991	-2111	Dilum	2 8-11	P. Cole	A. Munro	2-7F
1990	211112	Mac's Imp	2 8-11	W. O'Gorman	A. Munro	2-1F
1989	-2	Contract Law	2 8-11	W. Jarvis	B. Raymond	9-2

● After a period when the winners had not previously contested a Group race, the balance has now swung the other way – Sri Pekan, Dilum and Mac's Imp all won the Coventry at Royal Ascot and First Trump won Newmarket's July Stakes.

Schweppes Golden Mile Handicap 1m Goodwood July

	FORM	WINNER	AGE/WEIGHT	TRAINER	JOCKEY	SP
1994	01420-2	Fraam	5 9-9	A. Scott	W. Swinburn	10–1
1993	40-0234	Philidor	4 8-7	J. Eustace	N. Kennedy (3)	13–2
1992	-2101	Little Bean	3 8-2 (5ex)	G. Wragg	M. Hills	9–1
1991	10-2140	Sky Cloud	5 8-7	R. Akehurst	T. Quinn	20–1
1990	-014d	March Bird	5 7-8	J. Sutcliffe	N. Adams	15–1
1989	021-011	Safawan	3 8-0	M. Stoute	W. Carson	11–2

● In the 8 runnings of this event only the first winner, Waajib, and last year's winner, Fraam, carried more than 8st 7lb. Philidor fitted the pattern in terms of weight and number of runs (no more than 4 in the current season) but unlike Little Bean, Sky Cloud, Safawan and Waajib he hadn't won a major handicap as part of his build-up.

Vodafone Nassau Stakes (Group 2) 1m 2f Goodwood July

	FORM	WINNER	AGE/WEIGHT	TRAINER	JOCKEY	SP
1994	10-3132	Hawajiss	3 8-6	M. Stoute	W. Swinburn	4-1F
1993	-2111	Lyphard's Delta	3 8-6	H. Cecil	W. Ryan	10-1
1992	0111-32	Ruby Tiger	5 9-1	P. Cole	T. Quinn	2-1
1991	11-3011	Ruby Tiger	4 9-4	P. Cole	T. Quinn	11-4
1990	-110	Kartajana	3 8-6	M. Stoute	W.R. Swinburn	11-2
1989	101-242	Mamaluna	3 8-6	G. Harwood	G. Starkey	9-1

● Three-year-olds dominate, having won 13 of the last 16 runnings, but Oaks form can be a mixed blessing – the Epsom race has provided 5 winners in the last 12 years but also 6 beaten favourites. Winners can suddenly leave their spring form behind. The Ribblesdale Stakes is not a good trial.

Vodac Stewards' Cup Handicap 6f Goodwood July

	FORM	WINNER	AGE/WEIGHT	TRAINER	JOCKEY	SP
1994	0-30423	For The Present	4 8-3	T. Barron	J. Fortune	16–1
1993	11000-1	King's Signet	4 9-10 (7ex)	J. Gosden	W. Carson	16–1
1992	211-314	Lochsong	4 8-0	I. Balding	W. Carson	10–1
1991	0-0441	Notley	4 8-12	R. Hannon	R. Perham (5)	14–1
1990	043411	Knight Of Mercy	4 9-0 (7ex)	R. Hannon	B. Raymond	14–1
1989	000004	Very Adjacent	4 7-8	G. Lewis	D. Gibson (5)	12–1

● In the last 15 years there have been no discernible patterns to the draw. The Wokingham Stakes is the best guide, providing the winner 6 times in the last 11 years and not one of them had finished worse than 5th at Royal Ascot. The last 15 winners all made the frame on their previous run.

Ibn Bey Geoffrey Freer Stakes (Group 2) 1m 5f 61y Newbury August

	FORM	WINNER	AGE	WEIGHT	TRAINER	JOCKEY	SP
1994	22121	Red Route	3	8-5	H. Cecil	W. Ryan	11–10F
1993	21-1443	Azzilfi	3	8-5	J. Dunlop	W. Carson	5–1
1992	0-23020	Shambo	5	9-3	C. Brittain	M. Roberts	9–1
1991	14-0231	Drum Taps	5	9-5	Lord Huntingdon	L. Dettori	15–2
1990	133420	Charmer	5	9-2	C. Brittain	L. Dettori	4–1
1989	41-2011	Ibn Bey	5	9-8	P. Cole	T. Quinn	9–2

● Formerly a tremendous race for the 1st and 2nd in the market, Red Route was the last winning favourite since Bakharoff (1986). Form in Pattern race company at 1m 4f or more is essential. Older horses hold their own. Clive Brittain has 'farmed' the race, winning it 3 times in the last 7.

Great Voltigeur Stakes (Group 2) 1m 4f York August

	FORM	WINNER	AGE/WEIGHT	TRAINER	JOCKEY	SP
1994	4111	Sacrament	3 8-9	M. Stoute	W. Swinburn	6-1
1993	0411-10	Bob's Return	3 8-9	M. Tompkins	P. Robinson	16-1
1992	1-03021	Bonny Scot	3 8-9	L. Cumani	L. Dettori	11-8F
1991	0-11002	Corrupt	3 8-9	N. Callaghan	Pat Eddery	5-1
1990	1-1131	Belmez	3 9-0	H. Cecil	S. Cauthen	1-2F
1989	1112-13	Zalazl	3 8-9	H. Cecil	S. Cauthen	7-4

• Not as good a St Leger trial as it is perceived. Since 1974 only Reference Point and Bob's Return have gone on to win the Leger. Bob's Return was a rare shock winner – the biggest price in the previous 13 years was 6-1. Winners have generally been busy (at least 4 runs) and Goodwood's Gordon Stakes has provided 3 winners since 1980.

Juddmonte International Stakes (Group 1) 1m 2f 85y York August

	FORM	WINNER	AGE/WEIGHT		TRAINER	JOCKEY	SP
1994	0-0321U	Ezzoud	5	9-6	M. Stoute	W. Swinburn	4–1
1993	230-120	Ezzoud	4	9-6	M. Stoute	W.R. Swinburn	28–1
1992	1-41104	Rodrigo De Triano	3	8-12	P. Chapple-Hyam	L. Piggott	8–1
1991	0-12304	Terimon	5	9-6	C. Brittain	M. Roberts	16–1
1990	3-20114	In The Groove	3	8-9	D. Elsworth	S. Cauthen	4–1
1989	2-02122	Ile De Chypre	4	9-6	G. Harwood	A. Clark	16–1

• The trend for shock results has certainly returned – remember Roberto in 1972. Group 1 form is essential; the last 10 winners had all won or been placed in that grade, including 28–1 chance Ezzoud. Older horses do better than the Classic generation; 5 3-year-olds have met defeat here recently after finishing 2nd in the King George.

Aston Upthorpe Yorkshire Oaks (Group 1) 1m 4f York August

	FORM	WINNER	AGE/WEIGHT	TRAINER	JOCKEY	SP
1994	1104-00	Only Royale	5 9-7	L. Cumani	L. Dettori	8-1
1993	121-222	Only Royale	4 9-7	L. Cumani	R. Cochrane	10-1
1992	-1111	User Friendly	3 8-11	C. Brittain	G. Duffield	8-11F
1991	-03102	Magnificent Star	3 8-11	M. Moubarak	A. Cruz	16-1
1990	4-11	Hellenic	3 8-11	M. Stoute	W. Carson	100-30
1989	24-3321	Roseate Tern	3 8-11	W. Hern	W. Carson	11-2

● Older horses have been eligible only since 1992. In the decade prior to Only Royale's first win, only Hellenic had failed to contest either the English or Irish Oaks. Nassau Stakes runners have a poor record.

Scottish Equitable Gimcrack Stakes (Group 2) 6f York August

	FORM	WINNER	AGE/WEIGHT	TRAINER	JOCKEY	SP
1994	034	Chilly Billy	2 9-0	Mrs J. Ramsden	K. Fallon	12–1
1993	-11431	Turtle Island	2 9-5	P. Chapple-Hyam	J. Reid	5–2
1992	-3110	Splendent	2 9-0	P. Cole	A. Munro	8–1
1991	-212	River Falls	2 9-0	R. Hannon	B. Raymond	9–4
1990	-11	Mujtahid	2 9-3	R. Armstrong	W. Carson	1–2F
1989	-1111	Rock City	2 9-3	R. Hannon	W. Carson	1–2F

● Turtle Island became the 3rd in the last 9 years to make a quick winning reappearance after running in the Heinz 57 Phoenix Stakes. An even better trend is trainer Richard Hannon's record – 3 wins in the last 7. Ten of the last 13 winners had run in Pattern race company and all had raced exclusively over 5f and 6f, except Chilly Billy.

Tote Ebor Handicap 1m 6f York August

	FORM	WINNER	AGE/WEIGHT	TRAINER	JOCKEY	SP
1994	2124-22	Hasten To Add	4 9-3	Sir Mark Prescott	G. Duffield	13–2F
1993	31-0400	Sarawat	5 8-2	R. Akehurst	T. Quinn	14–1
1992	220210	Quick Ransom	4 8-3	M. Johnston	D. McKeown	16–1
1991	011114	Deposki	3 7-8	M. Stoute	F. Norton (5)	12–1
1990	011021	Further Flight	4 8-8	B. Hills	M. Hills	7–1JF
1989	4110-20	Sapience	3 8-4	J. FitzGerald	Pat Eddery	15–2

● Two trends emerge – the exposed horse with form in high-class handicaps and the lightly raced dark 'un. Out-and-out shocks are rare. Flint Jack (1922–3) was the last to win it back-to-back.

Keeneland Nunthorpe Stakes (Group 1) 5f York August

	FORM	WINNER	AGE/WEIGHT	TRAINER	JOCKEY	SP
1994	031202	Blue Siren	3 8-10	I. Balding	M. Hills	6-1
1993	344311	Lochsong	5 9-3	I. Balding	L. Dettori	10-1
1992	121111	Lyric Fantasy	2 7-8	R. Hannon	M. Roberts	8-11F
1991	0-1214	Sheikh Albadou	3 9-3	A. Scott	Pat Eddery	6-1
1990	2-01211	Dayjur	3 9-3	W. Hern	W. Carson	8-11F
1989	011-301	Cadeaux Genereux	4 9-6	A. Scott	Pat Eddery	11-10F

● The only Group 1 5f race in the calendar. Out of the last 13 winners only Handsome Sailor (1988) and Blue Siren had not won on either of their last 2 outings. During the same period there have been 7 winning favourites.

Traditionally the best trial has been the July Cup but it hasn't produced the winner now for 5 years.

Lowther Stakes (Group 2) 6f York August

	FORM	WINNER	AGE/WEIGHT	TRAINER	JOCKEY	SP
1994	12	Harayir	2 8-11	W. Hern	W. Carson	2–1F
1993	-141	Velvet Moon	2 8-11	P. Cole	A. Munro	10–1
1992	-11143	Niche	2 9-0	R. Hannon	L. Piggott	2–1
1991	-12	Culture Vulture	2 8-11	P. Cole	T. Quinn	85–40F
1990	-12	Only Yours	2 8-11	R. Hannon	B. Raymond	8–1
1989	-2112	Dead Certain	2 9-0	D. Elsworth	S. Cauthen	5–4F

• Win or placed form over the 6f trip is essential, and 12 of the last 16 winners have been either 1st or 2nd favourite. Royal Ascot's Queen Mary Stakes has proved the best trial, producing 3 of the last 6 winners.

Tripleprint Celebration Mile (Group 2)　1m　Goodwood　August

	FORM	WINNER	AGE/WEIGHT	TRAINER	JOCKEY	SP
1994	3-14133	Mehthaaf	3 8-11	J. Dunlop	W. Carson	5–2
1993	110423	Swing Low	4 9-3	R. Hannon	J. Reid	10–1
1992	310-102	Selkirk	4 9-3	I. Balding	R. Cochrane	1–2F
1991	32-2021	Bold Russian	4 9-0	B. Hills	W. Carson	100–30
1990	21-2413	Shavian	3 9-0	H. Cecil	S. Cauthen	5–2F
1989	1-13311	Distant Relative	3 8-12	B. Hills	M. Hills	2–1

● Only 2 of the last 13 winners had won their prep race; given that, surprise results are not uncommon. Eight of the last 9 winners, however, had won a Pattern race. Barry Hills has the best trainers' record, winning in 3 of the last 7 years.

Hazlewood Foods Sprint Cup (Group 1) 6f Haydock September

	FORM	WINNER	AGE/WEIGHT	TRAINER	JOCKEY	SP
1994	11-4023	Lavinia Fontana	5 8-9	J. Dunlop	J. Weaver	11–2
1993	-2242	Wolfhound	4 9-9	J. Gosden	M. Roberts	7–2
1992	124-134	Sheikh Albadou	4 9-9	A. Scott	B. Raymond	9–4JF
1991	22-1144	Polar Falcon	4 9-9	J. Hammond (Fr)	C. Asmussen	13–2
1990	2-12111	Dayjur	3 9-6	W. Hern	W. Carson	1–2F
1989	0-13413	Danehill	3 9-5	J. Tree	Pat Eddery	3–1

• Understandably, the July Cup (6f) rather than the Nunthorpe (5f) or the King's Stand (5f) has been the best trial, pinpointing 6 of the last 12 winners. Only 3 of the last 13 won their prep race but generally the winner comes from the market leaders.

Laurent-Perrier Champagne Stakes (Group 2) 7f Doncaster September

	FORM	WINNER	AGE/WEIGHT	TRAINER	JOCKEY	SP
1994	21111	Sri Pekan	2 9-0	P. Cole	M. Kinane	10–3
1993	-0112	Unblest	2 8-11	J. Fanshawe	G. Duffield	3–1
1992	-110	Petardia	2 9-0	G. Wragg	M. Hills	11–2
1991	-111	Rodrigo De Triano	2 8-11	P. Chapple-Hyam	W. Carson	11–8F
1990	-3	Bog Trotter	2 8-11	W. Haggas	N. Day	8–1
1989		Abandoned – course unsafe				

● Look to the lightly raced colts who have form in Listed or Pattern company, like 9 of the last 11 winners. Unbeaten horses have won 7 of the last 13. Henry Cecil has been out of luck in this event since 1980. The race produced 2 recent Two Thousand Guineas winners.

Coalite St Leger Stakes (Group 2) Doncaster September 1m 6f 132y

	FORM	WINNER	AGE/WEIGHT	TRAINER	JOCKEY	SP
1994	112003	Moonax	3 9-0	B. Hills	Pat Eddery	33-1
1993	411-101	Bob's Return	3 9-0	M. Tompkins	P. Robinson	3-1F
1992	-11111	User Friendly	3 8-11	C. Brittain	G. Duffield	7-4F
1991	1-3101	Toulon	3 9-0	A. Fabre (Fr)	Pat Eddery	5-2F
1990	322-22	Snurge	3 9-0	P. Cole	T. Quinn	7-2
1989	-131	Michelozzo	3 9-0	H. Cecil	S. Cauthen	6-4F
1988	20-1101	Minster Son	3 9-0	N. Graham	W. Carson	15-2
1987	1-11211	Reference Point	3 9-0	H. Cecil	S. Cauthen	4-11F
1986	111113	Moon Madness	3 9-0	J. Dunlop	Pat Eddery	9-2
1985	-11122	Oh So Sharp	3 8-11	H. Cecil	S. Cauthen	8-11F

● Contenders who won at least 2 of their last 3 races have supplied 9 of the last 12 winners, 7 of them having shown winning form in Pattern race company. During the same period Henry Cecil had 3 winners, while a trio of Oaks winners have also obliged. Great race for favourites – 8 of the last 12 came up trumps.

Tripleprint Flying Childers Stakes (Group 2) 5f Doncaster September

	FORM	WINNER	AGE/WEIGHT	TRAINER	JOCKEY	SP
1994	322114	Raah Algharb	2 8-11	M. Stoute	W. Swinburn	7–1
1993	141332	Imperial Bailiwick	2 8-6	M. Usher	J. Williams	12–1
1992	-310	Poker Chip	2 8-6	I. Balding	M. Hills	33–1
1991	-111212	Paris House	2 8-11	J. Berry	J. Carroll	4-6F
1990	-14122	Distinctly North	2 8-11	J. Berry	Pat Eddery	6-4F
1989		Abandoned – course unsafe				

• Between 1980 and 1991 there was only one losing favourite. All the winning favourites had either won or been placed in Pattern company and had plenty of experience.

Ladbrokes Ayr Gold Cup Handicap 6f Ayr September

	FORM	WINNER	AGE/WEIGHT	TRAINER	JOCKEY	SP
1994	310202	Daring Destiny (29)	3 8-0	K. Burke	J. Tate	16–1
1993	000210	Hard To Figure (8)	7 9-6	R. Hodges	R. Cochrane	12–1
1992	1-31411	Lochsong (28)	4 9-0 (7ex)	I. Balding	F. Arrowsmith	10–1
1991	301121	Sarcita (18)	3 9-1 (7ex)	D. Elsworth	B. Doyle	14–1
1990	221303	Final Shot (8)	3 8-2	M.H. Easterby	J. Lowe	12–1
1989	221400	Joveworth (6)	6 8-5	M. O'Neill	J. Fortune	50–1

● A low to middle draw is best; in the last 13 runnings on good to soft or worse, only 7 of the 52 to make the frame were drawn 18 or higher. In 1986, the race was run on firm, and the first 8 home were on the stands (high) side. Nine of the last 13 winners ran in either the Portland Handicap or the Great St Wilfrid. Peter Easterby has won it 3 times.

Rokeby Farms Mill Reef Stakes (Group 2) 6f Newbury September

	FORM	WINNER	AGE/WEIGHT		TRAINER	JOCKEY	SP
1994	11144	Princely Hush	2	8-11	M. Bell	M. Fenton	9–2
1993	-121	Polish Laughter	2	8-11	B. Hanbury	W.R. Swinburn	4–1
1992	-12	Forest Wind	2	8-11	M. Moubarak	L. Dettori	11–2
1991	-221	Showbrook	2	9-1	R. Hannon	W. Carson	4–1
1990	-143	Time Gentlemen	2	8-11	J. Dunlop	W. Carson	9–2
1989	-41	Welney	2	8-11	G. Wragg	G. Carter	9–1

● Eight of the last 12 winners had form in Listed or Group company but only 1 of them had to defy a 4lb penalty. Shocks are rare – in that same period, only 2 winners started at bigger than 11–2. Recent winning form is almost essential – 8 were 1st past the post in their prep race.

Fillies' Mile (Group 1) 1m Ascot September

	FORM	WINNER	AGE/WEIGHT	TRAINER	JOCKEY	SP
1994	1	Aqaarid	2 8-10	J. Dunlop	W. Carson	11–2
1993	-011	Fairy Heights	2 8-10	N. Callaghan	C. Asmussen	11–1
1992	-103	Ivanka	2 8-10	C. Brittain	M. Roberts	6–1
1991	-121	*Culture Vulture	2 8-10	P. Cole	T. Quinn	5–2F
1990	-012	Shamshir	2 8-10	L. Cumani	L. Dettori	11–2
1989	-1	Silk Slippers	2 8-10	B. Hills	M. Hills	10–1

● Henry Cecil has had 3 winners and 3 2nds in the last 11 years. Six winners in the 1980s maintained unbeaten records in the race. Ten of the last 14 winners had Pattern race form, 6 of them either winning or making the frame in the May Hill Stakes at Doncaster. Fairy Heights was the biggest-priced winner since the race began in 1973.

* Midnight Air finished 1st but was disqualified and placed last.

Queen Elizabeth II Stakes (Group 1) 1m Ascot September

	FORM	WINNER	AGE/WEIGHT		TRAINER	JOCKEY	SP
1994	022402	Maroof	4	9-4	R. Armstrong	R. Hills	50–1
1993	122213	Bigstone	3	9-0	E. Lellouche (Fr)	Pat Eddery	100–30
1992	21-0212	Lahib	4	9-4	J. Dunlop	W. Carson	8–1
1991	4-23341	Selkirk	3	9-0	I. Balding	R. Cochrane	10–1
1990	23-1414	Markofdistinction	4	9-4	L. Cumani	L. Dettori	6–1
1989	-1111	Zilzal	3	8-11	M. Stoute	W. R. Swinburn	Evens F

● A light campaign or perhaps a mid-season break seems popular; only Maroof, Bigstone and Tele-prompter (1984) in the last 12 years have had more than 5 runs in the current season. Michael Stoute has won it 3 times in the last 10 years. Bigstone was the 1st non-British winner since World Cup for Ireland in 1968. Three-year-olds have the best record.

Royal Lodge Stakes (Group 2) 1m Ascot September

	FORM	WINNER	AGE/WEIGHT	TRAINER	JOCKEY	SP
1994	211	Eltish	2 8-10	H. Cecil	Pat Eddery	7-4F
1993	-1310	Mister Baileys	2 8-10	M. Johnston	L. Dettori	100-30JF
1992	-02	Desert Secret	2 8-10	M. Stoute	Pat Eddery	12-1
1991	-1222	Made Of Gold	2 8-10	M. Moubarak	A. Cruz	4-1
1990	-231	Mujaazif	2 8-10	M. Stoute	W.R. Swinburn	11-2
1989	-21	Digression	2 8-10	G. Harwood	Pat Eddery	4-1JF

● Eltish was only the 4th winner in the last 14 years who had winning form in Pattern company, but he did fulfil the criterion for having form over at least 7f. Desert Secret was a very rare maiden winner. Henry Cecil and Michael Stoute have won 6 of the last 10 runnings between them.

Tote Festival Handicap 7f Ascot September

	FORM	WINNER	AGE/WEIGHT	TRAINER	JOCKEY	SP
1994	12113	Wizard King (23)	3 8-7	Sir Mark Prescott	G. Duffield	13–2F
1993	300104	Young Ern (17)	3 8-12 (5ex)	S. Dow	W. Ryan	25–1
1992	420401	Sharpalto (1)	5 9-3 (5ex)	Mrs M. Reveley	M. Kinane	11–1
1991	30-4410	Night Jar (9)	4 8-9	Lord Huntingdon	A. Munro	33–1
1990	101012	Pontenuovo (6)	5 8-8	D. Elsworth	W. Carson	7–1
1989	-42034	Runun (15)	3 8-4	C. Brittain	T. Quinn	12–1

● Only 2 winners in the last 11 years have been outside the 8st to 8st 13lb weight range. Young Ern was the 4th in 8 years to win at 20–1 or bigger. Wizard King was only the 3rd in the last 11 years to be drawn higher than 10, and a rare winning favourite. 3 penalized horses have won in the last nine years.

Ascot Handicap 1m 4f Ascot September

	FORM	WINNER	AGE/WEIGHT	TRAINER	JOCKEY	SP
1994	1022-43	Whitechapel	6 8-5	Lord Huntingdon	M. Hills	6–1
1993	230210	League Leader	3 8-10 (4ex)	M. Stoute	W. Carson	10–1
1992	202101	Quick Ransom	4 9-1 (4ex)	M. Johnston	D. McKeown	14–1
1991	000113	Tidemark	4 8-10	L. Cumani	L. Dettori	10–1
1990	203144	Secret Society	3 8-0	M. Camacho	M. Camacho	20–1
1989	-02111	Braashee	3 9-4 (4ex)	A. Stewart	Pat Eddery	8–1

● League Leader was the race's 4th penalized winner since its inception only 8 years ago. Look for in-form horses who have won at least 1 of their 2 prep races. Winners tend to be classy, improving 3-year-olds or top-class handicappers, emphasized by the fact that only 1 winner has carried less than 8st 5lb. Only 1 favourite has obliged.

Shadwell Stud Cheveley Park Stakes (Group 1) 6f Newmarket September

	FORM	WINNER	AGE/WEIGHT	TRAINER	JOCKEY	SP
1994	0123	Gay Gallanta	2 8-11	M. Stoute	Pat Eddery	14–1
1993	-1001	Prophecy	2 8-11	J. Gosden	Pat Eddery	12–1
1992	-211	Sayyedati	2 8-11	C. Brittain	W.R. Swinburn	5–2
1991	-111	Marling	2 8-11	G. Wragg	W.R. Swinburn	15–8F
1990	-1011	Capricciosa	2 8-11	V. O'Brien (Ire)	J. Reid	7–1
1989	-21121	Dead Certain	2 8-11	D. Elsworth	C. Asmussen	11–2

● French and Irish stables have won it 5 times in the last 14. Form at 6f is almost essential – the last winner to be switching back from 7f was Ma Biche in 1982. The Moyglare Stakes has pinpointed 5 winners in the last 14.

Newgate Stud Middle Park Stakes (Group 1) 6f Newmarket September

	FORM	WINNER	AGE/WEIGHT	TRAINER	JOCKEY	SP
1994	311142	Fard	2 9-0	D. Morley	W. Carson	33–1
1993	-11113	First Trump	2 9-0	G. Wragg	M. Hills	6–1
1992	-111	Zieten	2 9-0	A. Fabre (Fr)	S. Cauthen	5–2
1991	-1111	Rodrigo De Triano	2 9-0	P. Chapple-Hyam	W. Carson	Evens F
1990	-412	Lycius	2 9-0	A. Fabre (Fr)	C. Asmussen	13–8F
1989	320313	Balla Cove	2 9-0	R. Boss	S. Cauthen	20–1

● Twelve of the last 13 winners had run in Pattern company but only 6 had won. Winners tend to have been surprisingly busy; 9 of the last 13 had run at least 5 times, which may account for the numerous shocks – 5 winners since 1981 at 20–1 or higher! Fabre has saddled 2 winners and a 2nd in the last 5 runnings.

Sun Chariot Stakes (Group 2)   1m 2f   Newmarket   October

	FORM	WINNER	AGE/WEIGHT	TRAINER	JOCKEY	SP
1994	1	La Confederation	3 8-8	D. Loder	K. Darley	5–1
1993	124323	Talented	3 8-8	J. Dunlop	W. Carson	4–1
1992	210-041	Red Slippers	3 8-8	L. Cumani	L. Dettori	6–4F
1991	-142	Ristna	3 8-8	J. Gosden	W. Carson	4–1
1990	-11012	Kartajana	3 8-11	M. Stoute	W. R. Swinburn	11–10F
1989	3-11041	Braiswick	3 8-7	G. Wragg	G. Carter	4–1

● The market rules: there hasn't been a winner above 6–1 since 1980. Luca Cumani has won it 4 times in the last 11 years using 4 different jockeys. Three-year-olds dominate their older rivals, winning in 8 of the last 9 years. Only concern yourself with fillies who finished 1st or 2nd in their preps – they've won 12 of the last 14.

William Hill Cambridgeshire Handicap 1m 1f Newmarket October

	FORM	WINNER	AGE/WEIGHT	TRAINER	JOCKEY	SP
1994	040-11	Halling	3 8-8	J. Gosden	L. Dettori	8-1F
1993	313212	Penny Drops (18)	4 7-13 (5ex)	Lord Huntingdon	D. Harrison	7-1F
1992	-20111	Rambo's Hall (7)	7 9-3 (5ex)	J. Glover	D. McKeown	9-2F
1991	124042	Mellottie (27)	6 9-1	Mrs M. Reveley	J. Lowe	10-1
1990	0-1201	Risen Moon (2)	3 8-9	B. Hills	S. Cauthen	7-1F
1989	-30112	Rambo's Hall (19)	4 8-6	J. Glover	D. McKeown	15-1

● A race for specialists – Baronet won it twice (1978 and 1980) and was placed twice. Rambo's Hall has won it twice; perhaps that is why Rambo became one of only two winners since the late 1970s to defy a penalty. Lightweights struggle – only 2 winners below 8st 1lb since 1974. Every winner in the last decade had won at least 2 in the current season. Favourites have won 4 of the last 5 but before that the last winning favourite was Prince De Galles in 1969. The draw is anyone's guess.

Challenge Stakes (Group 2) 7f Newmarket October

	FORM	WINNER	AGE/WEIGHT	TRAINER	JOCKEY	SP
1994	3043-20	Zeiten	4 9-0	J. Gosden	L. Dettori	13-2
1993	101121	Catrail	3 8-11	J. Gosden	M. Roberts	4-5F
1992	1-10213	Selkirk	4 9-3	I. Balding	R. Cochrane	5-6F
1991	-11004	Mystiko	3 9-0	C. Brittain	M. Roberts	9-4F
1990	400132	Sally Rous	3 8-8	G. Wragg	G. Carter	11-4
1989	331113	Distant Relative	3 8-13	B. Hills	M. Hills	Evens F

● Look no further than the first 2 in the betting; favourites have won 11 of the last 16 and 2nd favourites 3 of the other 5. Four winners since 1982 had been placed in the Queen Elizabeth II Stakes, while 3 recent winners contested Goodwood's Supreme Stakes. It is a specialist trip so Pattern race-winning form over 7f almost essential.

Dewhurst Stakes (Group 1) 7f Newmarket October

	FORM	WINNER	AGE/WEIGHT	TRAINER	JOCKEY	SP
1994	11	Pennekamp	2 9-0	A. Fabre (Fr.)	T. Jarnet	5–2
1993	-131	Grand Lodge	2 9-0	W. Jarvis	Pat Eddery	9–4F
1992	-111	Zafonic	2 9-0	A. Fabre (Fr)	Pat Eddery	10–11F
1991	-12112	Dr Devious	2 9-0	P. Chapple-Hyam	W. Carson	3–1F
1990	-12301	Generous	2 9-0	P. Cole	T. Quinn	50–1
1989	-1131	Dashing Blade	2 9-0	I. Balding	J. Matthias	8–1

● In the last 7 years there has been a shift to proven Group race form. Results have an even mix of shocks and the predictable. Despite Dr Devious and Huntingdale (1985) it is vital to have won at least the last prep race. Good form at 7f is a major factor.

Dubai Champion Stakes (Group 1) 1m 2f Newmarket October

	FORM	WINNER	AGE/WEIGHT	TRAINER	JOCKEY	SP
1994	1230-01	Dernier Empereur	4 9-4	A. Fabre (Fr.)	S. Guillot	8-1
1993	11-1441	Hatoof	4 9-0	Mrs C. Head (Fr)	W.R. Swinburn	5-2F
1992	411041	Rodrigo De Triano	3 8-12	P. Chapple-Hyam	L. Piggott	11-8F
1991	1-24311	Tel Quel	3 8-12	A. Fabre (Fr)	T. Jarnet	16-1
1990	114130	In The Groove	3 8-9	D. Elsworth	S. Cauthen	9-2
1989	-11210	Legal Case	3 8-10	L. Cumani	R. Cochrane	5-1

● Until Rodrigo won in 1992 every running but one since 1976 had been won by a filly or the French. Before Dernier Empereur, the last 4-year-old colt to win was Brigadier Gerard in 1972, who the previous year was the last before Rodrigo to complete the Two Thousand Guineas–Champion double. At least 2 wins in the current season are usually required.

Tote Cesarewitch Handicap   2m 2f   Newmarket   October

	FORM	WINNER	AGE/WEIGHT	TRAINER	JOCKEY	SP
1994	0-20101	Captain's Guest	4 9-9	G. Harwood	A. Clark	25–1
1993	204-213	Aahsaylad	7 8-12	J. White	J. Williams	12–1
1992	1-1310	Vintage Crop	5 9-6	D. Weld (Ire)	W.R. Swinburn	5–1F
1991	002104	Go South	7 7-11	J. Jenkins	N. Carlisle	33–1
1990	13-2101	Trainglot	3 7-12	J. FitzGerald	W. Carson	13–2
1989	210431	Double Dutch	5 9-10 (4ex)	Miss B. Sanders	W. Newnes	15–2

● The race is dominated by improving 3-year-olds and run-of-the-mill handicappers. The latter group have provided the 5 20–1+ shocks in recent years, though the general trend is for fancied horses. Eight of the last 13 winners carried 8st 1lb or less, but none from more than 4lb out of the handicap.

Racing Post Trophy (Group 1) 1m Doncaster October

	FORM	WINNER	AGE/WEIGHT	TRAINER	JOCKEY	SP
1994	11	Celtic Swing	2 9-0	Lady Herries	K. Darley	Evens F
1993	-011	King's Theatre	2 9-0	H. Cecil	W. Ryan	9-2
1992	-11	Armiger	2 9-0	H. Cecil	Pat Eddery	5-4F
1991	-1213	Seattle Rhyme	2 9-0	D. Elsworth	C. Asmussen	2-1F
1990	-11	Peter Davies	2 9-0	H. Cecil	S. Cauthen	2-1JF
1989	-11111	By My Chief	2 9-0	H. Cecil	S. Cauthen	4-7F

● Should be renamed the Henry Cecil Trophy, he's won it 10 times in all and 7 times in the last 13 years. Cecil's winners have been a mix of Group scorers and lightly raced maiden winners. No Royal Lodge winner has done the double since 1982. Every winner in the last decade had won a race over 7f or 1 mile.

Ladbroke Autumn Handicap 1m Newmarket October

	FORM	WINNER	AGE/WEIGHT	TRAINER	JOCKEY	SP
1994	013212	Master Beveled	4 8-4	P. Evans	J. Stack	8–1
1993	031130	Cambara	3 9-4	M. Stoute	M. Roberts	16–1
1992	–01001	Cambrian	3 8-7 (5ex)	Mrs J. Cecil	G. Duffield	33–1
1991	000411	Scales Of Justice	5 7-13	J. Hills	R. Hills	9–2F

● Newly inaugurated; too early to determine any patterns.

William Hill November Handicap 1m 4f Doncaster November

	FORM	WINNER	AGE/WEIGHT	TRAINER	JOCKEY	SP
1994	041214	Saxon Maid	3 8-9	L. Cumani	J. Weaver	16-1
1993	100332	Quick Ransom	5 8-10	M. Johnston	J. Weaver	6-1F
1992	104241	Turgenev	3 9-0	J. Gosden	D. Holland	10-1
1991	311134	Hieroglyphic	3 8-13	J. Gosden	W. Carson	11-4F
1990	141-001	Azzaam	3 9-8	J. Dunlop	W. Carson	7-1
1989	344112	Firelight Fiesta	4 9-8	B. Hanbury	B. Raymond	9-2F

● Some decent hurdlers like Champion Hurdle challenger Swingit Gunner have used this race as a stepping stone. Recent trend since Firelight Fiesta (1989) has been for high-weighted winners – previous winner over 9st was Mr Bigmore in 1975. The pattern is for heavy campaigns, even among 3-year-old winners who have won 10 in the last 13. Nine straight losing favourites in the 1980s.

National Hunt

Mackeson Gold Cup Handicap Chase 2m 4½f Cheltenham November

	FORM	WINNER	AGE/WEIGHT	TRAINER	JOCKEY	SP
93/4	34223-1	Bradbury Star	8 11-8	J. Gifford	D. Murphy	13-2
92/3	120-411	Tipping Tim	7 10-10	N. Twiston-Davies	C. Llewellyn	11-2F
91/2	P13FF-2	Another Coral	8 10-1	D. Nicholson	R. Dunwoody	15-2
90/1	211220-	Multum In Parvo	7 10-2	J. Edwards	N. Williamson	12-1
89/90	2213F-1	Joint Sovereignty	9 10-4	P. Hobbs	G. McCourt	10-1
88/9	2U312-1	Pegwell Bay	7 11-2	T. Forster	P. Scudamore	6-1

● Apart from a 3-year burst in the mid-1980s, lightweights have the call – 4 of the last 7 winners came from the 10st 1lb to 10st 4lb range. Good prep run and winning form over 2m 4f are important, reflected in the fact that 12–1 is longest SP in the last 20 years. Only 3 of the last 20 winners have been older than 8.

Hennessy Cognac Gold Cup 3m 2½f Newbury November

	FORM	WINNER	AGE/WEIGHT	TRAINER	JOCKEY	SP
93/4	1112F-2	Cogent	9 10-1	A. Turnell	D. Fortt (7)	10-1
92/3	0U-4121	Sibton Abbey	7 10-0	F. Murphy	A. Maguire	40-1
91/2	11U2-	Chatam	7 10-6	M. Pipe	P. Scudamore	10-1
90/1	U2F12-1	Arctic Call	7 11-0	O. Sherwood	J. Osborne	5-1
89/90	2114-02	Ghofar	6 10-2	D. Elsworth	H. Davies	5-1
88/9	4FU0F3-	Strands Of Gold	9 10-0	M. Pipe	P. Scudamore	10-1

● Young, relatively inexperienced chaser needed with solid handicap form. Good, preferably winning form in prep races is essential – only Pipe in the last 12 years has trained a horse to win on its reappearance. Eight of the last 9 have carried 10st 8lb or less. Sibton Abbey, 21lb out of handicap, was a rare shock. Only Arkle has ever followed up.

William Hill Handicap Hurdle 2m 4f Sandown December

	FORM	WINNER	AGE/WEIGHT		TRAINER	JOCKEY	SP
93/4	131F-14	Land Afar	6	11-2	J. Webber	W. Marston	13–2
92/3	31401-1	Valfinet	5	10-2 (4ex)	M. Pipe	J. Lower	5–4F
91/2	113121-	Balasani	5	10-0	M. Pipe	M. Perrett	7–1
90/1	00040-F	Wonder Man	5	10-12	Mrs J. Pitman	M. Pitman	11–4F
89/90	10P4-24	Liadett	4	10-0	M. Pipe	J. Lower	12–1
88/9	3024P-4	Corporal Clinger	9	10-7	M. Pipe	M. Perrett	9–2

● Martin Pipe has won 4 of the last 6. Valfinet won the best trial, the Whitbread White Label Handicap at Cheltenham. Nine of the last 11 winners have carried 10st 12lb or less. The market is a good guide, 6 of the last 13 winners have been favourite. All bar Pipe runners need a 2nd prep race.

Tripleprint Gold Cup Handicap Chase 2m 5f Cheltenham December

	FORM	WINNER	AGE/WEIGHT	TRAINER	JOCKEY	SP
93/4	214220-	Fragrant Dawn	9 10-2	M. Pipe	D. Murphy	14-1
92/3	2340-22	Another Coral	9 11-4	D. Nicholson	R. Dunwoody	11-2
91/2	1111-31	King's Fountain	8 11-10	K. Bailey	A. Tory	7-4F
90/1		Abandoned – snow				
89/90	-12F11	Clever Folly	9 10-4	G. Richards	N. Doughty	4-1
88/9	U312-11	Pegwell Bay	7 10-13	T. Forster	B. Powell	7-2

● Market leaders dominate. It is almost essential to have finished 1st or 2nd in prep races, preferably over 2m 4f. Only Pegwell Bay has ever followed up in this race after winning the Mackeson.

Northumberland Gold Cup Novices' Chase (Grade 1)   2m ½f   Newcastle
December

	FORM	WINNER	AGE/WEIGHT	TRAINER	JOCKEY	SP
93/4	0422-11	Native Mission	6 11-7	J. FitzGerald	M. Dwyer	10–11F
92/3	1303-11	Sybillin	6 11-7	J. FitzGerald	C. Grant	15–8F
91/2	44-1111	Clay County	6 11-7	R. Allan	B. Storey	6–4F
90/1	001111	Moment Of Truth	6 11-7	P. Monteith	L. O'Hara	9–2

● All four winners of this newly inaugurated race have maintained their unbeaten records over fences. Each time the prize has stayed in the north.

Long Walk Hurdle (Grade 1)   3m   Ascot   December

	FORM	WINNER	AGE/WEIGHT	TRAINER	JOCKEY	SP
93/4	11F-222	Sweet Duke	6 11-7	N. Twiston-Davies	C. Llewellyn	7–2
92/3	P2P1-12	Vagog	7 11-7	M. Pipe	M. Foster	15–2
91/2		Abandoned – frost				
90/1	244340-	Floyd	10 11-7	D. Elsworth	G. Bradley	10–1
89/90	012313-	Royal Athlete	6 10-8	Mrs J. Pitman	D. Gallagher	33–1
88/9	3101-31	French Goblin	5 11-1	J. Gifford	Peter Hobbs	3–1

● Five of the last 11 winners have been able to score without a prep race, which helps to explain why only 2 favourites in 14 have triumphed. Plenty of shocks. Vagog was the latest of 5 recent winners to have shown winning form over an extended 3m at Cheltenham. Ascot's Racecall Hurdle (2m 4f) is a bad trial.

King George VI Tripleprint Chase (Grade 1) 3m Kempton December

	FORM	WINNER	AGE/WEIGHT	TRAINER	JOCKEY	SP
93/4	1F1P-11	Barton Bank	7 11-10	D. Nicholson	A. Maguire	9–2
92/3	1220-13	The Fellow	7 11-10	F. Doumen (Fr)	A. Kondrat	Evens F
91/2	211-11U	The Fellow	6 11-10	F. Doumen (Fr)	A. Kondrat	10–1
90/1	1131-24	Desert Orchid	11 11-10	D. Elsworth	R. Dunwoody	9–4F
89/90	111F-12	Desert Orchid	10 11-10	D. Elsworth	R. Dunwoody	4–6F
88/9	2211-11	Desert Orchid	9 11-10	D. Elsworth	S. Sherwood	1–2F

● The same faces keep coming back – the last 21 runnings have been won by just 12 horses. The best horse wins, after 2 or 3 prep races.

Tripleprint Feltham Novices' Chase (Grade 1) 3m Kempton December

FORM	WINNER	AGE/WEIGHT	TRAINER	JOCKEY	SP
93/4	See More Indians	6 11-7	P. Nicholls	G. Bradley	7–2
92/3	Dakyns Boy	7 11-7	N. Twiston-Davies	P. Scudamore	9–2
91/2	Mutare	6 11-7	N. Henderson	R. Dunwoody	11–8F
90/1	Sparkling Flame	6 11-7	N. Henderson	R. Dunwoody	7–2
89/90	French Goblin	6 10-11	J. Gifford	Peter Hobbs	15–8F
88/9	Sir Blake	7 11-4	D. Elsworth	B. Powell	8–11F

FORM column (by row): /-111, 144-311, 11020-1, -1, 11P4-1F, 41F1-11

● The market rules; since 1985 there hasn't been a winner bigger than 5–1. Winners haven't been busy but what they've done has been high-class.

Bonusprint Christmas Hurdle (Group 1) 2m Kempton December

	FORM	WINNER	AGE/WEIGHT	TRAINER	JOCKEY	SP
93/4	10113-3	Muse	6 11-7	D. Elsworth	M. Richards	3–1
92/3	13-1111	Mighty Mogul	5 11-7	D. Nicholson	R. Dunwoody	3–1
91/2	1332-21	Gran Alba	5 11-7	R. Hannon	G. McCourt	3–1
90/1	U011-1	Fidway	5 11-7	T. Thomson Jones	S. Smith Eccles	100–30
89/90	1110-1	Kribensis	5 11-3	M. Stoute	R. Dunwoody	4-6F
88/9	111-11	Kribensis	4 11-3	M. Stoute	R. Dunwoody	4-9F

● Ten of the last 12 winners won last time out, 8 of them being young, second-season hurdlers. Newbury's Gerry Feilden Hurdle is the best trial.

Castleford Chase (Grade 1) 2m Wetherby December

	FORM	WINNER	AGE/WEIGHT		TRAINER	JOCKEY	SP
93/4		Abandoned					
92/3	2211-12	Katabatic	9	11-10	A. Turnell	S. McNeill	Evens
91/2	1232-21	Waterloo Boy	8	11-10	D. Nicholson	R. Dunwoody	4–11F
90/1	324-023	Waterloo Boy	7	11-10	D. Nicholson	R. Dunwoody	6–4
89/90	P11-242	Ida's Delight	10	10-7	J. Charlton	B. Storey	17–2
88/9	F41-	Midnight Count	8	12-2	J. Gifford	P. Hobbs	15–8

● Designed as a trial for the Queen Mother Champion Chase, but since it switched from a handicap in 1990 the 3 winners have all subsequently failed at Cheltenham.

Coral Welsh National Handicap Chase 3m 5½f Chepstow December

	FORM	WINNER	AGE/WEIGHT	TRAINER	JOCKEY	SP
93/4	1U4FP-2	Riverside Boy	10 10-0	M. Pipe	R. Dunwoody	6-4F
92/3	1133-11	Run For Free	8 10-9 (4ex)	M. Pipe	M. Perrett	11-4JF
91/2	1F-1	Carvill's Hill	9 11-12	M. Pipe	P. Scudamore	9-4F
90/1	21442-3	Cool Ground	8 10-0	R. Akehurst	L. Harvey	9-2
89/90	F140P-1	Bonanza Boy	8 11-11	M. Pipe	P. Scudamore	15-8F
88/9	43230-1	Bonanza Boy	7 10-1	M. Pipe	P. Scudamore	9-4F

● Pipe and Pitman have won 8 of the last 12 between them: Pipe's usually win their 3m handicap prep (usually the Rehearsal Chase); Pitman's never win their prep and are often unplaced in the Hennessy. Run For Free was one of 4 recent winners who had run in the previous year's Sun Alliance Chase. Bad race for 10-year-olds and those more than 1lb out of handicap.

Finale Junior Hurdle (Grade 1) 2m ½f Chepstow December

	FORM	WINNER	AGE/WEIGHT		TRAINER	JOCKEY	SP
93/4	11	Mysilv	3	10-9	D. Nicholson	A. Maguire	11–10F
92/3	-11	Dare To Dream	3	11-0	R. Akehurst	D. Bridgwater	9–2
91/2	-1	Good Profile	3	11-0	G. Moore	L. Wyer	7–1
90/1	110111	Hopscotch	3	10-9	M. Pipe	J. Lower	9–4F
89/90	-302	Crystal Heights	3	11-0	Mrs J. Retter	B. Powell	33–1
88/9	-11	Enemy Action	3	11-3	M. Pipe	P. Scudamore	8–15F

● Twelve of the last 15 winners have been at 7–1 or less, Martin Pipe providing 3 successful favourites in the last 8 runnings. Recent winning form virtually essential.

Challow Hurdle (Grade 1) 2m 4f Newbury January

	FORM	WINNER	AGE/WEIGHT	TRAINER	JOCKEY	SP
93/4	101-211	Large Action	6 11-7	O. Sherwood	J. Osborne	4-5F
92/3	-11	Lord Relic	7 11-7	M. Pipe	P. Scudamore	15-8F
91/2	-1	Lift And Load	4 11-8	R. Hannon	G. McCourt	5-4F
90/1	-11	Tyrone Bridge	4 11-8	M. Pipe	R. Dunwoody	2-5F
89/90	211-01	Forest Sun	4 11-13	G. Balding	J. Frost	6-4F
88/9	2-11	Green Willow	6 11-13	J. Gifford	P. Hobbs	13-8

● Usually an uncompetitive single-figure field in which the form horse, and short-priced favourite, is dominant.

Tolworth Hurdle (Grade 1)   2m   Sandown   January

	FORM	WINNER	AGE/WEIGHT		TRAINER	JOCKEY	SP
93/4		Abandoned					
92/3	00-1211	Sun Surfer	5	11-7	T. Forster	C. Llewellyn	7–1
91/2	223-1	New York Rainbow	7	11-7	N. Henderson	J. Kavanagh	5–1
90/1	-12	Change The Act	6	11-7	O. Sherwood	J. Osborne	9–1
89/90	211-011	Forest Sun	5	11-12	G. Balding	J. Frost	8–11F
88/9	21031	Wishlon	6	12-0	R. Smyth	I. Shoemark	4–6F

● Nine of the last 10 winners won last time out. No shocks; all bar 2 of the last 16 winners have been at 5–1 or less. The first major race won by Desert Orchid.

Newton Chase (Grade 1) 2m 4f Haydock January

	FORM	WINNER	AGE/WEIGHT		TRAINER	JOCKEY	SP
93/4		Abandoned					
92/3	323-041	Gold Options	11	11-10	J. FitzGerald	L. Wyer	14-1
91/2	1211-1	Pats Jester	9	11-10	G. Richards	N. Doughty	7-1
90/1	44-1220	Sabin Du Loir	12	11-10	M. Pipe	M. Perrett	1-2F

● A relatively new race which has gone so far to specialist 2m 4f horses.

Cleeve Hurdle (Grade 1) 2m 5½f Cheltenham January

	FORM	WINNER	AGE/WEIGHT	TRAINER	JOCKEY	SP
93/4	0-43421	Flakey Dove	8 11-3	R. Price	R. Dunwoody	4-1
92/3	223-101	Muse	6 11-8	D. Elsworth	P. Holley	11-4
91/2		Abandoned – frost				
90/1	-121	Crystal Spirit	4 10-9	I. Balding	J. Frost	4-1
89/90	0111-31	Beech Road	8 12-0	G. Balding	R. Guest	1-3F
88/9	101221	Calapaez	5 11-10	Miss B. Sanders	S. Sherwood	6-4
87/8	110P-21	Cloughtaney	7 12-0	P. Mullins (Ire)	A. Mullins	5-2F

● Winners come from a small pool of in-form horses who have won at least their previous race. David Elsworth with Buckbe (1984) and Muse has won 2 of the last 9 runnings.

Scilly Isles Novices' Chase (Grade 1) 2m 4½f Sandown February

	FORM	WINNER	AGE/WEIGHT	TRAINER	JOCKEY	SP
93/4	111122	Baydon Star	7 11-6	D. Nicholson	R. Dunwoody	6-4F
92/3	402111	Young Hustler	6 11-6	N. Twiston-Davies	C. Llewellyn	5-2F
91/2	110111	Bradbury Star	7 11-6	J. Gifford	D. Murphy	6-5F
90/1	1P-0210	Tildarg	7 11-6	O. Sherwood	J. Osborne	11-2
89/90	Abandoned – waterlogging					
88/9	32-3011	The Bakewell Boy	7 11-6	R. Frost	J. Frost	6-1

● Favourites have a very good record; Killiney won it in 1973 at 10–1 on, and there have been only 4 winners bigger than 100–30 since 1965. Seven-year-olds have won 10 of the last 13 runnings.

Sandown Handicap Hurdle 2m 6f Sandown February

	FORM	WINNER	AGE/WEIGHT	TRAINER	JOCKEY	SP
93/4	011F01	Dark Honey	9 10-0	S. Dow	A. Dicken	8–1
92/3	202-311	Trainglot	6 10-2	J. FitzGerald	M. Dwyer	7–2F
91/2	02102-0	Black Sapphire	5 10-0	M. Tompkins	B. Powell	33–1
90/1	P-03044	Rouyan	5 10-0	R. Simpson	W. Morris	8–1
89/90		Abandoned – waterlogging				
88/9	2-0030	Special Vintage	9 10-12	J. FitzGerald	M. Dwyer	20–1

● The strongest trend is for a lightweight which is apparently out of form. Special Vintage is the only winner in the last 8 runnings to carry more than 10st 5lb. Trainglot was the first favourite to win; there have been some rare old shocks. Jimmy FitzGerald is the trainer to watch.

Tote Gold Trophy Handicap Hurdle 2m ½f Sandown February

	FORM	WINNER	AGE/WEIGHT	TRAINER	JOCKEY	SP
93/4	01-2111	Large Action	6 10-8	O. Sherwood	J. Osborne	9–2
92/3	1110-44	King Credo	8 10-0	S. Woodman	A. Maguire	10–1
91/2	311111	Rodeo Star	6 10-10	N. Tinkler	G. McCourt	15–2
90/1		Abandoned – frost				
89/90	011-423	Deep Sensation	5 11-3	J. Gifford	R. Rowe	7–1
88/9	14-0121	Grey Salute	6 11-5 (7ex)	J. Jenkins	R. Dunwoody	8–1

● Only 3 of the last 17 winners have carried more than 11st. A light campaign so as not to reveal too much and good form in a handicap seem the strongest trends. Form in the Ladbroke Hurdle doesn't seem to count for much.

Racing Post Handicap Chase 3m Kempton February

	FORM	WINNER	AGE/WEIGHT	TRAINER	JOCKEY	SP
93/4	022U14	Antonin	6 10-4	Mrs S. Bramall	J. Burke	7–1
92/3	02-1111	Zeta's Lad	10 10-10	J. Upson	J. White	11–1
91/2	11-2320	Docklands Express	10 11-10	K. Bailey	A. Tory	6–1
90/1	11-2123	Docklands Express	9 10-7	K. Bailey	A. Tory	7–2
89/90	1F-1211	Desert Orchid	11 12-3 (3ex)	D. Elsworth	R. Dunwoody	8–11F
88/9	140P-11	Bonanza Boy	8 11-1	M. Pipe	P. Scudamore	5–1

● This race is won by championship contenders or fast-improving handicappers. Eight of the last 10 winners have carried 10st 7lb or more. David Elsworth won it 3 times in 4 years with different horses and Kim Bailey won it back-to-back with Docklands Express. Five of the last 7 winners had won over the trip in the current season.

Smurfit Champion Hurdle (Grade 1)   2m ½f   Cheltenham   March

	FORM	WINNER	AGE/WEIGHT	TRAINER	JOCKEY	SP
93/4	421131	Flakey Dove	8 11-9	R. Price	M. Dwyer	9-1
92/3	1F1-223	Granville Again	7 12-0	M. Pipe	P. Scudamore	13-2
91/2	-211	Royal Gait	9 12-0	J. Fanshawe	G. McCourt	6-1
90/1	01-12P1	Morley Street	7 12-0	G. Balding	J. Frost	4-1F
89/90	110-111	Kribensis	6 12-0	M. Stoute	P. Dunwoody	95-40
88/9	0-4UF01	Beech Road	7 12-0	G. Balding	R. Guest	50-1
87/8	2-11112	Celtic Shot	6 12-0	F. Winter	P. Scudamore	7-1
86/7	-1	See You Then	7 12-0	N. Henderson	S. Smith Eccles	11-10F
85/6	-1	See You Then	6 12-0	N. Henderson	S. Smith Eccles	5-6F

● There were only 11 individual champions in the 20 years from 1968 to 1987 but we've had new champs in each of the last 6 years. Champions are rarely over-raced (up to 5 runs). Only Comedy Of Errors has ever regained his crown (1973 and 1975). Not since Sea Pigeon (1980) has a placed runner the previous year won the Champion.

Trafalgar House Supreme Novices' Hurdle (Grade 1) 2m ½f Cheltenham March

	FORM	WINNER	AGE/WEIGHT	TRAINER	JOCKEY	SP
93/4	4-10143	Arctic Kinsman	6 11-8	N. Twiston-Davies	C. Llewellyn	50–1
92/3	1112-12	Montelado	6 11-8	P. Flynn (Ire)	C. Swan	5–1
91/2	-1	Flown	5 11-8	N. Henderson	J. Osborne	13–2
90/1	-1	Destriero	5 11-8	A. Geraghty (Ire)	P. McWilliams	6–1
89/90	1-01111	Forest Sun	5 11-8	G. Balding	J. Frost	7–4F
88/9	-110	Sondrio	8 11-8	M. Pipe	J. Lower	25–1

● Lack of hurdling experience is not a problem. The Irish have won 2 of the last 4, reminding us of their heyday when they won for 7 successive years between 197/ and 1983. Only 3 favourites have won in the last 16 years. Only horses with near-unblemished records tend to be good enough these days.

Waterford Castle Arkle Trophy Chase (Grade 1) 2m Cheltenham March

	FORM	WINNER	AGE/WEIGHT	TRAINER	JOCKEY	SP
93/4	-11	Nakir	6 11-8	S. Christian	J. Osborne	9–1
92/3	20-1011	Travado	7 11-8	N. Henderson	J. Osborne	5–1
91/2	31-2121	Young Pokey	7 11-8	O. Sherwood	J. Osborne	4–1
90/1	2-11111	Remittance Man	7 11-8	N. Henderson	R. Dunwoody	85–40F
89/90	00-F11	Comandante	8 11-8	J. Gifford	Peter Hobbs	9–2
88/9	111112	Waterloo Boy	6 11-8	D. Nicholson	R. Dunwoody	20–1

● Fancied horses have been winning recently but only 2 outright favourites in the last 13 years. Even the form figures of the shock winners are littered with 1s and 2s. Plenty of experience is necessary, 4+ runs usually, and form over 2m 4f helps. Key prep races: James Capel (Ascot), Kempton over Christmas and Nottingham in February.

Sun Alliance Novices' Hurdle (Grade 1) 2m 5f Cheltenham March

	FORM	WINNER	AGE/WEIGHT	TRAINER	JOCKEY	SP
93/4	-13211	Danoli	6 11-7	T. Foley (Ire.)	C. Swan	7–4F
92/3	110222	Gaelstrom	6 11-2	N. Twiston-Davies	C. Llewellyn	16–1
91/2	-11131	Thetford Forest	5 11-7	D. Nicholson	R. Dunwoody	7–1
90/1	-1211	Crystal Spirit	4 10-12	I. Balding	J. Frost	2–1F
89/90	-1211	Regal Ambition	6 11-7	M. Pipe	P. Scudamore	3–1F
88/9	111311	Sayfar's Lad	5 11-7	M. Pipe	M. Perrett	12–1

● Brown Lad (1974), an 8-year-old, has been the only winner aged above 6. The Trial Hurdle at Warwick has been the best guide recently by pinpointing Sayfar's Lad, Thetford Forest and Rebel Song. Plenty of hurdling experience is necessary. Danoli was the first Irish winner since 1982. Only 5 favourites in the last 15 years have won.

Sun Alliance Novices' Chase (Grade 1) 3m 1f Cheltenham March

	FORM	WINNER	AGE/WEIGHT	TRAINER	JOCKEY	SP
93/4	F42111	Monsieur Le Cure	8 11-4	J. Edwards	P. Niven	15–2
92/3	111112	Young Hustler	6 11-4	N. Twiston-Davies	P. Scudamore	9–4
91/2	1114/11	Miinnehoma	9 11-4	M. Pipe	P. Scudamore	7–2F
90/1	114101	Rolling Ball	8 11-4	M. Pipe	P. Scudamore	7–2F
89/90	1-30212	Garrison Savannah	7 11-4	Mrs J. Pitman	B. de Haan	12–1
88/9	-22242	Envopak Token	8 11-4	J. Gifford	Peter Hobbs	16–1

● Warwick's Whitlenge Chase has provided 3 recent winners; The West Awake, Garrison Savannah and Rolling Ball. No Reynoldstown Chase winner has won this for more than a decade. Unless the horse is trained by Martin Pipe, experience is essential. Young Hustler was the youngest winner since Sweet Joe in 1978. 1st or 2nd placing last time out is imperative.

Queen Mother Champion Chase (Grade 1) 2m Cheltenham March

	FORM	WINNER	AGE/WEIGHT	TRAINER	JOCKEY	SP
93/4	11-2211	Viking Flagship	7 12-0	D. Nicholson	A. Maguire	4–1
92/3	212022	Deep Sensation	8 12-0	J. Gifford	D. Murphy	11–1
91/2	111-131	Remittance Man	8 12-0	N. Henderson	J. Osborne	Evens F
90/1	3-41231	Katabatic	8 12-0	A. Turnell	S. McNeill	9–1
89/90	11-F321	Barnbrook Again	9 12-0	D. Elsworth	H. Davies	11–10F
88/9	123-111	Barnbrook Again	8 12-0	D. Elsworth	S. Sherwood	7–4F

● Most recent winners have been equally good at 2m 4f, so had the necessary stamina for Cheltenham. Nine straight 1st or 2nd favourites won until the last 4 years. Only Royal Relief in the mid-1970s ever regained his title successfully. Champions regularly defend their crown.

Daily Express Triumph Hurdle (Grade 1) 2m 1f Cheltenham March

	FORM	WINNER	AGE/WEIGHT	TRAINER	JOCKEY	SP
93/4	11111	Mysilv	4 10-9	D. Nicholson	A. Maguire	2–1F
92/3	-2111	Shawiya	4 10-9	M. O'Brien (Ire)	C. Swan	12–1
91/2	-133	Duke Of Monmouth	4 11-0	S. Sherwood	M. Richards	33–1
90/1	-110	Oh So Risky	4 11-0	D. Elsworth	P. Holley	14–1
89/90	-002	Rare Holiday	4 11-0	D. Weld (Ire)	B. Sheridan	25–1
88/9	B14324	Ikdam	4 11-0	R. Holder	N. Coleman	66–1

● Oppose the favourite, Mysilv was the first to win since Attivo (at odds-on!) in 1974. Two long-standing trends have been broken in the last 5 years: Rare Holiday became the first maiden to win, and Shawiya the first filly. Eleven of the last 14 had run no more than 4 times.

Bonusprint Stayers' Hurdle (Grade 1) 3m ½f Cheltenham March

	FORM	WINNER	AGE/WEIGHT	TRAINER	JOCKEY	SP
93/4	40-0-41	*Balasani	8 11-10	M. Pipe	M. Perrett	9-2
92/3	10-302	Shuil Ar Aghaidh	7 11-5	P. Kiely (Ire)	C. Swan	20-1
91/2	32-223	Nomadic Way	7 11-10	B. Hills	J. Osborne	15-2
90/1	42-114	King's Curate	7 11-10	S. Mellor	M. Perrett	5-2F
89/90	22-4321	Trapper John	6 11-10	M. Morris (Ire)	C. Swan	15-2
88/9	231-F32	Rustle	7 11-10	N. Henderson	M. Bowlby	4-1

● Most winners have proven form over 3m. Only Crimson Embers has won it aged 10 or more. Five of the last 8 winners had either won at a Cheltenham meeting or been placed at the Festival previously. Best race for the Irish at Festival in recent years – 4 wins in the last 8. Shocks are rare.

* Avro Anson finished first but was disqualified and placed third.

Tote Cheltenham Gold Cup (Grade 1) 3m 2½f Cheltenham March

	FORM	WINNER	AGE/WEIGHT		TRAINER	JOCKEY	SP
93/4	40-3333	The Fellow	9	12-0	F. Doumen (Fr)	A. Kondrat	8-1
92/3	3-22111	Jodami	8	12-0	P. Beaumont	M. Dwyer	8-1
91/2	0P2101	Cool Ground	10	12-0	G. Balding	A. Maguire	25-1
90/1	02121-2	Garrison Savannah	8	12-0	Mrs J. Pitman	M. Pitman	16-1
89/90	11-0023	Norton's Coin	9	12-0	S. Griffiths	G. McCourt	100-1
88/9	1-11111	Desert Orchid	10	12-0	D. Elsworth	S. Sherwood	5-2F
87/8	-021	Charter Party	10	12-0	D. Nicholson	R. Dunwoody	10-1
86/7	11-0411	The Thinker	9	12-0	W. Stephenson	R. Lamb	13-2
85/6	-114	Dawn Run	8	11-9	P. Mullins (Ire)	J. O'Neill	15-8F
84/5	122121	Forgive 'N' Forget	8	12-0	J. FitzGerald	M. Dwyer	7-1

● Eight of the last 12 winners had won or been placed at the Festival, but The Fellow was the first for a decade to win this after being placed the previous year. No horse since L'Escargot (1970–1) has won back-to-back Gold Cups. Ten of the last 14 winners won their previous race at least. Only 2 winning favourites in the last decade, surprisingly for a championship.

Vincent O'Brien County Handicap Hurdle 2m 1f Cheltenham March

	FORM	WINNER	AGE/WEIGHT	TRAINER	JOCKEY	SP
93/4	0-00222	Dizzy	6 10-0	P. Monteith	A. Dobbin	12–1
92/3	0-12231	Thumbs Up	7 10-2	N. Henderson	R. Dunwoody	16–1
91/2	22-B23	Dusty Miller	6 10-6	S. Sherwood	J. Osborne	9–1
90/1	02-2100	Winnie The Witch	7 10-1	K. Bridgwater	D. Bridgwater	33–1
89/90	0-11041	Moody Man	5 11-2 (7ex)	P. Hobbs	Peter Hobbs	9–1
88/9	40-0311	Willsford	6 11-8	Mrs J. Pitman	M. Bowlby	11–1

● In-form horses necessary; 2 shocks in the last 4 years but previously no SP bigger than 14–1 since 1976. Moody Man and Floyd (1985) both doubled up after winning the Imperial Cup – a good trial. Look for a fresh horse; 8 of the last 11 winners had had 5 runs or less in the current season. Lightweights best; only 3 winners since 1974 have carried more than 10st 12lb.

Tetley Bitter Midlands National Handicap Chase 4m 2f Uttoxeter March

	FORM	WINNER	AGE/WEIGHT	TRAINER	JOCKEY	SP
93/4	3P-02F2	Glenbrook D'Or	10 10-0	A. Wilson	B. Gifford	10–1
92/3	30401F	Mister Ed	10 10-3	R. Curtis	D. Morris	25–1
91/2	33200P	Laura's Beau	8 10-8	F. Berry (Ire)	C. O'Dwyer	12–1
90/1	320202	Bonanza Boy	10 11-10	M. Pipe	P. Scudamore	15–8F
89/90	4112FP	Willsford	7 11-0	Mrs J. Pitman	M. Pitman	6–1
88/9	320-121	Gallic Prince	10 10-1	P. Hobbs	Peter Hobbs	12–1

● Despite the evidence of 3 of the last 7 years, the pattern is for lightweights to win. Before Knock Hill (1988), only 1 horse in 20 years (subsequent Gold Cup winner The Thinker) carried more than 11st to victory.

Mumm Melling Chase (Grade 1)   2m 4f   Aintree   April

	FORM	WINNER	AGE/WEIGHT		TRAINER	JOCKEY	SP
93/4	233-F10	Katabatic	11	11-10	J. Gifford	S. McNeill	14–1
92/3	120221	Deep Sensation	8	11-10	J. Gifford	D. Murphy	7–4JF
91/2	11-1311	Remittance Man	8	11-10	N. Henderson	R. Dunwoody	4–9F
90/1	211111	Blazing Walker	7	11-10	W. Stephenson	C. Grant	5–1

● Early days to be suggesting patterns for this new race, but generally in-form horses at the head of the market seem to have the advantage.

Martell Aintree Hurdle (Grade 1) 2m 4f Aintree April

	FORM	WINNER	AGE/WEIGHT	TRAINER	JOCKEY	SP
93/4	113211	Danoli	6 11-7	T. Foley (Ire.)	C. Swan	9–2
92/3	1-12300	Morley Street	9 11-7	G. Balding	G. Bradley	6–1
91/2	11-1120	Morley Street	8 11-7	G. Balding	R. Dunwoody	4–5F
90/1	-12P11	Morley Street	7 11-7	G. Balding	J. Frost	11–8F
89/90	01-2120	Morley Street	6 11-6	G. Balding	J. Frost	4–5F
88/9	4UF011	Beech Road	7 11-9	G. Balding	R. Guest	10–1

● Winners have without fail come on from the Cheltenham Festival but, of the last 7 Champion Hurdlers to come here, 3 were beaten (Flakey Dove, Granville Again and See You Then). Toby Balding has now won the race for 5 of the last 6 years, 4 of them with the moody but magnificent Morley Street. Favourites have won 5 of the last 8.

Martell Grand National Handicap Chase 4m 4f Aintree April

	FORM	WINNER	AGE/WEIGHT	TRAINER	JOCKEY	SP
93/4	223P-10	Miinnehoma	11 10-8	M. Pipe	R. Dunwoody	16-1
92/3		Race declared void				
91/2	1P-2200	Party Politics	8 10-7	N. Gaselee	C. Llewellyn	14-1
90/1	202131	Seagram	11 10-6	D. Barons	N. Hawke	12-1
89/90	0P-41304	Mr Frisk	11 10-6	K. Bailey	M. Armytage	16-1
88/9	240304	Little Polveir	12 10-3	G. Balding	J. Frost	28-1
87/8	31211F	Rhyme 'N' Reason	9 11-0	D. Elsworth	B. Powell	10-1
86/7	331F02	Maori Venture	11 10-13	A. Turnell	S. Knight	28-1
85/6	220001	West Tip	9 10-11	M. Oliver	R. Dunwoody	15-2
84/5	-12P	Last Suspect	11 10-5	T. Forster	H. Davies	50-1

• Not a lottery perhaps, but still fairly unpredictable. No winner has carried more than 11st for 11 years. Of the last 44 horses to make the frame, 33 have been in the handicap proper and only Little Polveir won from out of the handicap. Only 1 favourite (Grittar, 1982) has won in the last 19 years. Seagram was the 1st Cheltenham Festival winner to win in over 30 years.

Edinburgh Woollen Mills Future Champions Novices' Chase (Grade 1)
2m 4f   Ayr   April

	FORM	WINNER	AGE/WEIGHT	TRAINER	JOCKEY	SP
93/4	111115	See More Indians	7 11-8	P. Nicholls	R. Dunwoody	7–2
92/3	2-11121	Cab On Target	7 11-8	Mrs M. Reveley	P. Niven	4–9F
91/2	4211FP	The Illywhacker	7 11-8	Mrs J. Pitman	M. Pitman	6–1
90/1	1/03114	High Knowl	8 11-8	M. Pipe	G. McCourt	15–2
89/90	1112F0	Celtic Shot	8 11-13	C. Brooks	G. McCourt	5–2
88/9	221212	Southern Minstrel	6 11-13	W. Stephenson	C. Grant	5–4F

• Race distance changed to 2m 4f in 1991. All 7 winners had at least 2 chase wins to their credit and had run at either Cheltenham or Aintree (in Jim Thorpe's case, both).

Stakis Scottish National Handicap Chase 4m 1f Ayr April

	FORM	WINNER	AGE/WEIGHT	TRAINER	JOCKEY	SP
93/4	2112P0	Earth Summit	6 10-0	N. Twiston-Davies	D. Bridgwater	16–1
92/3	111202	Run For Free	9 11-10	M. Pipe	M. Perrett	6–1
91/2	121220	Captain Dibble	7 11-0	N. Twiston-Davies	P. Scudamore	9–1
90/1	U30-200	Killone Abbey	9 10-0	W. Stephenson	C. Grant	40–1
89/90	223-42P	Four Trix	9 10-0	G. Richards	D. Byrne	25–1
88/9	113111	Roll-A-Joint	11 10-0	C. Popham	B. Powell	4–1

● Astonishing race for lightweights; before Captain Dibble only 1 winner (Fighting Fit, 10st 10lb in 1979) had carried more than 10st 5lb to victory since Red Rum's triumph in 1974. In that time the 10st winners have been up to 14lb out of the handicap. Younger profile than Aintree National winners. Light campaign is useful; only 2 of the last 10 winners had run more than 6 times in the current season.

EBF Novices' Hurdle Handicap Final   2m 1f   Cheltenham   April

	FORM	WINNER	AGE/WEIGHT	TRAINER	JOCKEY	SP
93/4	030132	Gospel	5 11-7	N. Twiston-Davies	D. Bridgwater	7–1CF
92/3	203100	Country Lad	5 10-7	Mrs S. Williams	S. McNeill	33–1
91/2	22-10	Current Express	5 12-0	N. Henderson	R. Dunwoody	6–1
90/1	0-34211	Poetic Gem	6 10-0	G. Balding	R. Guest	9–2
89/90	20-1P41	Vazon Bay	6 12-0	Mrs J. Pitman	M. Pitman	7–1
88/9	20-111	For The Grain	5 11-10	J. Wilson	L. Wyer	14–1

● A win previously in a novice event is a must but a light, perhaps interrupted campaign is no drawback. Current Express (5th at Cheltenham) and Vazon Bay (winner at Aintree) both came here off excellent runs at the Festivals. Favourites have a bad record: only 1 made the first 3 in the 6 years before last year.

Whitbread Gold Cup Handicap Chase 3m 5½f Sandown April

	FORM	WINNER	AGE/WEIGHT	TRAINER	JOCKEY	SP
93/4	1F2P0U	Ushers Island	8 10-0	H. Johnson	C. Swan	25–1
92/3	003001	*Topsham Bay	10 10-1	D. Barons	R. Dunwoody	10–1
91/2	042P11	Topsham Bay	9 10-1	D. Barons	H. Davies	9–2
90/1	12131F	**Docklands Express	9 10-3	K. Bailey	A. Tory	4–1JF
89/90	133041	Mr Frisk	11 10-5	K. Bailey	M. Armytage	9–2F
88/9	4-12413	Brown Windsor	7 10-0	N. Henderson	M. Bowlby	12–1

● Grand National runners have a poor record – only 3 have made the first 3 in both races in the same season; Mr Frisk (1st in both), Lean Ar Aghaidh (3rd and 1st) and Nicolaus Silver (1st at Aintree and 2nd here). The last 8 to pass the post first all ran at the Cheltenham Festival. Lightweights dominate – 10 of the last 13 winners carried between 10st and 10st 6lb. Ushers Island was a rare shock result.

* Givus A Buck was 1st past the post but was disqualified and placed 2nd.

** Cahervillahow was 1st past the post but was disqualified and placed 2nd.

Swinton Handicap Hurdle 2m Haydock May

	FORM	WINNER	AGE/WEIGHT	TRAINER	JOCKEY	SP
93/4	1313	Dreams End	6 11-4	P. Hobbs	M. Hourigan	10–1
92/3	113-331	Spinning	6 11-0	I. Balding	J. Frost	3–1F
91/2	321213	Bitofabanter	5 11-1	A. Moore (Ire)	T. Taaffe	14–1
90/1	2-21101	Winnie The Witch	7 10-2	K. Bridgwater	D. Bridgwater	8–1
89/90	120201	Sybillin	4 10-1	J. FitzGerald	D. Byrne	8–1
88/9	-F1102	State Jester	6 10-0	W. Elsey	J. Quinn	14–1

● Six of the last 7 winners came on from either Cheltenham or Aintree and 3 of them won there. The last 8 winners all made the first 3 on their prep run and had relatively light campaigns. Spinning was the first favourite to win since Corporal Clinger (joint) in 1985.

Chapter Eighteen

How to Calculate Your Winnings

If the principles laid out in the earlier chapters have any merit, then the following section should become the most well-thumbed in the whole book – it shows how to settle your bets! All you need is a pocket calculator and the help of the decimal conversion section of the ready reckoner table in Appendix F.

WIN BETS

Win Single

E.g. £5 at 9–2: Cost £5.50 (inc. tax paid on stake).
  Convert odds to decimals; add 1 point; multiply by stake:
  $5.500 \times 5 = £27.50$ return.

Win Double, Treble, Accumulator

E.g. £2 treble at 7–2, 10–11, 7–4: Cost £2.20 (inc. tax paid on stake).
  Convert odds to decimals; add 1 point to each; multiply through, then multiply by stake:
  $4.500 \times 1.909 \times 2.750 \times 2 = £47.25$ return.

Alternative method for win double, treble, accumulator:
E.g. £2 treble at 3–1, 4–1, 7–4: cost £2.20 (inc. tax paid on stake).
  Add the two figures of the first price together: $3 + 1 = 4$.

Multiply by the stake and divide by the second figure: $4 \times 2 \div 1 = 8$.

Multiply by the total of the next price; divide by its second figure: $8 \times 5 \div 1 = 40$.

Multiply by the total of the next price; divide by its second figure: $40 \times 11 \div 4 = £110$ return.

EACH-WAY BETS

Odds for places are calculated as follows:

2–4 runners	No place betting
5–7 runners	1st and 2nd: one-quarter odds
8 + runners	1st, 2nd and 3rd: one-fifth odds
12–15 runners (handicap)	1st, 2nd and 3rd: one-quarter odds
16 + runners (handicap)	1st, 2nd, 3rd and 4th: one-quarter odds

Each-Way Single

E.g. £2 each way (win and place) at 11–2 in a 10-runner handicap: cost £4.40 (inc. tax paid on stake).

Calculate £2 at 11–2 as in a win single bet.

Convert odds to decimals; add 1 point; multiply by stake: $6.500 \times 2 = £13$ win return.

Calculate £2 place at 11–2.

Deduct stake from win portion of bet.

Multiply by the appropriate fraction (in this case one-fifth):

$11 \times 0.2 = 2.2$. Add stake:

2.2 + 2 = £4.20 place return. Add win return:
£13 + £4.20 = £17.20 total return.

Each-Way Double, Treble, Accumulator

E.g. £6 each-way treble on an evens winner (one-fifth odds, place); 6–1 2nd (one-quarter odds); 7–2 3rd (one-fifth odds): cost £13.20 (inc. tax paid on stake).

Win bet: lost because all three have to win.

Place bet: calculate place prices by converting odds to decimals and multiplying by the appropriate fraction:
1.000 × 0.2 = 0.2; 6 × 0.25 = 1.5; 3.5 × 0.2 = 0.7.

Add 1 point to each; multiply through; multiply by stake:
1.2 × 2.5 × 1.7 × 6 = £30.60 total return.

Alternative method for each-way double, treble, accumulator:
E.g. £3 each-way double on 7–1 and 13–2 winners (both at one-fifth the odds for a place): cost £6.60 (inc. tax paid on stake).

Calculate win double as in example above:
8 × 3 ÷ 1 × 15 ÷ 2 = £180 win return.

To calculate the place double:

Multiply the second figure of the first price by either 4 or 5 depending on the place odds paid (in this case one-fifth, therefore × 5); do likewise with the second price:
7–5 and 13–10.

Then do the same calculation on the win portion:
12 × 3 ÷ 5 × 23 ÷ 10 = £16.56 place return. Add win return:
£180 + £16.56 = £196.56 total return.

MULTIPLE BETS

Patent

Three selections combining for seven bets: three singles, three doubles and a treble.

For one winner, calculate as a win single.

For two or three winners, calculate by the following method. E.g. £10 win patent on a 7–4 winner, 2–1 winner and a loser: cost £77 (inc. tax paid on stake).

Convert odds to decimals; add 2 points to each; multiply through:

3.75 × 4 = 15. Subtract 1; multiply by stake:

14 × 10 = £140 total return.

Yankee, Super Yankee, Heinz

Yankee – four selections combining for 11 bets: six doubles, four trebles and a four-timer.

Super Yankee – five selections combining for 26 bets: 10 doubles, 10 trebles, five four-timers and a five-timer.

Heinz – six selections combining for 57 bets: 15 doubles, 20 trebles, 15 four-timers, six five-timers, and a six-timer.

For two winners calculate as a win double.

For three or more winners, calculate by the following method.

E.g £1 Super Yankee on a 2–1 winner, 8–11 winner, 7–4 winner, 13–8 winner and a loser: cost £28.60 (inc. tax paid on stake).

Convert odds to decimals: add 2 points to each; multiply through:

4 × 2.727 × 3.75 × 3.625 = 148.28062.

Subtract 1 = 147.28062 in order to subtract the singles; add 1 point to the original decimal conversion of odds; and *minus* through; multiply by stake:

147.28062–3–1.727–2.75–2.625 × 1 = 137.17862 = £137.18 total return.

Each-Way Patent, Yankee, etc.

Calculate as two separate bets, win and place.

E.g. 10p each-way Yankee on a 2–1 winner (one-fifth odds, place), 7–4 winner (one-quarter odds, place), 4–6 winner (one-fifth odds, place), 9–2 3rd (one-fifth): cost £2.42 (inc. tax paid on stake).

Convert to decimals; add 2 points to each; multiply through:
$4 \times 3.75 \times 2.667 = 40.005$.

Subtract 1 = 39.005 in order to subtract the singles; add 1 point to the original decimal conversion of odds; and *minus* through; multiply by stake:
$39.005 - 3 - 2.75 - 1.667 \times 0.10 = 3.1588 = £3.16$ win return.

Place bet: calculate place prices by converting odds to decimals and multiplying by the appropriate fraction:
$2 \times 0.2 = 0.4$; $1.75 \times 0.25 = 0.4375$; $0.667 \times 0.2 = 0.1334$; $4.5 \times 0.2 = 0.9$.

Add 2 points to each; multiply through;
$2.4 \times 2.4375 \times 2.1334 \times 2.9 = 36.193131$.

Subtract 1 = 35.193131 in order to subtract the singles; add 1 point to the original decimal conversion of odds; and *minus* through; multiply by stake:
$35.193131 - 1.4 - 1.4375 - 1.1334 - 1.9 \times 0.10 = 2.9322231 = £2.93$ place return. Add win return:
£2.93 + £3.16 = £6.09 total return.

Non-Runners

In all multiple bets, the odds of the non-runner are 0.

E.g. £5 win double on a 2–1 winner and a non-runner: cost: £5.50 (inc. tax paid on stake).

Convert odds to decimals; add 1 point to each; multiply through; multiply by stake:

$3 \times 1 \times 5 = £15$ total return.

BETTING TAX

Betting duty – more usually called 'betting tax' – was first imposed in 1960. Bookmakers originally spared the punter by paying the tax themselves. As the rate of tax increased the layers passed on the burden, but offered the punter two alternative ways of settling the charge: they could pay the tax and levy due on their returns, and risk losing a sizeable chunk of their winnings, or pay a minimal amount on their stakes.

Betting tax through the years

	Off course (%)	On course (%)
October 1966	2½	2½
March 1968	5	5
April 1970	6	5
July 1972	6	4
March 1974	7½	4
July 1981	8	4
April 1987	8	0
March 1992	7¾	0

Off-course betting is currently subject to a deduction of 10p in the £. The bulk of this burden is the 7¾ per cent tax; in addition a variable amount (approximately 1 per cent) is returned to the sport by way of the annual Horserace Betting Levy. The remaining deduction (approximately 1¼ per cent) disappears behind a nebulous phrase like 'tax on tax' or on betting shop overheads and VAT. It is, though, nothing more nor less than the price the bookmaker charges the punter for the privilege of betting.

The following two comments are taken from the Home Affairs Select Committee investigation of the betting levy in 1991:

'The bookmaker's liability to duty and levy is on his total turnover, and it is *his* liability, not the punters'. To call bookmakers' deductions "tax" is at the least disingenuous, at worst less than honest.'

'The use by the bookmakers of VAT as a justification for deductions is entirely indefensible.'

The bets highlighted in this chapter have all been 'tax paid', that is to say, the 10 per cent deduction has been paid on the stake money. Should you decide to bet 'tax unpaid' then a 10 per cent deduction will have to be made from your return.

Betting 'tax paid' is marginally advantageous to the punter, as the following example shows:

'Tax unpaid' bet: £10 on a 3–1 winner; return £40 less 10 per cent deduction = £36.

    'Tax paid' bet: £9 (+ 90p tax) at 3–1; return £36.

The return is identical but the cost of the 'tax paid' bet was 10p less.

To calculate your return on a 'tax unpaid' bet after tax has been deducted, multiply by 0.9.

Racecourse betting shops make a deduction of 6 per cent from returns. To calculate your return after 6 per cent 'tax' has been deducted, multiply by 0.94.

Appendices

Appendix A

Weight-for-Age-Scale – Flat

The table shows the number of pounds that it is deemed the average horse in each age group falls short of maturity at different dates and distances.

Distance	Age	JAN. 1–15	JAN. 16–31	FEB. 1–14	FEB. 15–28	MARCH 1–15	MARCH 16–31	APRIL 1–15	APRIL 16–30	MAY 1–15	MAY 16–31
5f	2	–	–	–	–	–	47	44	41	38	36
	3	15	15	15	15	14	13	12	11	10	9
6f	2	–	–	–	–	–	–	–	–	44	41
	3	16	16	16	16	15	14	13	12	11	10
7f	2	–	–	–	–	–	–	–	–	–	–
	3	18	18	18	18	17	16	15	14	12	11
1m	2	–	–	–	–	–	–	–	–	–	–
	3	20	20	19	19	18	17	16	15	13	12
	4	1	1	–	–	–	–	–	–	–	–
1m 1f	3	22	22	21	20	20	19	18	17	15	14
	4	2	2	1	1	1	–	–	–	–	–
1m 2f	3	23	23	22	22	21	20	19	18	16	15
	4	3	3	2	2	1	1	–	–	–	–
1m 3f	3	–	–	–	–	23	22	21	20	18	17
	4	4	4	3	3	2	1	1	–	–	–
1m 4f	3	–	–	–	–	24	23	22	21	19	18
	4	5	4	4	3	3	2	2	1	–	–
1m 5f	3	–	–	–	–	25	24	23	22	20	19
	4	5	4	4	3	3	2	2	1	–	–
1m 6f	3	–	–	–	–	26	25	24	23	21	20
	4	6	5	5	4	4	3	3	2	1	–
1m 7f	3	–	–	–	–	28	27	26	25	23	21
	4	6	5	5	4	4	3	3	2	2	1
2m	3	–	–	–	–	29	28	27	26	24	22
	4	7	7	6	6	5	5	4	4	3	2
2m 2f	3	–	–	–	–	31	30	29	28	26	24
	4	8	8	7	7	6	6	5	5	4	3
2m 4f	3	–	–	–	–	33	32	31	30	28	26
	4	9	9	8	8	7	7	6	6	5	4

JUNE		JULY		AUG.		SEPT.		OCT.		NOV.		DEC.	
1–15	16–30	1–15	16–31	1–15	16–31	1–15	16–30	1–15	16–31	1–15	16–30	1–15	16–31
34	32	30	28	26	24	22	20	19	18	17	17	16	16
8	7	6	5	4	3	2	2	1	1	–	–	–	–
38	36	33	31	28	26	24	22	21	20	19	18	17	17
9	8	7	6	5	4	3	3	2	2	1	1	–	–
–	–	38	35	32	30	27	25	23	22	21	20	19	19
10	9	8	7	6	5	4	4	3	3	2	2	1	1
–	–	–	–	37	34	31	28	26	24	23	22	21	20
11	10	9	8	7	6	5	4	4	3	3	2	2	1
–	–	–	–	–	–	–	–	–	–	–	–	–	–
12	11	10	9	8	7	6	5	5	4	4	3	2	2
–	–	–	–	–	–	–	–	–	–	–	–	–	–
13	12	11	10	9	8	7	6	6	5	5	4	4	3
–	–	–	–	–	–	–	–	–	–	–	–	–	–
15	14	12	11	10	9	8	7	7	6	6	5	4	4
–	–	–	–	–	–	–	–	–	–	–	–	–	–
16	15	13	12	11	10	9	8	8	7	7	6	6	5
–	–	–	–	–	–	–	–	–	–	–	–	–	–
17	16	14	13	12	11	10	9	8	8	7	6	6	5
–	–	–	–	–	–	–	–	–	–	–	–	–	–
18	17	15	14	13	12	11	10	9	9	8	7	7	6
–	–	–	–	–	–	–	–	–	–	–	–	–	–
19	18	16	15	14	13	12	11	10	9	9	8	7	6
–	–	–	–	–	–	–	–	–	–	–	–	–	–
20	19	17	16	15	14	13	12	11	10	10	9	8	7
1	–	–	–	–	–	–	–	–	–	–	–	–	–
22	21	19	18	17	16	15	14	13	12	11	10	9	8
2	1	–	–	–	–	–	–	–	–	–	–	–	–
24	22	20	19	18	17	16	15	14	13	12	11	10	9
3	2	1	–	–	–	–	–	–	–	–	–	–	–

Appendix B

Weight-for-Age-Scale – National Hunt

The hurdle races table shows the allowance in pounds that 3-year-olds and 4-year-olds will receive from 5-year-olds and upwards; the steeplechases table the allowance in pounds that 4-year-olds and 5-year-olds will receive from 6-year-olds and upwards

HURDLE RACES

Distance	Age	JAN.	FEB.	MAR.	APRIL	MAY
2m	3					
	4	12	10	8	6	5
2m 4f	3					
	4	13	11	9	7	6
3m	3					
	4	14	12	10	8	7

STEEPLECHASES

Distance	Age	JAN.	FEB.	MAR.	APRIL	MAY
2m	4					
	5	10	9	8	7	6
2m 4f	4					
	5	11	10	9	8	7
3m	4					
	5	12	11	10	9	8

JUNE	JULY	AUG.	SEPT.	OCT.	NOV.	DEC.
	20	20	18	17	16	14
5	3	3	2	1	–	–
	21	21	19	18	17	15
6	3	3	2	1	–	–
	23	23	21	19	18	16
7	4	4	3	2	1	–

JUNE	JULY	AUG.	SEPT.	OCT.	NOV.	DEC.
	15	15	14	13	12	11
6	3	3	2	1	–	–
	16	16	15	14	13	12
7	4	4	3	2	1	–
	17	17	16	15	14	13
8	5	5	4	3	2	1

Poundage Allowance for Distance Beaten

Lengths beaten		Race distance															
	5f	6f	7f	1m	1m 1f	1m 2f	1m 3f	1m 4f	1m 5f	1m 6f	1m 7f	2m	2m 1f	2m 2f	2m 3f	2m 4f
Neck/½	1	1	1	1	1	1	1	1	1	1	1	1	1	1	1	1
¾	2	2	2	2	1	1	1	1	1	1	1	1	1	1	1	1
1	3	3	2	2	2	2	2	2	2	2	2	2	2	2	1	1
1½	4	4	3	3	3	3	3	3	3	2	2	2	2	2	2	2
1¾	5	4	4	4	4	3	3	3	3	3	3	3	3	3	2	2
2	6	5	4	4	4	4	4	4	3	3	3	3	3	3	3	3
2½	7	6	6	5	5	5	5	5	4	4	4	4	4	4	3	3
3	9	8	7	6	6	6	5	5	5	5	5	5	5	5	4	4
3½	10	9	8	7	7	7	6	6	6	5	5	5	5	5	5	4
4	12	11	9	8	8	8	8	7	7	7	6	6	6	6	6	5
4½	13	12	10	9	9	9	9	8	8	8	8	7	7	7	7	6
5	15	14	11	10	10	11	11	10	10	9	9	8	8	8	8	7
6	18	17	13	12	12	11	11	10	10	10	9	9	9	9	8	8
8	24	22	17	16	16	15	15	14	13	13	12	12	12	12	11	11
10	30	27	21	20	20	19	18	17	16	16	15	15	15	15	14	14
12	36	32	25	24	24	22	21	20	19	19	18	18	18	18	17	17
15	45	39	31	30	30	27	26	24	23	23	22	22	22	22	21	21

Appendix D

Flat Programme Categories

PATTERN – Groups 1, 2, and 3.

LISTED – including 14 Rated Stakes.

RATED STAKES – valuable handicaps with a maximum 141b weight range.

CONDITIONS STAKES – races for horses below top class and which are not handicaps, maidens, sellers or claimers.

LIMITED STAKES – weight-for-age races with a maximum rating band of 75.

STANDARD HANDICAP – including nurseries.

MAIDEN HANDICAP – for maidens of limited ability (top rating 70) which have run at least four times.

OPEN MAIDEN – for maidens of any ability.

RATING-RELATED MAIDEN – rating defines eligibility; horses must have run at least three times.

AUCTION MAIDEN – for horses originally sold by auction at specified sales.

MEDIAN AUCTION MAIDEN – for progeny of stallions which established a median price for their yearlings at specified sales.

SELLER – winner must be offered for sale; every loser may be claimed for a specified price.

CLAIMER – every horse may be claimed for a specified price.

APPRENTICE/AMATEUR – confined to these groups of riders.

The seven PRIZE MONEY BANDS (minimum guaranteed prize money) are:

A. Pattern and Listed
B. £10,000; 2yo £9,000
C. £6,500 (£7,500 for apprentice or amateur race)
D. £4,500
E. £3,750
F. £3,250
G. £3,000

Appendix E

Expected Value Grid

The figures in the table show the return on a notional £10 stake.

Odds	1	2	3	4	5	6	7	8	9
				Number of expected wins in 10 runnings					
1–2					−2·5	−1	0·5	2	3·5
4–5				−2·8	−1	0·8	2·6	4·4	6·2
Evens				−2	0	2	4	6	8
5–4				−1	1·25	3·5	5·75	8	10·25
6–4			−2·5	0	2·5	5	7·5	10	12·5
7–4			−1·75	1	3·75	6·5	9·25	12	14·75
2–1			−1	2	5	8	11	14	17
9–4			−0·25	3	6·25	9·50	12·75	16	19·25
5–2		−3	0·5	4	7·5	11	14·5	18	21·5
11–4		−2·5	1·25	5	8·75	12·5	16·25	20	23·75
3–1		−2	2	6	10	14	18	22	26
7–2		−1	3·5	8	12·5	17	21·5	26	30·5
4–1	−5	0	5	10	15	20	25	30	35
9–2	−4·5	1	6·5	12	17·5	23	28·5	34	39·5
5–1	−4	2	8	14	20	26	32	38	44
11–2	−3·5	3	9·5	16	22·5	29	35·5	42	48·5
6–1	−3	4	11	18	25	32	39	46	
7–1	−2	6	14	22	30	38	46		
8–1	−1	8	17	26	35	44			
10–1	1	12	23	34	45				
12–1	3	16	29	42					
14–1	5	20	35						
16–1	7	24	41						
20–1	11	32							
25–1	16	42							
33–1	24								

Ready Reckoner

Figures are inclusive of £1 stake. To deduct tax at 10 per cent, multiply by 0.9.

Odds	Decimal conversion	Win	Place (1/5 odds)	Place (1/4 odds)	Dead-heat or jt-favs
1–5	0·200	1·20	1·04	1·05	0·60
2–9	0·222	1·22	1·04	1·06	0·61
1–4	0·250	1·25	1·05	1·06	0·63
2–7	0·286	1·29	1·06	1·07	0·64
30–100	0·300	1·30	1·06	1·08	0·65
1–3	0·333	1·33	1·07	1·08	0·67
4–11	0·364	1·36	1·07	1·09	0·68
2–5	0·400	1·40	1·08	1·10	0·70
4–9	0·444	1·44	1·09	1·11	0·72
40–85	0·471	1·47	1·09	1·12	0·74
1–2	0·500	1·50	1·10	1·13	0·75
8–15	0·533	1·53	1·11	1·13	0·77
4–7	0·571	1·57	1·11	1·14	0·79
8–13	0·615	1·62	1·12	1·15	0·81
4–6	0·667	1·67	1·13	1·17	0·83
8–11	0·727	1·73	1·15	1·18	0·86
4–5	0·800	1·80	1·16	1·20	0·90
5–6	0·833	1·83	1·17	1·21	0·92
10–11	0·909	1·91	1·18	1·23	0·95
20–21	0·952	1·95	1·19	1·24	0·98
evens	1·000	2·00	1·20	1·25	1·00
21–20	1·050	2·05	1·21	1·26	1·03
11–10	1·100	2·10	1·22	1·28	1·05
6–5	1·200	2·20	1·24	1·30	1·10
5–4	1·250	2·25	1·25	1·31	1·13
11–8	1·375	2·38	1·28	1·34	1·19
6–4	1·500	2·50	1·30	1·38	1·25
13–8	1·625	2·63	1·33	1·41	1·31

Odds	Decimal conversion	Win	Place (1/5 odds)	Place (1/4 odds)	Dead-heat or jt-favs
7–4	1·750	2·75	1·35	1·44	1·38
15–8	1·875	2·88	1·38	1·47	1·44
2–1	2·000	3·00	1·40	1·50	1·50
85–40	2·125	3·13	1·43	1·53	1·56
9–4	2·250	3·25	1·45	1·56	1·63
5–2	2·500	3·50	1·50	1·63	1·75
11–4	2·750	3·75	1·55	1·69	1·88
3–1	3·000	4·00	1·60	1·75	2·00
100–30	3·333	4·33	1·67	1·83	2·17
7–2	3·500	4·50	1·70	1·88	2·25
4–1	4·000	5·00	1·80	2·00	2·50
9–2	4·500	5·50	1·90	2·13	2·75
5–1	5·000	6·00	2·00	2·25	3·00
11–2	5·500	6·50	2·10	2·38	3·25
6–1	6·000	7·00	2·20	2·50	3·50
13–2	6·500	7·50	2·30	2·63	3·75
7–1	7·000	8·00	2·40	2·75	4·00
15–2	7·500	8·50	2·50	2·88	4·25
8–1	8·000	9·00	2·60	3·00	4·50
17–2	8·500	9·50	2·70	3·13	4·75
9–1	9·000	10·00	2·80	3·25	5·00
10–1	10·000	11·00	3·00	3·50	5·50
11–1	11·000	12·00	3·20	3·75	6·00
12–1	12·000	13·00	3·40	4·00	6·50
14–1	14·000	15·00	3·80	4·50	7·50
16–1	16·000	17·00	4·20	5·00	8·50
18–1	18·000	19·00	4·60	5·50	9·50
20–1	20·000	21·00	5·00	6·00	10·50
25–1	25·000	26·00	6·00	7·25	13·00
33–1	33·000	34·00	7·60	9·25	17·00
40–1	40·000	41·00	9·00	11·00	20·50
50–1	50·000	51·00	11·00	13·50	25·50
66–1	66·000	67·00	14·20	17·50	33·50

Appendix G

Odds Percentage Conversion Table

Odds	%	Odds	%
1–3	75·0	5–2	28·6
4–11	73·3	11–4	26·7
2–5	71·4	3–1	25·0
4–9	69·2	100–30	23·1
40–85	68·0	7–2	22·2
1–2	66·7	4–1	20·0
8–15	65·2	9–2	18·2
4–7	63·6	5–1	16·7
8–13	61·9	11–2	15·4
4–6	60·0	6–1	14·3
8–11	57·9	13–2	13·3
4–5	55·6	7–1	12·5
5–6	54·5	15–2	11·8
10–11	52·4	8–1	11·1
20–21	51·2	17–2	10·5
evens	50·0	9–1	10·0
21–20	48·8	10–1	9·1
11–10	47·6	11–1	8·3
6–5	45·5	12–1	7·7
5–4	44·4	14–1	6·7
11–8	42·1	16–1	5·9
6–4	40·0	18–1	5·3
13–8	38·1	20–1	4·8
7–4	36·4	25–1	3·8
15–8	34·8	33–1	2·9
2–1	33·3	40–1	2·4
85–40	32·0	50–1	2·0
9–4	30·8	100–1	1·0

Sources

BOOKS

Bennett, David, *Know Your Bets*, The Sporting Life, 1992
Bird, Alex and Manners, Terry, *Alex Bird*, Queen Anne Press, 1985
Lambton, George, *Men and Horses I Have Known*, 1924
Smith, Raymond, *The High Rollers of the Turf*, Sporting Book Publishers, 1992
Stafford, Tony, *All Weather Racing*, Raceform, 1991
Supernap, *Betting To Win*, Odhams, 1963
Sutherland, Dr Stuart, *Irrationality*, Constable, 1992
Anon, *Calc-U-Form*, Majica Publishing, 1988

PAPERS AND PERIODICALS

Raceform, *The Daily Express*, *The Daily Star*, *The Daily Telegraph*, *The Independent*, *The Racing Calendar*, *The Racing Post*, *The Sporting Life*, *The Stallion Focus*, *The Statistical Record*, *The Times*, *Timeform*.

A selection of non-fiction from Headline

THE DRACULA SYNDROME	Richard Monaco & William Burt	£5.99 ☐
DEADLY JEALOUSY	Martin Fido	£5.99 ☐
WHITE COLLAR KILLERS	Frank Jones	£4.99 ☐
THE MURDER YEARBOOK 1994	Brian Lane	£5.99 ☐
THE PLAYFAIR CRICKET ANNUAL	Bill Findall	£3.99 ☐
ROD STEWART	Stafford Hildred & Tim Ewbank	£5.99 ☐
THE JACK THE RIPPER A–Z	Paul Begg, Martin Fido & Keith Skinner	£7.99 ☐
THE *DAILY EXPRESS* HOW TO WIN ON THE HORSES	Danny Hall	£4.99 ☐
COUPLE SEXUAL AWARENESS	Barry & Emily McCarthy	£5.99 ☐
GRAPEVINE; THE COMPLETE WINEBUYERS HANDBOOK	Anthony Rose & Tim Atkins	£5.99 ☐
ROBERT LOUIS STEVENSON; DREAMS OF EXILE	Ian Bell	£7.99 ☐

All Headline books are available at your local bookshop or newsagent, or can be ordered direct from the publisher. Just tick the titles you want and fill in the form below. Prices and availability subject to change without notice.

Headline Book Publishing, Cash Sales Department, Bookpoint, 39 Milton Park, Abingdon, OXON, OX14 4TD, UK. If you have a credit card you may order by telephone – 01235 400400.

Please enclose a cheque or postal order made payable to Bookpoint Ltd to the value of the cover price and allow the following for postage and packing:

UK & BFPO: £1.00 for the first book, 50p for the second book and 30p for each additional book ordered up to a maximum charge of £3.00.
OVERSEAS & EIRE: £2.00 for the first book, £1.00 for the second book and 50p for each additional book.

Name ....

Address ....

....

....

If you would prefer to pay by credit card, please complete:
Please debit my Visa/Access/Diner's Card/American Express (delete as applicable) card no:

Signature .... Expiry Date ....